Born to
SHOP
TOKYO

Bantam Books of Related Interest
Ask your bookseller for the books you have
  missed.

BORN TO SHOP: France
BORN TO SHOP: Italy
BORN TO SHOP: London
BORN TO SHOP: Hong Kong
BORN TO SHOP: Tokyo

Born to SHOP

TOKYO

▼

SUZY GERSHMAN
and
JUDITH THOMAS

Introduction by
Shu Uemura

BANTAM BOOKS
TORONTO • NEW YORK • LONDON
SYDNEY • AUCKLAND

BORN TO SHOP: TOKYO

A Bantam Book / April 1987

Cover art by Dave Calver.

All rights reserved.
Copyright © 1987 by Suzy Kalter, Judith Evans Thomas and
Appletree Productions.
This book may not be reproduced in whole or in part, by
mimeograph or any other means, without permission.
For information address: Bantam Books, Inc.

Library of Congress Cataloging-in-Publication Data

Gershman, Susan.
    Born to shop.

    Includes indexes.
    Contents: —[2] Italy —[3] London —   —[5] Tokyo.
    1. Shopping—Directories.   I. Title.
TX335.T45   1986   380.1'025   85-48224
ISBN 0-553-34353-X

Published simultaneously in the United States and Canada

PRINTED IN THE UNITED STATES OF AMERICA

FG   0 9 8 7 6 5 4 3 2 1

The BORN TO SHOP Team:

authors: Suzy Kalter Gershman
         Judith Evans Thomas
editor: Jill Parsons
executive editor: Toni Burbank
assistant to executive editor:
         Andrew Zega
copy editor: William D. Drennan
cover artist: Dave Calver
maps by: Judith Evans Thomas
         Lauren Dong
book design by: Lynne Arany

Acknowledgments

You are not planning on reading the acknowledgments. In fact, you are not planning on reading most of the front of the book. You're going to skip around to find the parts about bargains.

You're making a big mistake.

Not only is this book packed with information you are going to need, but we are now weaving information into the acknowledgments. So there. You may not care about all the people we have to thank, but we care about them! So to make it that much more interesting for you, we've got a few extra tips that are strategically placed just to get your attention. And they don't appear anywhere else!

Ready? Good.

Now then, this book would not have been possible without the help of family and friends . . . and even a few strangers. Koichi Tsuchida, and the beloved Nori, have never met us or shopped with us, but they took our manuscript to heart and checked every word, every turn and every train schedule to make sure this book was accurate. Buddha bless you.

We also must thank Bobbi Schlesinger, Werner Leighren, and our friends at Varig since we mostly fly back and forth from L.A. to Tokyo on Varig Airlines—Varig has the only flight that can get you into Tokyo in time to get in some shopping, so we call it the "Born to Shop Airline"—after all, after ten hours on a plane and two on a bus, when you get into town what you most need to do is shop. Right? Right! Varig makes it all possible.

And if you shop as much as we do, you'll understand why we stay at the Keio Plaza, which is an Inter•Continental Hotel, and appreciate it so much—it's located right in the heart of Shinjuku, which is shoppers' heaven. Our thanks to Masaru Yu Fukuda of Inter• Continental International in L.A. and Koichi Hirose at the Keio in Tokyo. The Keio, by the way, provides all those business and tourist services you need help with when you are less than sure of yourself in Japanese. (*Domo* to all.) The coffee seems expensive at first, but you get a second cup free which makes the hotel one of the bargain spots of Tokyo—dear to locals as well as tourists. (A local told us this—it's not just a silly plug!)

Yes, Suga does have a haircutting salon in Tokyo. It's on Omotesando.

One of the reasons we have so much fun in Tokyo is that each trip is another opportunity to visit the Far East branch of the Joseloff family. Suzy Joseloff knows everything there is to know about Tokyo, or knows how to find it out, and even provides two children for us to hug when we grow lonely for our own; Gordon Joseloff may be one of CBS Network's rising stars, but luckily for us—he's just part of our family. Thank you, Gordon, Suzy, Anna-Lisa, Benjamin, and Reiko for everything!

We also have to thank all our friends at the Japan National Tourist Organization for making us part of their family, both in L.A. and in Tokyo, and everyone at the TIC (Tourist Information Center). At Mitsukoshi, Munehiro Kumada spent several hours with us discussing Japanese retailing methods.

You can get a charge card from Mitsukoshi in New York at your convenience and use it any place in the world. Or any place they have a store, which is every place. This will impress your friends and win you extra bows while in Tokyo.

At the Tokyo Women's and Children's Wear Manufacturers Association, Keiko Shinomiya has been most helpful in providing Fashion Week background information; thank you, Dick Harbig, for one of the highlights of Tokyo, friendship with Hiro and Aiya, that's Hiromasa Murata—and his charming wife—who are always available to explain the inscrutable to us.

Thanks also to our trusty translator, Uniko Harada, who was essential in many a transaction; Sachi Irwin who connected us with her friends in Tokyo and even let us bite her pearls; Jun Shimuzu; Mucci Taylor, Simon David and Mitsue Sasaki and all the other friends and friends of friends who turned us on to sources and secrets.

If you have jet lag, don't toss and turn or reach for the sleeping pills . . . hop out of bed and hightail it over to the Tsukiji Market . . . you can go on the subway and be perfectly safe. Who said all stores were closed in the middle of the night?

At Bantam, we want to thank the entire Born to Shop team. Last but not least, we want to thank our husbands and children for being so understanding of all our travels and the serious nature of our work. We love you!

CONTENTS

Editorial Note

Currency in Japan is the yen, which has been fluctuating madly. When we began going to Japan regularly, the yen was at 225 to the dollar. Lucky us! There are rumors in the business and banking communities that the Japanese plan to keep the yen down at 150 to 180 to the dollar. So watch out. We have used the rate of exchange in this book as $1 U.S. = 180 yen. Obviously, this exchange rate may change; please recalculate prices accordingly.

We have visited each shop listed in this book at least once, usually more than once. Our description of the stores, the locations, and the bargains offered herein is purely our opinion. It was never our intent to list every shop in Tokyo; those included represent our selections per the purpose of this book. The length of a listing is meaningless in terms of endearment. Stores open and close, merchandise comes and goes—we cannot promise beyond a shadow of a doubt that a resource has not changed since our last inspection and before our revision of this edition.

Born to Shop is a series of books. Each book is divided into two parts: text and listings. While the subtitles of the text chapters are the same in some of the books, the information varies from book to book due to differences in countries, cultures, cities, and customs. There may be some overlap of material in some of the text portions of the books. On the whole, however, you will find this book striking different from the other *Born to Shop* b since shopping in Japan is such a unique experience. We set out to make Tokyo less confusing for you; we've given you more tours and more neighborhood information with fewer addresses to track down—simply because finding specific addresses in Tokyo is virtually impossible. Read, shop, enjoy!

Introduction

I am pleased to be able to convey this message of greetings to you and to welcome you to Tokyo. This is not going to be one of those introductions where I tell you how well I know the authors and how much fun we have together eating sushi every time they come to Tokyo. I do not really know the authors.

I wrote this introduction for one simple reason: they asked me.

And since I have just been welcomed so enthusiastically to the United States with marvelous kinds of attention for my makeup boutiques, I want to welcome you to Tokyo in the same way.

But also, I like this book.

It is so refreshingly American that it is a pleasure. It is brash and honest and not so subtle. Few Japanese authors would say the things these women say. Their outlook is uniquely American and their eye for fashion, style, and a good buy is unerring. They have spotted and reported and explained the most essential Tokyo stores and neighborhoods within these pages.

They rave about my cosmetics.

I rave back about their book.

This is possibly called a mutual admiration society.

In the 1950s I lived in Hollywood and worked as a makeup artist at Universal Studios. I have known Americans well over many years. But I chose to return to Tokyo to oper my own beauty school and boutiques. T' original Shu Uemura Beauty Boutique opened in 1983 in Omotesando, on To' leading fashion street. Currently there are 40 boutiques throughout Japan, two in Hong Kong, one in Paris, etc. We will soon open in more American locations as well as other Far Eastern and international cities. I hope Mrs. Gershman and Mrs. Thomas write books for all those cities, too. Perhaps they will let me write the introduction for their book about Singapore, as well. Very good shopping in Singapore.

Many times I think this book is much like one of my shops—there is a little bit of everything under one roof; many colors and many styles; much to sample and much to enjoy. You can wander into this book, like my shop, and have fun and buy nothing. Or you can spend all your salary. Everything I do, I try to make unique and exclusive—just like this book.

You have a home away from home within the walls of my shops and in the pages of this book when you are visiting Japan. Please come to visit, to take back to America some memories of something very different and yet very international. I welcome you. This book is a fine beginning for a trip you will never forget.

Shu Uemura
Tokyo

Preface

Nippon.

We fell in love the minute *Pacific Overtures* began.

Fell in love again, the minute *Shōgun* was over.

After several trips, we're still in love. And we're still laughing.

Laughing, because just about everyone we know was wrong about Tokyo.

For years we've heard people complain about the costs of a trip to Tokyo, that a cup of coffee costs $2.50 (it often does), that a Coke is $2.00, that Scotch can be as much as $30.00 a glass. Some friends even laughed aloud when we told them we were going to report the bargains of Tokyo. "Pretty short book," they said with a smirk, and all that.

The joke's on them. And on anyone who judges a place by the price of a cup of coffee. Yes, coffee and Coca-Cola are expensive in Tokyo. Taxis also are expensive, and imported designer goods are outrageous. But there are designer bargains galore in ready-to-wear, crafts, gifts, and toys—you just have to know where to look for them. No matter how high or how low the yen bows or stretches, there still are some 12 million people in Tokyo alone who have to wear clothes. Who have to go shopping. There is much merchandise to be had for less than American prices.

You just have to know the magic words "made in Japan."

It also helps if you have a good sense humor. On your trip to Tokyo you can e to get lost every day, maybe several t day. You can expect to see some very high prices on some very ordinary merchandise. You can expect to shake your head in wonder at much of what you see. But you can also expect to come away with sizable savings.

This book will guide you around Tokyo through walking-shopping neighborhood tours and specific directions for getting lost and found again. There is no better way to enjoy Tokyo. You'll note that in our other books we solicit tips; in Tokyo we do not. We think our job in Tokyo is to guide you to the bargains, to show you how to have fun shopping, to prevent you from suffering the dreaded Tokyo Overdose. We don't want to list every store in town, every store in the Ginza area. We list far fewer addresses in this book than in any other. The way to enjoy Tokyo is to find a neighborhood and go with the flow. Let it take you someplace, rather than vice versa.

So toss off your high-heeled sneakers, get rid of your uptight Western ways. Whether you are in Tokyo for a week or a year, you'll find that every day is a new adventure. The only way to make the most of it is to clutch your subway map to your bosom and toss care to the four winds. Bow three times to Fuji-san and remember the only rule of shopping in Tokyo: *If you wanted Christian Dior, you should have gone to Paris.*

Suzy Gershman
Judith Thomas
Spring 1987

I ▾ THE SHOPPING EXPERIENCE

Shopping in Japan

Many people go to Europe just to shop.
Few go to Japan just to shop.
Foolish, foolish, foolish.
Japan is shopping heaven. It's confusing, it's different, it's expensive, it's cheap. And Tokyo has been maligned as the most expensive city in the world. There are bargains galore in Tokyo, and we think it just may be the new fashion capital of the world. If you're talking innovative, Tokyo can make Paris look boring. If you're talking bargains, Tokyo can make Sears look expensive.

Okay, rent for an apartment in Tokyo is even pricier than in Manhattan. But who said anything about moving in? Yes, coffee costs a fortune. But caffeine is bad for you, it stunts your growth and all that. Besides, don't you get naturally high when you find a bargain? Who needs coffee, anyway? Consider these facts:

▾ Perry Ellis shoes are $60 a pair, as opposed to double that in the United States.

▾ Joseph Tricot sweaters go on sale for $30 each. You'll pay $200 for a similar sweater in New York.

▾ A genuine Chanel handbag—with papers and everything but a birth certificate and French passport—is $385, just about half its U.S. price and a full $100 cheaper than its French price.

Tokyo is not the most beautiful city on earth. Tickets to the Kabuki are outrageously expensive (like $45 for an orchestra seat!). But you want to see part of the Kabuki and d mind standing, you can see the same pla

$4 an act. Shopping in Tokyo is like that. You just have to know the ins and the outs. And if you like shopping, you will be in paradise.

Shopping is the national sport of Japan. Welcome to heaven.

Shoppers Unanimous

Of course, not everyone wants to go to Japan to shop. There are shoppers and there are *shoppers.* We all buy a few things. The amount you buy may be governed by finances, storing limitations, or whatever. But the enthusiasm with which you pursue your purchase separates the *shopper* from the mere shopper.

This book is for the *shopper.* This book is for the person, male or female, who considers a good shopping experience to be equal to a stimulating religious or sexual experience . . . possibly better. That doesn't mean that he or she got a bargain, or even bought anything. The experience was psychologically exciting, innervating, uplifting, and creative. The true *shopper* may be exhausted physically after a hard day on the pavement but will be mentally exhilarated.

The shopping experience should satisfy all the senses—there will be interesting and often beautiful things to look at, touch, smell; new pieces of information to learn, bits of history, sociology, marketing, and behavioral science all wrapped up together (with a bow and a bow). The experience is topped only if something of value to the shopper can be purchased, and purchased well within budget.

Some shopping is done for the glory of seeing what is available; some shopping is done see what beautiful and wondrous things can quired within means; some shopping is taken on as a challenge, kind of a can-you-top-this need deep within the bosom that only Monty Hall or your best friend would understand.

To many, the thrill of the chase is to bring home a prized item at a low price. After all, anyone with the money to do so can walk into a Fifth Avenue, Rodeo Drive, or even Ginza-dori store, lay out some cash, and walk away with an item of taste and beauty. It's easy. What isn't so easy is finding the same item in a less obvious place but getting a big discount on it. Some shoppers do not enjoy their splurges unless they shop the top of the line. There are people who hate crowds, big stores, sales, and public transportation. To them, a quiet specialty store where they are known and will get the most intimate service is worth any price. (We love good service, but we are not that kind of person.) There are people who go to Tokyo and do not venture beyond any of the big and luscious department stores—they are afraid of getting lost. They are afraid of adventure.

To us, shopping is both a sport and an art. We value our time, so we would not spend a day to save $10. We do, however, take serious pride in saving money, in going two for one, or in coming home with a 50% saving. For the same money our friend spent in the fancy shop, we like to have gone to the discounter and bought *two* of the item (or have saved *half* the money). We believe in mixing merchandise so that we look like a million without having spent it. And we always quit shopping when it ceases to be fun. But we like the thrill of the chase; we like getting lost. We have learned that by getting lost you always get found. And usually you find something to buy at the same time.

We call ourselves—unofficially, of course shoppers unanimous. Unanimously, shop is our first choice. Our feelings about ping are akin to those others have about cigarettes, maybe even drugs. (Haven't you found that a really good bargain gives you an incredible high?!!) We are addicted not only to spending a portion of our income, but also to spending it in the ways that amuse and satisfy us the most. Luckily for us, almost everyone in Tokyo is a member of our elite club. You will never see so many shoppers anywhere else in the world; nor will you ever see so much merchandise for sale.

Kanji Shopping

E very shopping area is filled with signs, colors, and the words of retailing we have all come to know and love—sale, bargain, exit, elevator, up, down, etc. The words that give directions, tell amounts, and provide information are taken for granted in our own stores because we absorb them so greedily. When you shop in Japan you will feel like an illiterate child in need of a grown-up to take you through the real world. Almost all signs in Tokyo are in *kanji*, the cuneiform symbols or characters that make up the Japanese language. *Kanji* is not based on an alphabet system, so you cannot sit down and learn the basics in a few hours, as you can Greek or Russian. If you're really quick-witted, you might learn the symbols for the men's room or the ladies' room, but that's about it. When you shop in Japan you will be very sorry you can't read *kanji* and very sorry that more signs are not also in Roman letters.

Not only will you not always know how ~~mu~~ch something costs or if it's on sale, but ~~some~~times you won't even know the names of ~~sh~~ops you are patronizing. You will find ~~in~~ a guidebook a location that sounds ~~like a gre~~at place to visit, only you'll never be able to read the name of the place once you get there, to verify that you are there. It's very upsetting and often frustrating.

After spending two hours (actually more) looking for one address, we have come up with our own way of dealing with *kanji* shopping, and we pass it on to you:

▼ If there is a placard on a display or bin that has large numbers or is bordered in red, the item is either featured or on sale (or both).

▼ The Japanese use Arabic numbers, so use a pen and pad to have someone write down a price for you. Don't mistake the yen figure for an additional "1," which we did once; not everyone draws a perfect ¥.

▼ Hand motions will help you for directions. *Toilet* seems to be understood by all. Escalators don't always run in up-and-down pairs; be prepared to ask where the down is by pointing.

▼ Show your array of credit cards as if you were playing "Go Fish," and let a clerk take one from the pile if you want to use a credit card. Don't be surprised if she shakes her head "no."

▼ Shopping bags are a Western invention; the Japanese tie everything in fabulous bundles. All big stores now provide bags, but you may have to ask for one with mime.

▼ Bowing is essential to the transaction. Please be polite and bow all the time, especially when merchandise is brought out for you, when you are led to a dressing room, or whatever.

▼ It is possible to get street and subway maps written in English and *kanji*. A map that is just in English may be fine for you, but it won't help your taxi driver.

▼ Take a business card from favorite sh and keep it; you may never be able to find way back without the card. Most card with maps, which are almost essential

Chome Shopping

T he word *chome* (cho-may) means "block." When you look at a Tokyo address, there are three numbers separated by hyphens. The first number designates the *chome,* or block. While we don't give many addresses in this book and don't want you to spend a lot of time tracking down buildings by location, it's fun to pick an interesting *chome* or two and just wander around there. The best-known *chomes* of Ginza are 1 through 9—which is the whole stretch of the commercial zone—but we highly recommend 5 through 7.

The third *chome* in Shinjuku is also filled with good stores. The first *chome* of Ayoma isn't as interesting as it sounds.

When you study maps and subway signs, look for the word *chome* as part of the name—it is your clue to where you will be. Also, if you take the time to learn to count a few numbers, you'll cut down on your lost-and-found time. The number, written out and next to the word *chome,* often is a subway stop: Hence, *nishi-chome* means first block, *san-chome* means third block, etc.

(It's almost as easy as 1, 2, 3—*ichi, ni, san*—but you will see the number one written as *ichi* or *nishi,* depending on what is being counted. All subway stops with a 1-*chome* in it use nishi.)

The *Koban* Experience

our shopping adventures in Tokyo will include several visits to the *koban,* which not one of those communal bathhouses have been reading about in your guide- e *koban* is the police station, or police box. It's a small (maybe 15-by-15-foot) building on the main drag of every district; it has a seal that looks like a gold star over the doorway. The Ginza *koban* is very chic; others reflect their neighborhoods.

If—or should we say when—you get lost, find the *koban,* which usually is near the subway station. There are one or two police officers there who know where everyplace in the district is. Of course, they may not speak English, or understand your Japanese, but hey—no one's perfect. Always ask for big buildings, famous stores, or show a logo. You can try pointing to a phone number in one of your guidebooks and insisting that they call for you, but you will find that the more you ask at the *koban,* the more time you spend there, and the less time you are out enjoying being lost. We give ourselves ten minutes to be lost, *then* go to the *koban.*

First-timer's Fever

The first time you go shopping in Tokyo, you may be overwhelmed. Try to arrange your schedule so you can just observe on the first time out. Do your actual buying after you get the lay of the land. Don't do too much; don't be upset if you get lost or find yourself confused. Once you relax, you'll have a great time. You have nothing to fear except fear itself—and maybe a sharp letter from American Express when you can't pay all of the bill on time.

After the first day's first-timer's fever, you may settle into what we call Tokyo Overdose—too much of a good thing. The first time walk into a *depato,* you think, "Hey, isn't great—eight floors of wonder!" But after you begin to get a giant headache. Afte done one of the Parco buildings, you may find it inconceivable that there are two more around the corner. The way to handle Tokyo Overdose best is to know that it exists and can happen to anyone. Pace yourself against it. Tokyo Overdose is a mental collapse, so you need to alternate what and where you shop so you don't have a breakdown. If you love yourself, you won't do five *depatos* in one day. If you respect yourself, you'll walk into some buildings and say to yourself, "This is a great place, but I don't really need to do this."

Pick your choices carefully, and allow yourself to get plenty of fresh air. You may want to look at our tours (see page 302), which were devised to prevent you from cracking up. In Tokyo, the mind gives out far before the feet. Protect yourself and enjoy yourself!

Booking Japan: Part One

Hopefully, your bargain-hunting in Tokyo began at home when you were able to purchase a special-fare airline ticket. One of the best tricks we learned from several people who travel to Tokyo regularly is to compare ticket prices between the United States and Tokyo and the United States and Hong Kong. The Hong Kong plane stops in Tokyo, and you can get off there. Because so many more tourists go to Hong Kong than to Tokyo, often you can get a bargain ticket for less than the ticket to Tokyo. You just throw away give away the Tokyo-to-Hong Kong part of ticket, or spend a weekend in Hong Kong. about a four-hour flight.)

high seasons in Hong Kong and in e different, so winter bargains do not method as much as summer trips.

Also, be sure that your luggage is checked to Tokyo rather than to Hong Kong.

Another way to ensure the best deal in travel to Tokyo is to find an airline that few people know about. Often we fly Varig from Los Angeles to Tokyo because it caters to Brazilian businessmen (few Americans know of the business and cultural ties between Brazil and Japan—but they are deep). The plane stops in Los Angeles to refuel and offers just about the best service we've had anywhere. They do everything but give you samba lessons. And no one knows this secret—yet. Varig does not go on to Hong Kong, so you can't tear off the back half of the ticket, but they do have business and promotional fares that are worth looking into. They will put you in touch with a *wholesaler*! And remember, all planes headed to Tokyo leave from one of the four West Coast gateway cities (Los Angeles, San Francisco, Portland, or Seattle), so if you have to change planes anyway, you might as well get yourself the best deal possible.

Sometimes we call all the carriers to see how full the flights are; for the same price you might as well be on a less full plane and be more comfortable. Bargain shopping begins at home!

Booking Japan: Part Two

P art of everyone's preparation for a foreign trip is a visit to a bookstore. We own just about every guidebook ever published on Tokyo, so we have a few suggestions. First, you don't need every book ever published on Tokyo. There are truly hundreds of them. Because Tokyo is such a difficult city to get around, more guidebooks are written for it than perhaps for any other city.

think there is one book that is so far superior to the others (besides ours) that we heartily recommend it: *Tokyo City Guide* by Judith Connor and Mayumi Yoshida. It's available in most U.S. bookstores and in hotels and bookstores in Tokyo—in English.

Some people also like *Tokyo Access* by Richard Saul Wurman, with its plethora of maps.

Do not feel compelled to buy a subway book—it's a fabulous book and we love it, but you will be given a free subway map at your hotel (and by many retailers)—it's all you need. Save the $6 and spend it at Itoya.

If you live in New York, or are visiting New York while planning a trip to Japan, you might want to stop by the Kinokuniya bookstore in Rockefeller Plaza. (10 W. 49 St.) It is devoted totally to books about Japan (in English and Japanese), and you will want to spend the amount of your airfare just on books. Prices are high here; most of the books are available for less in Japan, and you don't need all these books—but it is a fun place.

We don't suggest you schlep a lot of book weight around with you, but we do want to point out that Japanese book publishing is very exciting and very different from that in the United States. You can buy gorgeous books, with a multitude of color pictures, for not much money. All the big bookstores have foreign floors where the English-language books are sold.

The Pursuit of Excellence

For centuries, the Japanese were quite happy without any outside interference in their island kingdom, but once the black ships arrived in Yokohama Bay, their lives ~nged forever. They very quickly became ~est shoppers in the world.

Thanks to the trading companies, products from all over the world are now available in Japan, and branded and designer goods are held in the highest regard. If it's designer, it must be good—and excellence is of the utmost importance to the Japanese. The Japanese, as well as people all over the world, have proved that they were willing to pay homage to a name by paying more for it.

That point has been made absurdly clear with the arrival of designer everything. Often the same merchandise is available with and without the designer name, the only difference being the price tag. Yet people seek out the designer name for the confidence it provides them. If you think Americans are designer-conscious, wait until you get to Tokyo.

It's clearly psychological: With the pursuit of excellence there had to be a way to measure just who and what were excellent. In Japan, everything is excellent. So imported goods of excellent quality gained in status because they were so rare. Name brands and then designer logos became a source of identifying the haves from the have-nots. With this social measurement came the pursuit of status. Status became the ability to prove that you had the financial wherewithal, and often the personal panache, to wear, use, or eat the very best.

Undoubtedly, the pursuit of excellence will lead you to many famous names and addresses. We find the true Japanese merchandise to be the most excellent buys in the country, but you will find all categories of excellence in this very competitive marketplace. We ask only that you evaluate with a steady hand and a businesslike head each purchase you make. Keep in mind:

▼ Just because the Japanese think the "name" is worth a lot of money doesn't mean you should. Many French and Italian designers who are ultrachic in Tokyo do not even sell in United States or are barely known here example, Renoma is a tony French tailor who some American men of upper-class wealth are familiar with; in Tokyo, the name Renoma is splashed over everything and appears to be an even bigger deal than Gucci.)

▼ You will not have saved any money if you rush through Tokyo and buy everything in sight, whether you need it or not.

▼ You can buy cheaply made merchandise anyplace in the world.

▼ It's possible that you can get a better buy in the item you desire through a private-label or unbranded manufacturer. Check it out. After all, how many different ways can they make aspirin?

▼ Fakes of everything—from Oriental masters to Louis Vuitton luggage—abound; you may get taken if you aren't careful. Although the Japanese say they disdain fakes, the Korean market in fakes in Japan is outstanding. With pressure to own status items so severe, there are plenty of fakes to be found.

The Moscow Rule of Shopping

T he Moscow Rule of Shopping has nothing to do with shopping in Moscow and a lot to do with shopping while on vacation, especially in Tokyo.

Now: The average shopper, in his or her pursuit of the ideal bargain, does not buy an item he wants when he first sees it because he's not convinced he won't find it elsewhere for less money. This is human nature. He wants to see everything available, then return for the purchase of choice. This is a normal thought process, especially in Tokyo, where every store seems to have exactly the same merchandise. If you live in Moscow, however, you know that you must buy something the minute you see it because if you hesitate—it will be gone. Hence the title of our international law.

When you are on a trip, you probably will not have the time to compare prices and then return to a certain shop; you will never be able to backtrack cities, and if you could, the item might be gone by the time you got back, anyway. What to do? The same thing they do in Moscow: Buy it when you see it, with the understanding that otherwise you may never see it again. But since you are not shopping in Moscow and you *may* see it again, weigh these questions carefully before you go ahead:

1. Is this a touristy type of item that I am bound to find all over town? Are there scads of shops selling this kind of stuff, or is this one a unique model that few other vendors seem to have?

2. Is this an item I can't live without, even if I am overpaying?

3. Is this a reputable shop, and can I trust what they tell me about the quality of this merchandise and the availability of such items?

4. Is the quality of this *particular* item so spectacular that it is unlikely it could be matched anywhere else, or at this price?

CAVEAT (*ichi*): The Moscow Rule of Shopping breaks down totally if you are an antiques or bric-a-brac shopper, since you never know if you can find another of an old or used item, if it's in the same condition, or if the price will be higher or lower. It's very hard to price collectibles, so consider doing a lot of shopping for an item before you buy anything. At a certain point, you just have to buy what you love and not worry about the price. After all, you are on vacation, aren't you?

CAVEAT (*ni*): If you are shopping for cameras, watches, or high-ticket electronics, you always will see it again in Tokyo. However, if you see an item in another city in Japan—or another part of the Orient—you may not find the same item later on when you shop in Tokyo. This makes comparison shopping very difficult.

CAVEAT (*san*): Because of the national need to look alike, buyers stock their stores with fashion merchandise that appears to be the same. As you examine it more carefully, you'll see variations on a theme. You may never see that same variation again, while you will see much look-alike merchandise.

The best way to decide on future purchases in Tokyo is to spend a full day shopping without buying anything. Do this just to judge availability, to learn to differentiate what appears the same but is different. If you have only two hours to shop in Tokyo, it doesn't matter, anyway. Just hit the Seibu on Ginza and smile. Moscow was never like this.

The Tokyo Rule of Supply

This retailing trick was taught to us by a retailing master at Mitsokoshi, one of the oldest and most famous department stores in Tokyo: Stores in Tokyo do not necessarily expect to make their money on the merchandise sold, because the competition is so keen.

In other words, stores provide all life-style services—including many cultural events as well as services such as child care, banking, travel bureaus, and optometry—so that a shopper will do all his or her business with one or two stores. The stores *know* that there is a finite amount of merchandise out there in the world.

You will see more merchandise for sale in Tokyo than anyplace else; however, the stores accept that you can buy this merchandise in many different places. For locals, the stores want long-term life-style business; for tourists, they just want you to be so comfortable and happy in their store that you do all your buying there.

Be Prepared

We thought we left homework the day we graduated. But the bargains go to the shopper who is ready to recognize them, and that means doing some homework.

▼ If you have favorite designers or targets of acquisition for your trip, shop the major department stores and United States-based boutiques (if in your city) for comparison prices. Don't assume you will get a bargain on every purchase; keep a notebook with European and U.S. prices of your favorite designers handy, so you can judge if the Japanese price is a bargain or not. If you don't have access to European prices, just write down the U.S. prices. It's no fun to get to the Chanel shop and get a headache trying to figure out if this is a saving or not.

▼ Do some shopping through *Vogue* and *Harper's Bazaar*. In the ads for the designer boutiques, you'll find phone numbers. Call and ask about prices and sales. Don't be afraid to explain that you are contemplating a shopping trip and are doing some comparison pricing

▼ Realize that you might not recognize nese designer big names (see page 198 because you haven't heard of a designer mean he or she isn't good, popular, or worth the price of admission. Few American stores carry more than a half-dozen Japanese designers, yet thousands of Japanese resources make incredible goods you are going to want to buy.

▼ The converse is true: Just because the Japanese are willing to pay a lot of money for a name doesn't mean that the name is worth it in your community. The relationship between status and big-name designers is based on the covetability of the name: If your friends don't recognize a name, then you have made a poor investment *if you were buying only for the sake of recognition.*

▼ Understand the licensing process (see below). The YSL shoes you buy in Tokyo are different from the YSL shoes you get in Paris. Both are fabulous—but they have different makers.

▼ If you are on a whirlwind tour of the Orient, know your goods, services, and marketplaces before you set foot on land. Are you wondering if you can get a better price on electronics in Tokyo, Hong Kong, or your hometown? The time to find out is before you leave—not while you are standing in the Sony showroom (see page 243). Tokyo is great for certain types of bargains, but it is not Hong Kong. You need to know the difference in what to expect, so you can shop wisely.

Licensing as Big Business

icensing is the selling of a person's name or likeness to another company for the production of goods made in association with the licensee. The licensee always is a ...turer, usually one you have never heard In foreign licensing, a deal may be available in some countries but not in ours. Therefore it's possible to buy European-licensed goods in Japan that you've never seen in Europe or the United States.

A designer will make his reputation, but not his fortune, in couture. But once the public is clamoring for the goods, the designer will sell his name to manufacturers who can produce and distribute his creations. Within this system, there will be a wide range of quality, of prices, and of merchandise. Pierre Cardin is the king of the license, with over 150 items with his name on them. Yves Saint Laurent has a bevy of licensees, as do the Girbauds, who are much newer to the game. Needless to say, licensing deals are only made with nationally—or internationally—known names.

The designer (or the licensor) may be very involved or barely involved with the licensee; sometimes the person whose name is on the item gave his approval to another designer's sketches, sometimes he actually worked it all out himself. How involved he is in the design process usually is secret. Since people are paying for the goods of a big-name designer, the system wouldn't work if word got out that the designer had nothing to do with the whole thing and just laughed his way to the bank.

Licensed items may be made wherever the licenseholder has his factories and then exported for international distribution. Thus a sketch may go from Christian Dior (who happens to be very dead) in Paris to a firm in New York that will send it to Brazil for manufacture. If the designer has a tight rein on his manufacturers, he will make sure that nothing is ever made that does not follow through with his design concept and quality standard. However, the bigger designers are running empires, and often they are not as careful as we would like them to be.

While designers obviously are in the licen game for money, usually they make their bu on the long haul—in royalties. Most li deals include an advance, but generally it is in the $50,000 to $100,000 range (it can be even less) and not the millions of dollars you expect. The millions come in on multiple sales because the designer will be paid 4 to 7% of the wholesale price of each item the manufacturer sells.

In Tokyo, there is a large demand for fashion goods, big-name designers, and high-quality merchandise. The working person wants to look like a fashion plate. Social pressure and status demand the best. As a result, there is a large market for licensed goods. Add to this the practical aspects—Japan is so far from the United States or France that it makes sense to make goods in Japan rather than have them shipped there, and the size factor (the Japanese body is smaller than the Western body)— and you'll understand why licensing is such big business.

Private Labels

P rivate labels are the opposite of designer labels but are now becoming competitive and exciting. Almost all big American department stores have private labels— many of which are made in Hong Kong. The private-label business is one of direct contracting, whereas the license business is one of indirect contracting.

The manufacturer who owns a license has to charge a higher price for his designer goods than his regular merchandise because he is paying out a piece of the action to the designer. The manufacturer can make that exact same merchandise and sell it without the label ▼ the logo and charge much less. He can put own company name on it for some product gnition and brand following, or he can department-store label in it and let the store take the responsibility for convincing the public that the item is of good quality. More and more department stores are going into the private-label business, connecting their fine reputations with the quality of the merchandise they have contracted for. Thus Neiman-Marcus can promote its own line of goods, which will retail for less than designer goods even though they may have been made in the same factory as the designer goods.

Japanese department stores want to do the same thing. They call the private-label business "private brands." Each big store has its own line, such as Mitsokoshi's Five Star, which is based on quality and design and is marketed to locals as an impressive alternate. Each big department store has an in-house label.

Japanese private-brand merchandise must compete with designer goods and has strict production rules applied to manufacture:

▼ the best ingredients in food with freshness dates on goods

▼ country-of-origin tags

▼ dye lots that match

▼ polyfilament thread because it is the strongest kind available

▼ exact color match of zipper

▼ no puckering in stitching

Exclusive Labels

Because the market is so competitive in Tokyo, department stores and big stores try to lure customers by offering exclusive merchandise. This is also done the United States, but in a slightly diff manner. In the United States, say B asks a designer to run a suit from the line in a different color, exclusively for them. No problem. In Tokyo, the department store will ask the designer to produce an exclusive item, or—more likely—the store will ask for the right to produce the items it wants and to put the designer's name on them. Thus while many stores will carry Oscar de la Renta, only Mitsokoshi has an exclusive line of unique Oscar de la Renta merchandise. This is endorsed by de la Renta himself, but you will not find it for sale in America.

Value-Added Tax

There is a value-added tax in Japan, and it is between 13 and 15%. It is refunded, however, only on certain luxury items—such as some electronics goods, photographic supplies, and pearls. The refund is granted automatically at the time of purchase, but you must fill out a certain form in some stores—particularly the department stores. This paperwork takes less than five minutes. There is no tax on antiques.

You will see discreet signs, in English, in major department stores on the counters or in some departments, advising you of the tax-free discount if you spend a certain amount of money. Usually the sign is on the pearl counter, and the amount you must spend for the discount is 37,500 yen ($185). This is not a storewide discount, as you may be used to in Europe. The discount applies only to the merchandise sold at that counter.

Camera and electronics shops are plainly ·layed in English to guide you to their duty- ⁻loor. (Usually it's two, but you can't this; once we walked directly to the ⁻loor in a noted electronics goods shop and came face to face with refrigerators only.)

Many stores refer to the tax-back system as a "discount." You may believe the retailer is granting you a 13 to 15% (this seems to be negotiable) discount because he's so pleased to have your business. He may indeed be pleased to have your business, but when he says "discount," he means value-added tax. Trust us. Use this to your advantage when you discuss price and terms and see if you can get an additional discount.

Store Catalogues

The catalogue business is alive and well—thriving—in Japan. All the major *depatos* have spring and winter catalogues that are much like American ones. Seibu publishes a catalogue that is the size of a small phone book, is filled with colored pictures, and can be bought in the United States for $20. (It costs $5 in Seibu in Japan.) All the stores have smaller catalogues that are free handouts, usually on first-floor counters.

The good news about catalogues: They have colored, pretty pictures of fabulous merchandise.

The bad news: All the text is in Japanese.

If you see something you want in a catalogue, go to the information booth and ask for directions to the floor. The price is in numbers you can read; this will give you an immediate idea if you are interested or not.

Charge and Send

Mail order is popular with the Japanese but not an option for you—unless you speak and read Japanese. Use the combination of *depato* delivery service (free) and hotel shipping to get your packages to you or your relatives in the United States best. While all the big department stores and many of the tourist-oriented smaller shops are used to international mailing, it will take a lot longer than simply speaking those magic words "Charge and send and thank you."

Customhouse Brokers

If you are sending home more than $250 worth of goods, or will not be home and have no one to accept your packages for you, you will probably need a customhouse broker to help you. If you live in a port of entry (New York, Charleston, New Orleans, Galveston, Los Angeles, San Francisco, Seattle, etc.), there will be a bounty of them listed in the yellow pages. Most customhouse brokers deal with businesses, so you may have to shop around a bit to find one that will take a personal shipment.

To make life even more convenient, many customhouse brokers also are associated with freight companies, shippers, and express package delivery services.

The customhouse broker will charge a flat fee, a percentage, or both, depending on what you are bringing in and for what purposes. Expect to pay a $30 flat fee to an express package delivery service and $50 to $100 for a broker who must go to Customs to retrieve your package.

If your shipment is being sent to you through a customhouse broker, ask the company you contract about the correct way to send in the package. Usually it is addressed to them rather than to you, then they deliver it for you. They do not like to store your packages. If the broker asks for power of attorney, find out why.

Packers and Craters

There is another service business that shoppers should know about that may be provided through your shipper or contracted for separately—the actual pickup, packing, and crating of your many purchases. You can go around town waving your charge cards like magic wands and then have everything picked up for you, packed, and sent home. You never even return to your hotel with so much as a shopping bag. Or you can schlep everything to your hotel and leave it there to be picked up, packed, crated, and then delivered to your shipper or sent air freight. Ask the concierge about these services, or check the yellow pages. Packing services are very popular in Tokyo; your hotel probably will have one.

Make sure you have insurance—this usually is a separate transaction and another price. Insurance rarely is included in the price of packing!

If you are arranging shipping, ask specifically if packing is included in the charge or i billed separately. For antiques, breakables a serious works of art, the actual packaging be quite involved.

Aunt LaRue's Packing Secret

Aunt LaRue is a master shopper—she knows all and sometimes tells all. When she travels, she, too, takes an empty suitcase—like all of us. But her empty suitcase isn't quite empty. She fills it with rolls of "bubble wrap." She buys the bubble wrap at a gift-wrap shop in Encino, California—but you can save yours from packages you receive during the year, or buy it at a stationery or gift-wrap shop. It costs about $5 a roll.

Anyway, Aunt LaRue, who often buys collectibles, doesn't do that much shipping because she has all her supplies right there with her and feels that her suitcases are pretty safe once her newly purchased items have been packed by Uncle Lennie in the bubble wrap. If you buy just clothes on your trips, you probably don't need this tip. But if you might buy something breakable and want to save on wrapping, packing, and shipping, remember Aunt LaRue!

Insurance

Insurance usually is sold by the package by your shipper. Do not assume that it is included in the price of delivery, because it isn't. There are several different types of insurance and deductibles or all-risk (with no deductible), so you'll have to make a personal choice based on the value of what you are shipping. Remember when figuring the value the item for insurance purposes to include the price of the shipping. If you bought a desk for $00 and it costs $500 to ship it home, the value for insurance purposes is $1,500. If you have replacement-cost type of insurance, you should probably double the price, since that is approximately what it would cost you to replace the item in the United States.

Shipping

S hipping from Tokyo is not as expensive as you might think but can be much more difficult than you ever expect it to be— unless you get everything back to your hotel where shipping becomes much less of a hassle. The language and communication problem will be so immense in over 90% of the stores where you shop that you will not be able to make arrangements you feel safe with. But remember, Japan is an island, and islands always know a lot about shipping. So where there's a will, there's a way.

If you anticipate buying an item that needs shipping, do your homework before you leave the United States. You may need a family member to claim the item at Customs if you will still be out of the country, or you may even need a Customs agent (see page 22). You will also want to know enough about shipping costs to be able to make a smart decision about the added cost of your purchase. To make shipping pay, the item—with the additional cost of shipping, duty, and insurance (and Customs agent, etc., if need be)—should still cost *less* than it would at home, or be so totally unavailable at home that any price makes it a worthwhile purchase. If it's truly unavailable (and isn't an antique or a one-of-a-kind art item) at home, ask yourself why. There may be a good reason—such as it's illegal to bring such an item into the country! If you are indeed looking for a certain type of thing, be very familiar with American prices. If it's an item of furniture, even an antique, can a decorator get it for you with a 20% rather than 40% markup? Have you checked out all the savings angles first? Are you certain the item is genuine and is worth the price of the shipping?

There are basically two types of shipping: surface and air. (Air can be broken down two ways: unaccompanied baggage and regular air freight.)

Surface mail (usually by ship in a transpacific transaction) is the cheaper. Surface mail may mean through the regular mail channels— that is, a small package of dolls would be sent through parcel post—or it may require your filling an entire shipping container or at least paying the price of an entire container. Many people make the mistake of assuming that the weight of an item will matter in the shipping. While weight matters, there may be a five-hundred-pound difference per price bracket! A piano may weigh more than two Chinese Chippendale chairs, but they may cost the same to ship. Surface mail may take three months; we find two is the norm.

If you're shipping by container but can't fill a container, you might want to save even more money by using groupage services. Your goods will be held until a shipping container is filled. The container will then go to the United States to only one of four ports of entry (Los Angeles, New York, San Francisco, or New Orleans), where you can meet the container at the dock, be there when your items are unpacked, and then pay the duties due. A full container is 1,100 cubic feet of space (or 8 feet, 6 inches by 8 feet, 6 inches by 20 feet long—big enough for about 100 pieces of furniture) and will not be delivered to your door (no matter how much you smile). Expect a full container to cost you about $6,000 total (without insurance) to Los Angeles. Packing usually is priced apart from shipping, so if you are not shipping chairs and need lots of packing, the container could cost you $6,000. The Japanese pack beautifully, by the way.

Air freight is several times more expensive than surface but has the assurance of a quick delivery. We can't think of anything that would have to be flown to us in the States; if it were so delicate and so important to need to be flown, it may indeed need an international courier, who is a person who hand-carries the item for you (often this is done with pieces of art or valuable papers). There is also an overnight air package service (much like Federal Express) that delivers within a day or two. This area is growing just the way overnight U.S. services expanded in the past three years, so check out the latest possibilities.

Here's a sampling of some airline air freight prices to give you an idea of what you're in store for:

▼ United Airlines Cargo: $3.85 per pound; $8.49 per kilo

▼ Northwest Orient Airlines: $5.14 per pound

If you want to price a few local freight offices, we have used these with great success:

▼ General Express Co. Ltd. (with offices in several Tokyo hotels)

▼ Nippon Express (up to 44 pounds): 03-572-0789

General Express Co. Ltd. has nicely set up offices in all the major Tokyo hotels (including Keio Plaza and Okura) to make life much easier for you. They will ship air parcel post, sea parcel post, and air cargo as well as unaccompanied baggage and overweight baggage. One of the best shipping tricks we learned in Tokyo is that people who buy furniture, or even loads of things, prefer to take a large additional package with them on the airpla Many of the leading antiques dealers will r for the airport. Likewise, General Express packs for the airport, and your airline will not be surprised if you arrive with additional items to check.

The problem with using air freight (or air cargo—it's the same) is the hassle. Businesses are competing for the same space and regular accounts may get that space before you. You must deliver (or pay to have delivered) your package to the freight office of the airline at Narita Airport—this is not the same address as where you will check in for your flight. The package must be properly wrapped or crated. You will be charged additionally for Customs clearance out of Japan and into the U.S.

We spoke to a representative of Nippon Express in Los Angeles at great length and he advised us to pay additional baggage charges rather than use air freight. A 25-pound package coming from Tokyo to L.A. would cost $118.73 (calculated at 180 yen to one U.S. dollar) in shipping (insurance is additional) and an estimated $100 to clear Customs in both countries—maybe more. Add on more if you must pay for "in-land transference"—getting the package from a store or hotel in Tokyo to Narita Airport. The most important tip he gave us regards duty—if the item you want to ship in is in a high duty range (most ready-to-wear and kimonos would be taxed at 30%), you do far better to bring the item in as baggage and stay within the $1,400 range so that you will pay $100 or less in duty.

If you want to buy an additional suitcase (you can buy a cheap one for $25 or have your hotel pack a box for you that will fly as baggage), you can take it with you when you leave and check it with your own baggage at a relatively inexpensive rate. Varig Airlines charges $72 per extra piece, the piece not to weigh more than 50 pounds. Northwest charges $77 per extra bag, not to weigh more than 70 pounds.

While postage charges vary, use these figures as a guideline if you are planning to use General Express and mails rather than airlines:

▼ packing charge: $10.00 a box

▼ handling charge: $10.00 a box

(Packing and handling are two different things; expect to pay both charges.)

Postage rates for a ten-pound box:

▼ air postage: $50.00

▼ sea postage: $17.50

For air parcel post you will be asked to fill in a Customs declaration that describes the contents and value of the goods in the box.

Overnight carriers such as Federal Express are becoming more and more popular on the international front, and prices are dropping.

Federal Express will charge you $125 for a 25-pound box shipped from Tokyo to the U.S. They have two offices in Tokyo:

▼ Federal Express KK 15-1 Kaigan, 1-Chome, Minato-ku, Tokyo (432-3200)

▼ Federal Express KK 3-1 Marunouchi 3-Chome, Chiyoda-ku, Tokyo (201-4331)

Both addresses are relatively convenient—the first is near Akasaka and the second is near the main Tokyo station between Ginza and Marunouchi. Both offices are open seven days a week, but have different opening and closing hours, so call ahead. Weight limit on a per-package-basis is 70 pounds; if the total shipment will exceed 500 pounds, please contact the office by noon on the day of shipment. You must have an export declaration on goods exceeding $1,000 in value or a U.S. shippers export declaration. All audio-visual commodities must have a commercial invoice describing the contents and reason for importation.

Don't forget that when you "overnight" something from Tokyo, it arrives in the United States on the same day because of the international date line. (But it takes two days for something to get to Tokyo from the States with overnight delivery.) Emery and Nippon Express both have built up overnight and regular delivery service—door-to-door. Someone who speaks English will be able to answer your questions if you call.

Unaccompanied baggage may be sent home whenever you want—you take it with your luggage to the airline desk and make the arrangements there. Often it goes on the same flight you do but is cheaper than being checked as an extra piece of luggage. Of course, if the baggage is going home and you're going on to Paris, it will not be on the same plane as you. If your returning baggage has no new possessions in it, tag it "Returning American Goods" so the Customs people know what it is. (They will still open it if they want to.)

Shop Ships and More

You can have items shipped directly from shops for you, but in everyplace we tried this (except Bingoya), the communications problems were so great that we gave up on the attempt. We found some museum-quality wedding kimonos on sale at a large department store and asked to have them shipped. The store was unable to find the personnel who spoke enough English to accomplish the task; after waiting forty-five minutes, we gave up. We ended up buying less and schlepping more. But because so few of a store's customers are American tourists, there is little call for good service in this area.

Several shops, however, specialize in the tourist business. We like some of them, avoid others specifically, but must explain that because it can be so difficult for an American to make himself understood, an entire stratum of business often is run by Americans living in Tokyo who enjoy taking care of the tourist business. Almost all the shops in the International Arcade, off the Ginza, ship to the United States and have help who speak excellent English. There are also Americans in the pearl business and the antiques business.

We don't go to Tokyo to shop in tourist shops, and we have found that by far the easiest thing to do, if you have time, is to get the department store (or boutique) to deliver your purchase to the hotel for you. Most do this free within two to three days. One-day service may cost $3. Once all your goodies are assembled in your hotel, you can arrange for shipping and insurance from there. All the big business and tourist hotels have a shipping department.

Try to pay for the purchase with a credit card; that way if it never arrives, you'll have an easier time getting a credit or a refund. Be sure to ask when the store will be able to ship out the goods.

If you want to save a little money, and if the item is of manageable size, consider shipping it yourself. Get the materials from a stationery store and go to the local post office. The Japanese mail system is incredibly efficient, and someone in the post office will speak English. There are neighborhood post offices just as in the United States; in Shinjuku, the post office is virtually across the street from the Keio Plaza, which means it's also convenient to the Hyatt and the Hilton. Japanese postal rates are listed in the Yellow Pages, an English version of the Tokyo phone book that almost every hotel room keeps for American and other English speaking tourists. For packages up to f pounds, the sea mail price is $14.50.

The U.S. Postal Service automatically sends all incoming foreign mail shipments to Customs for examination. If no duty is being charged, the package goes back to the post office and will be delivered to you. If duty is required, the Customs officer attaches a yellow slip to your package, and your mailman will collect the moneys due when the package is delivered to you. If you feel the duty charge is inappropriate, you may file a protest, or you don't have to accept the package. If you don't accept it, you have 30 days to file your objection so the shipment can be detained until the matter is settled.

Be sure to keep all paperwork. If you use a freight office, keep the bill of lading. If the shop sends your package, keep all receipts.

▼ Ask the policy for breakage from any shop that ships for you.

▼ Know the Zip Code where you are shipping to in the United States.

▼ Remember that you can ship unsolicited gifts valued up to $50 duty free.

Luggage Insurance

After you've bought all these fabulous things and packed them à la Aunt LaRue's famous bubble-wrap method, what would you do if your luggage were lost or stolen? Cry. Airlines do not pay much for lost suitcases—about $750 maximum.

Ask your personal insurance broker if you covered for this loss.

▼ Consider Safe Travel Network, a package offered by Bank America that costs only $5 if you buy your travelers checks from them and provides a raft of travel insurance (including health-related insurance, twenty-four-hour English-speaking doctor service, etc.) and pays about $2,000 for lost luggage.

▼ While flight insurance is easy to get at airports, luggage insurance is not. Don't wait until the last minute and then ask your airline for some extra coverage. They will not be amused.

U.S. Customs and Duties

H ave you ever noticed that when you get off the plane in a foreign city, you more or less breeze through Customs? Yet when you return to the United States, you may go through a rather involved system that may or may not include inspection of your luggage and a barrage of questions, some of them personal or even insulting? Well, if it makes you feel any better, all nationals go through more or less the same procedures when they return to their own countries. In fact, in recent years, the United States has been changing its welcoming ceremonies to the red light/green light system that is an imitation of the European system that's been in operation for years.

To make your re-entry into the United States as smooth as possible, follow these tips:

▼ Know the rules and stick to them!

▼ Don't try to smuggle anything.

▼ Be polite and cooperative (up until the point when they ask you to strip, anyway . . .).

Remember:

▼ Currently you are allowed to bring in $400 worth of merchandise per person, duty free. Before you leave the United States, verify this amount with one of the U.S. Customs offices (see the list on page 39). This amount does change (recently it was raised from $300), and if you miss the news item in the paper, you may be cheating yourself out of a good deal. Each member of the family is entitled to the deduction; this includes infants (but not pets).

▼ You pay a flat 10% duty on the next $1,000 worth of merchandise. This is extremely simple and is worth doing. We're talking about the very small sum of $100 to make life easy—and crime free.

▼ Duties thereafter are based on a product-type basis (see the list on page 37 for more specific information). They vary tremendously per item, so check out the list before you shop! (Look at the hefty levies on hand embroidery!)

▼ The head of the family can make a joint declaration for all family members. The "head of the family" need not be male. Whoever is the head of the family, however, should take the responsibility of answering any questions the Customs officers may ask. Answer questions honestly, firmly, and politely. Have receipts ready and make sure they match the information on the landing card. Don't be forced into a story that won't wash under questioning. If you tell a little lie, you'll be labeled a fibber and they'll tear your luggage apart.

▼ You count into your $400-per-person everything you obtain while abroad—this includes toothpaste (if you bring the unfinished tube back with you), gifts, items bought in duty-free shops, gifts for others, the items that other people asked you to bring home for them, and—get this—even alterations.

▼ Have the Customs registration slips for your personally owned goods in your wallet or easily available. If you wear a Cartier watch, for example, whether it was bought in the United States or in Europe ten years ago, should you be questioned about it, produce the registration slip. If you cannot prove that you took a foreign-made item out of the country with you, you may be forced to pay duty on it!

▼ The unsolicited gifts you mailed from abroad do not count in the $400-per-person rate. If the value of the gift is more than $50, you pay duty when the package comes into the country. Remember, it's only one unsolicited gift per person, and you cannot mail them to yourself.

▼ Do not attempt to bring in any illegal food items—dairy products, meats, fruits, or vegetables. Liquor-filled chocolates are a no-no for some reason, but coffee is okay. Generally speaking, if it's alive, it's *verboten*. Although you will be tempted to do so, do not bring in any roe from Tokyo.

▼ We don't need to tell you it's tacky to bring in drugs and narcotics.

▼ Antiques must be a hundred years old or older to be duty free. Provenance papers will help (so will permission to export the antiquity, since it could be an item of national cultural significance).

▼ Dress for success. People who look like hippies get stopped at Customs more than average folks. Women who look like a million dollars, who are dragging their fur coats, have first-class baggage tags on their luggage, and carry Gucci handbags but declare they have bought nothing are equally suspicious.

▼ Any bona fide work of art is duty free whether it was painted fifty years ago or just yesterday; the artist need not be famous.

▼ With Japanese-made goods, the duty may vary during a short period of time because the United States tries to protect its own industries from Japanese competition. If you are considering the purchase of electronics goods or gadgets, call your district office for the latest guidelines. Cellular telephones are just the type of thing that can go from low duty to high duty depending on the trends of the marketplace.

▼ The amount of cigarettes and liquor you can bring back duty free is under federal regulation. Usually, if you arrive by common carrier, you may bring in duty free one liter of alcoholic beverages. You may bring in an additional five liters on which you must pay duty. The IRS taxes you at $10.50 per gallon on distilled spirits, so obviously you don't want to go over your allowance unless you are carrying some invaluable wine or champagne. If you drive across borders, the regulations may vary, but it's unlikely you will drive home from Japan. (If you do, please write and tell all.)

You may also bring back a hundred cigars and one carton of cigarettes without import duty, but there will be state and local taxes on the smokes. You cannot trade your cigar-cigarette-liquor quota against your $400 personal allowance, so that even if all you bought while abroad was ten gallons of champagne (to bathe in, no doubt), you probably will not have paid $400, but you still will have to pay duty and taxes. Also, please note that you must be twenty-one or over to get the liquor allowance, but you may be any age for the puffables; thus an infant gets the same tobacco allowance as an adult. No cigars from Cuba, please.

▼ Some no-nos are governed on a statewide basis, so check your Customs officials at your planned port of entry. A few tips:

1. Asian elephant ivory is not allowed in the United States, but African elephant ivory

in souvenir form is okay if accompanied by a permit. Now then, if you did not make an A in fifth-grade science, you will need to know: You can tell the difference between an African elephant and an Asian elephant by the size of the ears (the African elephant's ears are larger). Most ivory sold in the Orient is Asian.

2. Tortoiseshell is a no-no—no matter where it comes from (unless, that is, it comes from a plastic tortoise).

▼ If you are planning on taking your personal computer with you (to keep track of your budget, perhaps), make sure you register it before taking it out of the country. If you buy a computer abroad you must declare it when you come in.

The Department of the Treasury was kind enough to give us their latest list of duty rates, which we are passing on to you in case you want to memorize it. Do read it carefully, since the variables are rather amazing. You pay this tariff after your personal exemption and after the flat 10% on an additional $1,000 worth of goods. We don't know just how much of Tokyo you're planning on buying, but here goes, just in case you need to know the tariffs:

Antiques: a hundred years old or older (prior to entry) admitted duty free. Have proof of antiquity from seller.

Automobiles: passenger, 2.7%

Bags: hand, leather, 6.5 to 10%

Beads: imitation of precious and semiprecious, 4.7 to 9.1%; real ivory (when allowed), 6.3%

Binoculars, opera glasses, and field glasses: free

Books: free

Cameras: motion picture over $50 each, 5.1%; still, over $10 each, 4.7%; cases, leather, 8.8%; lenses, mounted, 8.8%

Chess sets: 5.92%

China (other than tableware): bone, 8.8%; nonbone, 2.3 to 14.1%

China tablewear: bone, 11.6%; nonbone, valued not over $56 per set, 30.7%; nonbone, valued at $56 or over per set, 11.9%

Cigarette lighters: pocket, 10.1 to 15.6%; table, 7.5%

Clocks: valued over $5 but not over $10 each, 46 cents plus 10%; valued over $10 each, 70 cents plus 10%

Drawings: by hand, free

Figurines: china, 14.1%; if by professional sculptor, 3.4%

Film: exposed, free; unexposed, 4.2%

Fur: wearing apparel, 6.5 to 11.6%; other, 3.4 to 7.4%

Furniture: wood chairs, 5.3 to 6.5%; other than chairs, 3.4%; Bentwood, 8.8%

Gloves: fur, 6.2%; horsehide or cowhide, 15%

Handkerchiefs: linen, hemmed, 7.3%

Jade: cut but not set, suitable for jewelry, 2.3%; other articles, 21%

Jewelry: silver chief value, valued not over $18 per dozen, 27.5%; other, 8.6%

Leather: flat goods, wallets, 5.6 to 8%; other, 2.7 to 7.4%

Music boxes: 5%

Paintings: by hand, free

Pearls (loose or temporarily strung without clasp): natural, free; cultured, 2.3%; imitation, 12.5%; permanently strung/temporary but with clasp, 8.6 to 17.2%

Perfume: $3 per pound plus 5.9%

Postage stamps: free

Printed matter: free to 6%

Radios: solid-state radio receivers, 7.7 to 9.2%

Shavers: electric, 5.2%

Shell arts: 3.4%

Skis and ski equipment: 5.2 to 6.8%

Stones (cut but not set): diamonds, free; others, free to 2.3%

Sweaters: wool over $5 per pound, 19 cents per pound plus 18.5%

Tape recorders: 4.5%

Toys: 10.9%

Watches: mechanical type, $2.00 to $5.37 (depending on jewels) plus 10% on value of gold case and 22% on value of gold bracelet; digital type, 4.9%

Wearing apparel: embroidered or ornamented, including beaded, 12 to 38.8%; not embroidered or ornamented: cotton, but not knit, 8 to 21%; cotton knit, 14.5 to 21%; linen but not knit, 5.3%; silk but not knit, 11.8%; wool knit, 19 cents per pound plus 11.5 to 23 cents per pound plus 25.1%; wool but not knit, 13 cents per pound plus 19% to 31 cents per pound plus 21%

Wood carvings: 6.2%

District Customs Offices

Anchorage, Alaska: 907-271-4043

Baltimore, Md.: 301-962-2666

Boston, Mass.: 617-223-6598

Bridgeport, Conn.: 203-579-4606

Buffalo, N.Y.: 716-842-5901

Charleston, S.C.: 803-724-4312

Chicago, Ill.: 312-353-6100

Cleveland, Ohio: 216-522-4284

Dallas/Fort Worth, Tex.: 214-574-2170

Detroit, Mich.: 313-226-3177

Duluth, Minn.: 218-727-6692

El Paso, Tex.: 915-543-7435

Galveston, Tex.: 713-763-1211

Great Falls, Mont.: 406-453-7631

Honolulu, Hawaii: 808-546-3115

Houston, Tex.: 713-226-4316

Laredo, Tex.: 512-723-2956

Los Angeles, Calif.: 213-548-2441

Miami, Fla.: 305-350-4806

New York, N.Y.: 212-466-5550

Nogales, Ariz.: 602-287-4955

Norfolk, Va.: 804-441-6546

Ogdensburg, N.Y.: 315-393-0660

Pembina, N.D.: 701-825-6201

Port Arthur, Tex.: 713-982-2831

Portland, Me.: 207-780-3326

Portland, Oreg.: 503-221-2865

Providence, R.I.: 401-528-4383

St. Albans, Vt.: 802-524-6527

St. Louis, Mo.: 314-425-3134

St. Thomas, V.I.: 809-774-2530

San Diego, Calif.: 714-293-5360

San Francisco, Calif.: 415-556-4340

San Juan, P.R.: 809-723-2091

Savannah, Ga.: 912-232-4321

Seattle, Wash.: 206-442-5491

Tampa, Fla.: 813-228-2381

Washington, D.C.: 202-566-8511

Wilmington, N.C.: 919-343-4601

2▼THE BUSINESS OF BARGAINS

Getting the Most

Getting the most for your money is an old American trait. Our country was founded, for the most part, by people who left behind one way of life and started over— many of them with more brains and brawn than cash or credit. Value was an important ingredient in their lives. The Japanese also appreciate value. They equate quality with value, service with quality, and they bring new dimensions to consumerism. You can expect to get more than what you pay for when you buy from the Japanese.

And that is, after all, what we're all looking for. The search for value probably has been passed on through your family as a way of life. No matter how wealthy we may become, few of us feel good about throwing away money needlessly. You don't have to be cheap to be smart. In recent years, value has taken on an added meaning for the baby boomers, who have watched inflation erode their standard of living and their expectation of acquiring a piece of the American Dream. To the shock and annoyance of many of us, the simple things we took for granted in our childhoods may now be out of reach. The quality items we thought we were entitled to, that we never questioned would be available for our children, are often priced higher than we enjoy paying. The only way to get the value we think we deserve is through careful shopping—couponing, comparison pricing, and using sources who discount, who wholesale, or who act as go-betweens to sell off-price merchandise.

While there are numerous ways to stretch

the dollar at all levels of retailing in America, you probably haven't realized how much value your money has in Japan. This is not a political or even a socioeconomic statement, but merely the fact that because Japanese consumers expect more, we all benefit. The cost of living in Tokyo is high, but the cost of visiting Tokyo and improving your life with what you buy is very reasonable.

Millions of Americans now annually visit the Land of the Rising Sun. Although the American dollar lost 25% of its face value between the years 1985 and 1986, American tourists have not stopped to worry about it. Yes, some go to Tokyo merely for business, but tourists are learning that the bargains—and the value for the dollar—in Japan are dramatic and that Japan has become one of the best-kept secrets of the Orient. Some people (we won't name names) are going *for the sole purpose of snapping up the bargains.*

London, Paris, and Rome particularly have been overrun with Americans who are not buying touristy junk in memory of a European fortnight, but who came with shopping lists in hand, comparison price lists tucked in notebooks, and serious notes on how to buy quality goods at a fraction of their American retail price. Some tourists are also arriving at the realization that Japan is a wonderful place to visit. Tokyo also has bargains. It's not nearly as cramped with Americans (maybe because it's so cramped with Japanese) because the word is just slowly leaking out, but Japan is the place to buy and to save . . . if you know what to buy.

Your trip to Tokyo will more than pay for itself if you shop wisely. If you are the same size as the average Japanese person, you will be amazed at the amount of fashion you can buy for so little money. If you are a large-size American, you'll be amazed that so much fits you—even though it's marked "size 9." If you think that your size-9 days are way behind you, don't despair—Japanese designers provide clothes in junior sizes that go all the way up to 23. We can't tell you precisely what size a 23 is, but it's a lot bigger than a size 9. In fact, the only person who won't find clothes to fit in Japan is the American man with the body of a football player and the feet of a—well, of an American man.

Inscrutable Japanese Prices

e've found that there are three distinct price categories of goods in Japan, and seemingly they make no sense to the tourist shopper or the outsider:

▼ Some goods are twice the price in Tokyo that they are in the United States.

▼ Some goods are 30 to 40% cheaper than they are in the United States.

▼ Some goods are exactly the same price as they are in the United States.

What is going on?

Well, it's a system. And as you see how the system works, you'll know which goods are real bargains and are worth your attention and which should be shunned. "I didn't come to Japan to buy *that*!" you can tell yourself when you run up against the outrageously priced items. What you came to Japan to buy are either licensed goods (see page 16) or Japanese-made goods—everything else is priced too high. It's just that simple. Remember:

▼ Licensed goods bear internationally famous designer names but are made in Japan and sold there and are cheaper there than those same name goods in the United States.

▼ Japanese designer goods cost less in Japan, but not much—expect a saving of perhaps $50 on a high-ticket item of clothing.

▼ Japanese prices often are artificially raised because the Japanese *like* expensive merchandise.

If this seems contradictory and ridiculous, welcome to Japan. We'll try to sort some of it out for you, but remember: One of the secrets of the Orient is that it's inscrutable.

American Prices vs. Japanese Prices

Japanese-designed and -produced goods are more expensive in America than in Japan due to transportation costs and duties. Usually they are only 25 to 30% more expensive, however, as opposed to European-made goods, which often are 100% more expensive in the United States.

Likewise, American-made and -designed goods are more expensive in Japan than in America unless you happen upon a licensed deal. American-designed but made-in-Japan clothes can be great bargains. For example, Norma Kamali clothes are very hot in Tokyo and are sold in most of the major department stores. They are slightly less expensive than in the United States. Why? Because they are made in Japan. Furthermore, they are made from "markers" (patterns) contoured for the Japanese body.

Actual made-in-America merchandise must be more expensive in Japan than it is in the United States. If you find items that are competitively priced, they probably are licensed. If the shoe fits, wear it!

U.S. Sale Prices vs. Japanese Sale Prices

While an American sale is a great place to get a bargain, and nothing beats the finds at Filene's Basement, it takes a real Japanese retail fair to deliver the best buys on Japanese designer merchandise. While the Japanese do have sales, and two distinct sale periods during the year (July and December), they have something better than the sale: the once-a-year fair. The fair is where they sell all the merchandise that didn't sell at the sale, and usually it's held outside the store. Watch for ads in newspapers; ask your concierge to call department stores and ask about these events. Even if you are told that only charge customers can attend, go. Chances are you will get in. (We did, as tourists. We pulled no strings.)

One of the biggest differences you will find between American and Japanese clothing racks is the sale merchandise. While the Japanese like sales as much as we do, they like them the way the British do—as big, brassy events. They don't want items marked down too fast, because that takes away the status and cachet. And status is much more important in Japan than just about anyplace else in the world. In fact, Europeans and Japanese do not like in-store sales and rarely mark merchandise down by more than 25%. The British very specifically like once-a-year or, at the most, twice-a-year sales. The Japanese have their sales as one type of event and their fairs as another.

Both sales and fairs are run much like a circus. Under normal circumstances, the Japanese are tremendously polite, refined, and civilized. They bow to each other all the time in the course of an average conversation. At sales, they can let it all out. Shouting, shoving, and grabbing are *de rigueur*. It's a marvelous release for everyone.

Americans also love sales. But they want instant gratification. Therefore the manager of a designer boutique in the United States will mark down merchandise that is slow after two months. If that doesn't move it out, he'll mark it down again. Fall merchandise that goes into stores in August will not be marked down in Japan until December or January but will be marked down in America by the end of October or the beginning of November. Very often you can get Japanese designer clothes in America, on a second markdown, for less than they would cost in Japan.

To cash in further, look for buying mistakes. If the shopowner or shop manager has misjudged what his market will buy, he will be stuck with a lot of quality merchandise that he will mark down to just about giveaway prices. He cannot send it back to Japan; he must sell it to the public or to a jobber, and the jobber will pay him very, very little. The manager needn't have made a buying mistake to be stuck with merchandise—a trend that's big in Japan may fizzle in the United States, so the shopowner has to mark down his goods. There are not a lot of free-standing Japanese designer boutiques in the United States. In fact, most Japanese fashion in the United States is sold through department stores. This merchandise will go on sale with the rest of the department store's goods because it is expected to turn over quickly. Americans do not seem to be buying Japanese fashion at the same rate as American or European fashion, so a department store may well have overbought. Their mistake is your gain . . . on sale, of course.

American Sale Prices vs. Regular Japanese Prices

As a rule of thumb, the American sale price on the first markdown equals a 20 to 25% reduction in price. On the second markdown, the cut is 40 to 50% of the original price, thus putting you at the wholesale price, or less. With Japanese designer merchandise, the first markdown will cover duties and shipping, the second markdown will bring you to the "landed" price. Since the price in Japan has been artificially raised on these same goods, you may get a better price in America.

For the most part, Japanese designers are not as big in the United States as European designers are. Few Japanese designers have their own boutiques; most of their goods are sold through department and specialty stores. One of the best tricks to remember is that the store does not want to spend the money to ship its unsold merchandise *back* to the country of origin. Thus they may have very unusual sales. The first markdown may be a traditional 20 to 25%, giving you no great bargain. But after a second markdown, the store may go to a third markdown or a reorganization of the shop, so that the merchandise from a passing season is under a sign that says "50 to 75% Off" or something like that. High-fashion clothes have a very short life-span. Usually the shopkeeper would rather sell the clothes at a fraction of their value than have to store them or sell them to a jobber. Ask to get on a mailing list; ask for sale dates. Don't be embarrassed to be a "sale only" customer of certain famous names—stores value this customer when she is steady. Stores will seek your patronage when they have merchandise to clear out.

Japanese Merchandise in America

Many of us operate under the fantasy that if we see a foreign-made or foreign-designed item in an American store, the item will be cheaper in the country of origin. Sometimes this is true. Very often, however, it is not. In fact, you may not even see the same merchandise.

Consider this shocker: One day we were in Robinson's in Beverly Hills. We saw the Matsuda boutique and were drawn to it. We know Matsuda is a very exclusive Japanese designer, with the average item priced at $200 to $400. Everything in this U.S. boutique was very reasonable. A to-die-over silk blouse was $136. Just as we were about to buy one in every color, we remembered we were en route to Tokyo and decided to wait, figuring a $136 U.S. price should be $75 in Tokyo. Sorry, folks, wrong number!

Matsuda in Japan was as expensive as ever and far more expensive than at Robinson's. We later discovered that the merchandise in Robinson's is a special line made for U.S. customers and is priced accordingly. The U.S. line is "Matsuda"; the Japanese line is "Matsuda for Nicole." This is a huge difference, and the best bargain on this Japanese designer was right in our backyard—much to our chagrin!

The bargains in Tokyo very often are on merchandise you cannot get in the United States; so if you are expecting to shop in a U.S. store and then find the same goods for less money in Tokyo, you may not be rewarded for your efforts.

Japanese Prices vs. European Prices

There are two pricing systems on European designer goods in Japan. Merchandise that is licensed is less expensive than in the United States and may be less expensive than in Europe. It is also merchandise you won't find in Europe.

Imported European designer merchandise is much more expensive than in Europe and usually much more expensive than in the United States. If you've ever wondered why the Japanese tourists were having so much fun at Hermès, Gucci, or Rive Gauche, it's because the prices on these items in Tokyo are outlandishly high. The Hermès scarf, which costs $100 in Paris and $117 in the United States, is $200 in Tokyo. That's not even funny. The famous Burberry raincoat, the one that costs $295 in London—is $1,400 in Tokyo!

A genuine Ungaro ready-to-wear outfit that would cost $2,000 for three pieces (jacket, blouse, skirt) in the United States is $3,000 in Tokyo. Yet a stunning pair of YSL shoes (licensed) are only $90. To figure out what's what, look for the country-of-origin label.

When European and American designer merchandise goes on sale in Tokyo, it is marked down to the full retail price in the United States. If you get to a big bargain fair, however, where a second markdown is offered, you may get a good or reasonable price on European merchandise. It will not be returned to Europe, that's for sure—so check out the intense sale periods with these bargains in mind.

Markdowns, Leftovers, and Write-offs

I n the average life of a garment at retail, especially in a big American department store, the buying and selling process goes something like this:

▼ The retailer buys the goods in bulk at wholesale prices and marks them up the full retail price, which is the price on the tag. If retail is 100%, the wholesale price is "retail less 40%." A few stores use 46%. The merchandise goes on the floor at the beginning of the season.

▼ Sometimes the manufacturer will make a special group of clothes or items for the retailer at a special promotional price, so the new clothes will go on sale with a full markup, but a promotional ticket or an ad will advise that because of Columbus Day or Mother's Day or some special occasion, these special garments are 20% off. Invariably this merchandise is made in another color than the rest of the line and has something distinctive about it so the maker knows it is a promotional item. It is not inferior merchandise by any stretch of the imagination, but it was never intended to be sold at full price.

▼ Whatever merchandise has not sold after a period of time (this differs from store to store) will be marked down. The first markdown also differs from store to store, with 20 to 25% as the usual figure. The second markdown will be around half the retail price, or wholesale, so the retailer is no longer making money and just wants to get rid of the piece. If the second markdown is less than half the original retail price, the manufacturer is "giving away" the garment just to clean house. Few retail establishments go to a third markdown, although small specialty stores may sometimes use this procedure when large department stores would not. Large department stores would rather their customers not know they are eating the merchandise. A few large department stores have hidden rooms where they "dump" their unsold second markdowns and where you are free to find a bargain. Bonwit Teller used to have the "Finale Room" in their Fifth Avenue store; Giorgio's has a discreet circular rack in the back corner of the store where one may find a Chloé for $200—a fraction of its original price; Neiman's sponsors "Last Call."

▼ When the unsold merchandise is removed from the racks, it either goes to a jobber or to a warehouse, where it will be combined with more unsold merchandise from other stores. Other department stores sell to famous jobbers, such as Filene's Basement (Boston and New York), that take the goods to another state, or to local jobbers who operate small, bargain-basement types of stores and who pay often as low as $1 a hanger for the clothes. (You pay considerably more than $1 a hanger but not nearly as much as the last markdown.) In Pasadena, there's a store called Jerry Piller's that sells merchandise from many of the Rodeo Drive and Beverly Hills boutiques. Piller's is a difficult store to work because the merchandise is piled densely and unartfully and you need patience and strength to get through it all. Many shoppers don't find the bargain worth the price.

▼ If you deal with a Filene's or a Piller's type of operation, be aware that the merchandise may no longer be in perfect condition. The more incarnations a garment goes through, the older it is and the more worn it becomes. Also, it gets hard to find your size or to find a complete outfit—if it's sportswear or separates you're trying to match up. But on a piece-by-piece basis, you can get very lucky and find a piece of very expensive European designer merchandise at a very low price. This type of shopping is only for the very patient, the very strong, and the true devotee of the bargain.

In Japan, the system is only slightly different:

▼ Much merchandise is sold on consignment in Japan. That doesn't affect you particularly, but it does affect the way the merchandise is marketed. And because it can be returned to the manufacturer, the store does not feel an urgency about selling it or marking it down at a sale or fair.

▼ The trading companies control the buying.

▼ Because the Japanese do not like out-of-style, old, used, or damaged merchandise, there is only a small substratum to retailing. Of those stores that do specialize in discount clothing, the clothes are always in perfect condition—they just haven't sold when first offered to the public. If the Japanese want inexpensive or fake merchandise, they buy Korean-made goods.

▼ Japanese people know that the goods that aren't sold during the regular season will be available at an end-of-season sale or fair. They will do some private shopping at this time, but they don't brag about their bargains. They are so concerned with status that they prefer you think they went hungry but bought a garment at the full price.

Discount Is Not Wholesale

Discounters do not sell at wholesale prices, despite the fact that they may advertise that they do. This kind of advertising is geared to those who do not understand the actual retailing process. Discounters expect to make a 20% markup rather than a traditional 40% markup, that's all. They buy their merchandise directly from the manufacturer, just like everyone else. The pieces they offer for sale have never hung in a store before (although an identical piece hangs in a store).

Discounters have become increasingly popular in America—so popular, in fact, that now there are even discount malls where each shop sells a type of merchandise at prices equal to 20 to 50% below regular retail cost. Paying full retail price for an item is not an acceptable practice to a huge segment of the population.

In Tokyo, there are two types of discounters: discounters who sell electronics/cameras, and those who operate from market stalls. Tokyo shoppers know to go "under the railroad tracks" (to Ameyoko—see page 181 for details) for discounted merchandise. But they would usually rather pay the full price at a *depato* (department store). While many, many people know about the discounters under and around the tracks, very few shop there. They giggle about it as if it were a taboo subject.

When the manufacturer hates the idea of selling his leftovers to a discounter, he opens his own shop to sell his own leftovers. These are called factory outlets and usually offer very good prices. Max Factor owns a little shop in downtown L.A. called the Cosmetic Connection; Dansk operates several retail discount outlets all over the country. Factory outlet retailing is booming in the United States and is starting to blossom in Europe. It does not exist in Japan. While tourists are encouraged to take factory tours, these tours are to see how goods are made. Japan pushes its factory tours as organized events and even advertises them. There is no factory outlet as a reward for the tour; there is no place to buy merchandise at a discounted price.

The true wholesale price is the trade price offered to retailers. Generally speaking, the item costs the manufacturer X dollars to produce; he must make 20 to 25% on the wholesale price to stay in business. His markup is the manufacturer's share, to pay for expenses, overhead, and profit. The retailer then marks up the goods again, for expenses, overhead, and profit. It is almost impossible for an individual to buy on a one-item basis from a wholesaler (except at special sample sales in trade marts). That doesn't mean, however, that you can't buy wholesale. You just have to get organized. To buy wholesale in Japan you certainly need a translator and usually need to use a buying office. While there are wholesale marts, admission is by badge only. We have one or two strictly wholesale sources where you can meet the minimum requirement, but there are not many of these. (See pages 104 to 114.)

There are also numerous wholesale districts in Tokyo (see page 105) where you may or may not be allowed to shop on a per-unit or even a per-dozen basis; this seems to be at the discretion of whoever is on duty when you stop by. We have been turned away from some shops, granted shopping privileges by others. We also think that the prices charged us were chosen totally at random.

Japanese who have the funds to be serious discount shoppers fly to Hong Kong or Seoul for the big bargains. If you are on a tour of the Orient and will be going to these places, you may want to limit your shopping in Japan to the items that can't be bought anywhere else— locally designed and locally made goods. If you like seconds and damaged merchandise, you will not find much of it in Japan.

Temple Sales, Flea Markets, and Bargains

I f you like used merchandise, you may be very happy at any of the various temple sales and building bargain days held once a month or on certain days of the month. Because the Japanese do not like used merchandise (except antiques), there is not a large resale business. But tourists have proven there is a market in used kimonos, and locals have been known to do some of their best shopping at pawnshop sales, which they tell few people about.

A temple sale is the Japanese version of a flea market. Vendors sell out of cars, trucks, wagons, or on blankets from the street and sidewalk near the entrance to a shrine. The steps and main walking area into the shrine are wall-to-wall junk—and it is wonderful. There are no vendors inside the gates of the shrine, however, so you can shop until you're ready to drop and then find some peace and quiet within the serenity of the shrine. If you are truly blessed, you may be able to watch a wedding.

There is a rather strict schedule for temple sales so that everyone knows when and where they are; you should also check with TIC (Tourist Information Center) for their free mimeographed page of paper with all the temple sales and special flea markets for the month. Also ask your hotel concierge and your interpreter, if you hire one. Our interpreter, Uniko, told us about the most wonderful pawnshop sale that no one else seemed to know about. Not only was it fascinating (and a great place for fur bargains), but also it was held right near the Sumo wrestling hall, so we got to be tourists and shoppers at the same time.

Also ask about the monthly sale at the Roi Building in Roppongi. The Roi sales are less junky and more sample- and antiques-oriented.

And don't forget, every now and then you may luck into a national sale holiday such as Boro-Ichi or the Trash Market. This is held at the end of the year so people can clean out what they don't want to carry into the new year and can get money for paying old debts, as it is not nice to carry an old debt into the new year. The Boro-Ichi has a four-hundred-year-old tradition behind it. It lasts all day, from 9:00 A.M. to 10:00 P.M., and has various rhythms moving with the flow of the day. While a lot of trees and plants are sold, and there are many items you can't use, you can pick up used kimonos and a few knicknacks.

When you shop a temple sale, remember these things:

▼ No one will speak very much English.

▼ The kimono may be cheap ($6 to $10), but it is also dirty. For $25 you can buy a clean one in a plastic bag at the Oriental Bazaar.

▼ Bargain like mad.

▼ Pay cash.

▼ Don't be upset if there is some anti-American pushing and shoving around some of the better antiques.

▼ Dealers work these sales and get there early. They are Japanese dealers who speak Japanese. If you are serious about this kind of work, take an interpreter with you.

Standing Monthly Schedule of Temple Sales

▼ First Sunday: Togo Shrine in Harajuku; Arai Yakushi Temple in Araiyakushi

▼ Second Sunday: Nogi Shrine in Roppongi

▼ Third Saturday and Sunday: Sunshine City/ Alpha Shopping Arcade B1 in Ikebukuro; Hanazono Shrine in Shinjuku

▼ Fourth Sunday: Togo Shrine in Harajuku

▼ Last Thursday and Friday of month: Roi Building in Roppongi

The Trading Companies vs. the Bargains

Long ago and far away—in Japan, to be exact—there was the Mitsui family. The Mitsui family was very rich and very powerful. As Japan emerged from its isolationist period, the government asked the Mitsui family to act as a middleman and deal with the outside businesses—and empires—that wanted to do business with Japan. The Mitsuis became the first official middlemen. In 1876 they opened Japan's first trading company, also called a *sogo shosha.* Several other trading companies emerged—many of them with big names you would recognize, such as Mitsubishi and Sumitomo. The trading companies worked very simply and with one complete rule: Anything going into Japan had to be bought and sold by them. They bought from the outside and resold to the inside, to Japanese resources. Two things happened: The trading companies became rich and powerful, and the price of imported goods fluctuated wildly.

After World War II, trading companies were officially disbanded. But the buying offices have remained, and the system in Japan still works pretty much the way it used to. Thus if you are an American designer who wishes to sell her goods in Japan, you do not go knocking on the door of your favorite department-store buyer, but go to a trading company. Your success in the land of the Rising Sun rises and sets on your acceptance by a good trading company. It's a lot like getting an agent.

Selection in department stores is based on centuries-old connections with trading companies, as is selection in all stores. A trading company is handed down from generation to generation; there is no breaking away from it or from its dictation. There is little independent retailing, there are no bargains without permission from trading companies.

Seconds Stores

We all make mistakes, so it's easy enough to understand that manufacturers make mistakes as well. But in Japan, workmanship is an important matter of pride. Japanese workers are under cultural pressure to make fewer mistakes because Japanese consumers do not like to buy merchandise that is in any way inferior.

In almost any other culture, seconds stores represent a substratum of retailing. Manufacturers are able to dump their mistakes at outlets that sell less-than-perfect merchandise. If a thousand units go down an assembly line, one of them will not be perfect enough to pass inspection. Yet the manufacturer can rarely afford to toss out the baby and the bath water. Instead, he collects all those slightly imperfect items and sells them to a store that doesn't mind slightly faulty merchandise.

In the industry, this merchandise is called seconds, irregulars, or imperfects. In Japan there is no business in seconds, irregulars, or imperfects.

But there are stores that sell overruns, closeouts, and out-of-season stock. There are also stores that sell merchandise from other businesses that have gone bankrupt.

Family Secrets

The biggest secrets in retailing are the ones usually reserved for members of the owner's family, employees, and their trusted friends. Some of our greatest bargains in Tokyo have come from the kindness of strangers who have allowed us to participate in their employee sales. Simply because Americans were such a curiosity to them, and they all wanted to be friendly, they let us in. The Japanese seem to get a big giggle out of our presence. We, in turn, play dumb (not hard, since we speak no Japanese) and keep motioning to ask if we can come in. Perhaps we were admitted because the doorkeepers got tired of telling us "no."

You may also wander into an employee special sale and not know what it is. That's okay, too. But basically, it's simple: Once or twice a year, usually on a Sunday, a store or outlet or buying office will open up just for employees and offer them fabulous discounts. Usually these sales are timed to coincide with the two national gift-giving times (June/July and December/January). Employees are permitted to buy goods at wholesale or cost, a privilege they have only at these special sales.

Most sales are held in the wholesale districts. (See page 105.) But not necessarily. We went to one that was in the ultrachic Imperial Hotel. We just wandered into a gigantic sale of closeouts for Diamura—a large department store—charge customers only. The first time we tried to get in, we were turned back and told, in halting English, "Charge customers only." We came around to another door, asked if we could come in, and the doorkeeper bowed and beckoned. We bought plenty (paid by American Express, not store charge) and never heard another word.

Used-Clothing Outlets

Mostly, the Japanese hate used anything. There is no business in used cars (*gaijin*—foreigners—buy them, however—see page 221), and only small business in used household goods and clothing. The Japanese buy valuable items and pass them down in their families. Kimonos never go out of style; futons wear out and eventually are replaced. Life can be simple.

There is a small fashion business in used military uniforms and in American used clothes; the shops that sell these items are clustered around the train station in Harajuku. Don't forget shrine sales, temple sales, and sample sales at the Roi Building for more possibilities. "Antiques" from the 1950s are quite the rage right now.

Street Bargains

There isn't a big pushcart business on the street in Tokyo, as there is in Hong Kong, nor are you likely to find ad hoc retailers hawking their wares in Tokyo. Those who do sell out of trucks or boxes congregate in train stations (Shinjuku is a favorite), usually on weekends, or at temple sales.

The Japanese consider themselves smart shoppers (as indeed they are) and make note of dates and special sales—such as the once-a-month sale in the Roi Building in Roppongi. Their method is to pursue the bargain rather than to let the bargain come to them.

Newspaper Bargains

One of the best ways to find out about sales—of any type—is through the newspapers. There are four English-language newspapers in Tokyo. Most hotels deliver one under your door each morning. (It's free!) Each newspaper offers you at least two sources of inside information: columns and ads. While many *gaijin* may be devoted to reading all the newspapers, we made do splendidly with the *Japan Times*—which is the freebie the Keio Plaza gave us. We did buy the *Mainichi Daily News* once or twice and discovered a few excellent columns but it was not imperative to read more than one newspaper.

It was through the newspaper that we learned about the Takashimaya kimono sale. Let us first mention that in our research we heard from only one person that the most incredible shopping experience of her life was to be at this sale at a department store that was selling off its supply of wedding kimonos. A wedding kimono is very elaborately embroidered (see page 235) and costs upward of $350 to many thousands of dollars. Since they are so expensive, department stores have a big business in renting them to brides. Once a year, they sell off their used rentals. We got lucky in our timing and were smart enough to know what the small ad ONCE-YEARLY KIMONO SALE meant. The P.S. to the story is that we were able to buy museum-quality wedding kimonos priced from $50 to $150—a fraction of their true value.

There are several Western women (mostly British and American) who pride themselves on their fashion and shopping tips and pass them on through their regular columns in the English-language newspapers. Check each day and read the entire column, since many listings and items may be run together in long paragraphs.

Another type of advertising that's fun to read and may be profitable as well is the classified section. *Gaijin* who have lived in Tokyo for a while and are leaving, often have to sell their furniture and personal belongings or collections. Our friend Tilda bought two tansu chests from an American who was being sent to, of all places, Moscow. If you happen to be moving to Tokyo, you can furnish your whole life with the items sold in the classified.

Gaijin Retailing

There are a few advantages to being a *gaijin* in Tokyo. The best one is that Japanese think that *gaijin* are crazy. This gives you the freedom not to be embarrassed about your actions. If you ask for directions five times, the Japanese will not realize their directions weren't clear, nor will they think you are stupid. They will merely place you in that great classification of weirdo—the *gaijin*.

Most *gaijin* do not have the education or cultural background to think like a Japanese, or even to guess what a Japanese is thinking. This makes business negotiations difficult but does not particularly affect tourists. We try to use our ignorance to our advantage. We smile, we bow, we are dedicated to manners that would make Miss Manners proud. We represent our mothers and our country in the best light possible—but we also try to calculate the cultural differences and use our unique position as *gaijin* in our favor. For example, we try to gain admittance to wholesale resources by pretending to not understand when we are being asked to leave. We just act like aggressive, crazy American *gaijin* and stand back to see if it worked.

The Japanese are incredibly nice to *gaijin*, probably because we amuse them so much. Often they will grant you favors just because you are a stranger. Don't knock it; just bow.

3▾ TOKYO IN STYLE

Shopping Adventures in Trendland

E veryone in Tokyo loves to go shopping. All 12 million people seem to be out on the street, or jammed into the stores. But because it's recreational shopping, everyone is polite and calm, bowing to friends, laughing, and having a good time. There's even an expression in Japanese for this entertainment form; it translates into "cruising the department stores." The Japanese may like shopping better than sex.

Stores are open almost every day of the week, and Sunday is considered the peak shopping day. Department stores close for one day (see page 79), but it's always during the week, and they aren't all closed on the same day—so there is never any down time when you are visiting Japan. To be a good guest in Japan, you are expected to go shopping.

Shopping also is a wonderful escape from rush-hour crowds. As in any big city, rush-hour traffic is a nightmare. We tried to ride the subway during rush hour (after all, we are veterans of ten years of living in Manhattan) but made it for only one stop. It was actually a life-threatening experience. So what do you do after a business appointment but before dinner? Go shopping, of course. If you keep occupied in a store from five to six-thirty, you'll find traffic oh, so much better and your nerves all the more strong. (You could also go out for a drink or go to the movies, but we always prefer shopping.)

Stores traditionally open at 10:00 A.M. and close at 7:00 P.M. However, in the two big shopping areas—Ginza and Shibuya—stores may not open until 11:00 A.M. Stalls, like the ones under the railroad tracks, are open much earlier in the morning and later at night and catch a lot of the after-work business. Because most Japanese businesspeople are workaholics, they often do not leave their offices before 7:00 P.M., then do their shopping and head home. Many go directly from office to dinner or dates and return home. But their late hours are good news for shoppers—some stores are open until 10:00 P.M.!

A Short History of Shopping in Tokyo

We're not really certain when the Japanese got to be such great shoppers. Possibly it was in 1543, when the first Westerners arrived. The Portuguese were the first foreigners to trade in Japan, which also explains the tight relationship between Brazil and Japan. The ships stopped in Rio before they went around Cape Horn and up to Nippon.

Guns were the first hot items, and silks were the trading ingredient. After a while, the Dutch moved in on the Portuguese. Note that we haven't mentioned *Shōgun* once. But you may want to know that there was a true-to-life English pilot on a Dutch ship; his name was Will Adams, and he was the original Anjin-san. A few hundred years later, things got more serious, and just about every seafaring nation was dying to trade with Japan. In 1853, Commodore Perry arrived with his famous black ships and pried open the doors of Japan. The next year, the Dutch, Russians, French, and British arrived. Shopping bags were invented shortly thereafter.

A Short History of Japanese Fashion

The Japanese fashion industry is a relatively new one. While kimonos are ancient and glorious and make quite a fashion statement, they weren't considered the hot new look that ruled the world after World War II. As recently as ten years ago, Japanese fashion designers who really wanted to make it had to leave their country and go to the United States or Europe. Kenzo became the rage of Paris, not Tokyo; Issey Miyake first worked in Paris and New York before he became rich and famous in Japan. Likewise, the Japanese liked to import others as their fashion gurus. In 1970, the hottest designer in Japan was the American Rudi Gernreich.

By 1980, it was all different. Issey Miyake, a protégé of Gernreich's, was the undisputed international master of Japanese fashion, and a dozen Japanese designers were commanding the attention of fashion mavens the world over. As Japanese designs, fabrications, and creations became "hot" more and more buyers realized they had been missing a large portion of the world's creative energy and started shopping the Tokyo market.

Today Tokyo is possibly the most fashionable city in the world and is ranked by members of the fashion industry on a par with New York, Paris, and Milan. The boutiques of Harajuku are considered *must* shopping for those looking for the next trends, while the subways of Tokyo boast the most eclectic breadth of fashion as women in kimonos sit next to trendies with pink spiked hair and unlaced lavender shoes. *Vive la différence.*

Trend-Spotting

Many American and European fashion editors and designers come to Japan just to trend-spot. Indeed, in the past five to ten years, Tokyo has become the recognized home of the advanced, the avantgarde, the with-it, and the amusing. Experts flock to parks on Sundays just to see the locals parade—to get ideas that will translate into wearable fashion on another continent. In Tokyo, half the fun is in just looking.

While we can't go anywhere without buying anything, you may want to do what the fashion editors do and take in the visual sights and sounds of retailing and fashion before you decide what you're looking for. Several areas close off a main street to cars on Sunday and become a parade ground. Half the people go there to be seen; the other half go there to see them.

On the Ginza, you can walk the main drag (Chuo-dori is closed to traffic on Sundays) as the perfect spot either to mingle, or to go to a cafe where you can look out a second-story window and observe the panoply below. Or you may want to try Hibiya Park, which is across from the Imperial Hotel and surrounds the Imperial Palace; the area on Hibiya-dori stretching to the Imperial Palace moat is prime for trend-spotting. You may care to jog this area—which seems to be what everyone else is doing. In Harajuku (marked Shibuya on the map TIC gives you), you get the best of teen fashions in Yoyogi Park, where there's even dancing to rock 'n' roll on Sundays. The Meiji Shrine and the Togo Shrine also are nearby, so if it's a temple sale day, you owe it to yourself to be there.

With or without a temple sale, if you begin your trip to Tokyo with a weekend, a day's worth of observing may help you get the feel for everything.

Culture shock in Tokyo can be so great that you truly don't know what to do first or where to go first—or even what to buy first. You'll adjust most easily if you go slowly and spend some time just gawking. It's okay. It's even free. And don't feel uncomfortable about it—people go to these locations to be seen. (You may also be stared at!)

Tourist Information Center

After your gawking period and before you jump right in to boost the Japanese economy personally, please stop by a little storefront called the TIC—the Tourist Information Center. We are big believers in do-it-yourselfing, but Tokyo is very, very difficult, and you will need all the help you can get. The TIC is one of the few places where experts are paid to (a) speak English and (b) know where to shop.

The TIC will have a bulletin board posted with special events of the month. This includes a notice about all flea markets, temple sales, and special selling events. (They will give you a copy of the sheet if you ask.) TIC also keeps lists of their favorite shops, so if you want to buy pearls or folk art or a very specific thing and you can't find it in this book, or if you want more resources than we have listed, ask the TIC for some choices. The TIC does not editorialize the way we do, nor do they leave anyone out because of quality (like we do), but they are very friendly. They will write the name of a store in *kanji* for you to give to a taxi driver, or will telephone someone for you and get some information you may want before trekking to a certain location.

We always make it a point to visit the TIC on our first day on the streets of Tokyo (it's right off the Ginza, which certainly will be your first stop, anyway). The TIC is on Harumi-dori Street, near the elevated JNR tracks.

Shopping Services

The TIC does not offer guided tours or shopping services, but your hotel does. Because of the difficulties with language and culture, many people think they cannot go shopping without using a shopping service. (This is not true.) As a result, there is a big business done through hotels, which provide English-speaking escorts who will pick you up at your hotel and take you to the stores you request. If you don't even know where you want to go, they will make suggestions or take you to the department stores.

If this sounds like exactly what you had in mind, we must warn you that the service costs about $500 a day! And you pay for meals and taxis (or transportation). We use a translator ($150 a day plus expenses) named Uniko Harada (03-354-2822) when we are going to the wholesale districts or anticipate some heavy negotiations, but otherwise we like to go out on our own. If you're feeling wild and crazy and very rich, use a car and driver—but we don't think you need a shopping service.

The department stores, by the way, have some English-speaking help. If you are stuck, stand at the counter and insist that you need someone who speaks English. It may be a fifteen to twenty minute wait, but someone will be sent to your rescue. With a lot of smiling and bowing, you can probably convince the store guide to go to several departments with you to help you with your purchases and the paperwork for tax discounts.

Vending Machines

As you walk around Tokyo, you will be amused to see the snazziest vending machines—selling just about everything. The usual soft drinks are available, of course, but anything else that you might buy at your neighborhood 7-Eleven or liquor store is in a vending machine in Japan. Entire bottles of beer or booze are right there. Prices are excellent.

While you are checking out what the vending machines sell, don't be surprised if you find condoms for sale. This brings us to a delicate matter. We have never discussed shopping for intimate articles before, but here goes. While you're having a Japanese shopping adventure, you just might want to sample the Japanese condoms. The Japanese do not like IUD's or birth-control pills because they don't think they are healthy, so they have pioneered condoms which are much, much thinner than their American counterparts. We know people who go to Japan to stock up on this very item. You read it here first.

Shopping Arcades

A nation of shoppers cannot live without several shopping arcades. Most of the shopping arcades in Tokyo are not like the huge malls in Hong Kong nor like the tiny *passages* of Paris. They are one- or two-story buildings with thirty to fifty shops. Most are clustered near train stations.

▼

THE INTERNATIONAL ARCADE: If you use guidebooks to study Tokyo before your trip, you will see many mentions of the International Arcade—so many mentions that you won't believe this little strip of shops is the place you have been dreaming of. Located directly under the train tracks and almost across the street from the Imperial Tower (part of the Imperial Hotel), the International Arcade is popular with many tourists because of its excellent location and the fact that almost everyone there speaks perfect English. There are about two dozen open-style shops in this arcade. If you are a kimono devotee (see page 235), be sure to stop here.

▼

NISHI-GINZA: Under the tracks and at the corner of one of the world's busiest intersections, Nishi-Ginza has a mishmash of fashion boutiques—including a Benetton. It's much more modern and snappy than the International Arcade and feels like a shopping center in the States.

▼

SUKIYABASHI SHOPPING ARCADE: Located right over the Ginza subway stop and maybe where you exit. There's nothing like coming out right in a store to start the shopping trip off nicely. The merchandise here is more low-end than spectacular, but you'll find good resources for imitation Chanel handbags, glitzy costume jewelry, and some designer merchandise—such as Miss Chloé, which is made in Japan.

▼

ODAKYU ACE: This is either part of the Shinjuku station or part of the Odukayu department store; essentially it's impossible to tell, and it doesn't really matter. The Odakyu Ace store in Shinjuku is in segments, anyway. The Ace arcade is not Gumps, but it's a good resource for young, fun Japanese fashion. There are also restaurants and shops.

▼

SUBNADE: The day we got lost between My City and Takano (two *depatos*) we discovered Subnade, a shopping arcade that is totally underground and is partially connected to the Shinjuku station but is also below a department store or two (Pepe). You may enjoy being lost down here for an hour—we found Godzilla mittens here, and a few more cute and inexpensive fashion outlets. There are over a hundred shops in Subnade.

Train-Station Retailing

The ultimate shopping arcade is the train station. In many cities, the river is the lifeblood of the town. In modern Tokyo, it is the train. The huge work force commutes from home to office mostly by train. As a result, the primary retailing thrust has been at train stations. Many of the department stores, in fact, are named for the station where they first set up shop.

Each big train station has at least one of the mega*depatos* (department stores), and several arcadelike wings filled with boutiques. There are also food vendors, grocers, and newsstands. Anything you need to survive—not just survive, but thrive with dignity—can be bought in a big train station. Not all train stations were created equal, of course, but major stations have as many as three floors filled with shops. The shops are open from early morning until after rush hour in the evening.

Our favorite train station for retailing is Shinjuku. Shinjuku is such a major intersection that it has an east and a west exit. We have been lost here for hours, which is why we know it so well and can sing its praises. The Shinjuku station has about four or five major department stores with access to the station, as well as two shopping arcades on the west side. If you go out the other side (east), you'll bump into a major retailing part of town that is actually another story! Besides the department stores and the arcades (Odakyu Ace), there are three levels of shops. On weekends, vendors sell from boxes and pushcarts. Just about anything you ever wanted to buy in Tokyo is available in the Shinjuku station on a weekend.

If you are looking for imitation designer merchandise (made in Korea), check out any of the major train stations on a weekend. Ralph Lauren would pass out.

Besides the actual train station as a center of retailing, there is the immediate neighborhood to the station. Shinjuku has two neighborhoods—one on either side of the vast train station (east or west—always check the signs on the train platform and at the stairwells or you may end up lost . . . again). The Ikebukuro station is attached to Seibu but provides the anchor to a cluster of marvelous stores—including a Habitat (Conran's is the U.S. name of this home-furnishings store), a Tokyu Hands, a Parco, etc.

The essence of train-station retailing is terrain-station retailing—everything must be convenient to the station so the person who uses that station frequently can do all his shopping right there. Within a one-mile radius of any big train station, you will find everything you need to live happily ever after.

When you are in Tokyo for a short time, study the various neighborhoods and the train stations that service them to see how many birds you can hit with one charge card. Because there will be a large amount of crossover merchandise, you don't need to go to every area and every branch of every store. But careful planning of your day will ensure that you see the most without spending too much down time.

Faces of Japanese Fashion

There are two—well, actually three—styles of Japanese fashion:

1. traditional (kimonos)

2. Western

3. Japanese

We adore kimonos and discuss them separately (see page 235), as we talk about the traditional costume and uses for these items in your own fashion wardrobe. But the two principal styles are Western—the cut and kind of clothes you find in America and Europe—and Japanese, available in America and Europe but still considered a bit unusual in those places. The Japanese-style garments use fabric in a dramatically different manner—comfort and drape are important, artificial restraints of style are not so important.

You will find good fashion buys in both Western- and Japanese-style clothing, and you may soon find yourself combining the two looks to make your own personal statement.

The most famous of the European Japanese designers are Kansai Yamamoto, Rei Kawakubo, and Kenzo Takada. Kenzo, the best known, left Tokyo in the late 1960s for Paris, where he became an almost immediate sensation. He is now considered a French designer, but his clothes are available in Tokyo—of course. Rei Kawakubo designs in Paris also and is famous for the Commes des Garçons line, which she took over from François and Marithe Girbaud. Kansai has shops all over the world and made his first big splash in Paris. He is most famous for an appliqué Western-style sweater with an Oriental design on it, but he has branched out more so that his ready-to-wear now is sort of crossover Euro-Japanese.

Issey Miyake is the most famous of the Japanese-style designers. Although Miyake left Tokyo after graduating from college and worked in Paris and New York, his cut is the perfect example of what is considered the best of Japanese-style fashion. While there are other Japanese-style designers to choose from, if you have ever wanted to try the look, you owe it to yourself at least to try on some Miyake. No one drapes body with more soul. Prices in Tokyo are also about 30% cheaper than in the United States.

The Hot Houses

Not all the designers work under their name, of course. While it would be impossible to mention every hot house, we have a few favorites that you will automatically bump into in the department stores and that will provide exactly the kind of fashion and design excitement you came to Tokyo to buy.

Milk

Half Moon

Persons

Pink House

Studio V

Workshop

Melrose

Moldy Fig

Batsu

Zelda

Hot houses usually sell through little boutiques in the department stores, and only a few of them have their own shops.

Department Stores

If we teach you only one word of Japanese (we know only about four words ourselves), we think you should learn—and use—the word *depato*, which means department store. We say *depato* a lot because it's a great word—

it's shorter and handier and conveys the meaning of the phenomenon more quickly than the words "department store." Rightly so, the *depatos* of Tokyo are far more than mere department stores. We have done Harrods, Ka De We, Bloomingdale's, and Macy's. We love them all. They are single examples of some of the best department stores in the world. Tokyo has twenty-four such stores right in its metropolitan area. Then there's Sogo Yokohama, which we discuss at great length (see page 215), but that can only be termed a miracle of modern science and retailing.

We have interviewed a lot of American visitors to Tokyo, and an abnormally high percentage of them told us they did all their shopping in department stores. The department stores are wonderful, they're easy, they always take credit cards, they are Western, and someone who speaks some amount of English can always be found. From our own personal experiences on the street (lost again, found again), we know that department stores also offer a security factor in that you can't get totally lost in one building. (Although you'll be proud to know we have done it . . . at Isetan in Shinjuku.) We don't want you to spend all your time exclusively in *depatos,* but we do want you to partake in the visual, psychic, and spiritual feast that awaits you in many of the *depatos.*

One word of warning: Not all *depatos* were created equal. In fact, of the top ten names, each strives to have a different image to attract a different type of shopper or a different facet of the population. Of the big stores, there are flagship stores (the best of the fleet), and branch stores that may not be so wonderful. How you feel about a store may be directly related to which branch you visit.

And one other word: Hong Kong. Most of the *depatos* have a branch store in Hong Kong. The Hong Kong store may be entirely different from the Tokyo branch. For easy reference, check out *Born to Shop: Hong Kong* (of course, we wrote it), or stroll into a few stores to decide for yourself. But do not let Tokyo color your feel for Hong Kong or vice versa when it comes to choosing a *depato*.

Most of the department stores are clustered around major train stations; some of the department stores have access through the subway or train station. The Shinjuku station has five different department stores attached to it and is smack dab in the center of another five. You can get out at Shinjuku—do the whole neighborhood—and end up at Shinjuku San Chome; then you won't have to backtrack. Or you can start at San Chome and go the other way. If you are staying in a hotel in the Shinjuku area, try the first method. If you are visiting Shinjuku for a day or a half day, get out at San Chome. The stores near here will be of top priority to the others, and you may get worn out. (See page 125 for a complete Shinjuku rundown.) Ikebukuro is another popular area, and Ginza—well, Ginza is the highway to heaven for all shoppers.

Some things to remember about all *depatos:*

▼ They are open on Sunday but do close one day a week. All branches of that store are closed on that one day, but closing days vary, although usually they are Wednesdays or Thursdays. Each department-store listing in this book notes the closing day. *Please* make note of this day, although if you screw up, don't worry too much—probably other stores in the neighborhood are open.

▼ All stores take plastic. If you have a charge card from Au Printemps in Paris (doesn't everyone?), you may use it in Tokyo.

▼ Merchandise that has a value-added tax (pearls, cameras, electronics) can be yours tax free when you wave your passport in the air and say, "tax free" a few times to your salesperson. You will be given some forms to fill out for the discount, which will be processed right on the spot, although you have to turn in a copy to Immigration when you leave Japan.

▼ If you are not given a shopping bag, ask. If you want one with handles, ask. This can be done with mime.

▼ You are entitled to free gift wrapping. If you are shopping during the Christmas season and do not want Christmas wrap, tell your clerk. You can have plain gift wrap. If you truly want to take advantage of the wonders of free gift wrapping, carry a package of Post-It's (TM) in your handbag and attach one to each gift-wrapped package so that you know what it is when you get home, or when you go through Customs.

▼ All department stores deliver free. Ask about this service and make sure the delivery to your hotel will be within the time you are in town. Delivery may take two or three days. Some stores may make same-day delivery for you, for a small fee ($2.50 to $5.00). If paying a fee grates on your nerves, think of how much you will save in cab fares if you don't have to return to the hotel with your bundles.

▼ You can exchange merchandise, just as in an American department store, but must be able to mime the reason for the return. There will not be any damaged goods, and not liking it isn't going to wash on a return. Good luck. For the most part, the fact that no one will understand you will work in your favor. Be firm and politely insistent. The store wants to accommodate its customers and probably will make the exchange.

▼ Try everything on! Clothes sold in Japan are, for the most part, made with special patterns cut to the proportions of the Japanese body. This is great if you are a petite American. Otherwise, try on everything. Even neckties!

▼ For some uncomprehensible reason, there are no checkrooms in *depatos,* so you are stuck with your coat and your packages. Don't ask or look for one; we've spent hours working on the problem.

▼ On the other hand, Japanese department-store bathrooms are huge, clean, and almost luxurious. None parallels the old bathroom in I. Magnin in San Francisco with its antiqued mirrors and crystal chandeliers, but you'll find changing tables for your baby, a urinal for your little boy (yes, in the ladies' room), and plenty of toilet paper. One or two stalls will be marked "Western," which is the kind of toilet we are used to; the regular Japanese toilet is the stand-up-and-squat style. Many of these toilets are made by a company called Toto, so that every time we are confronted with a Japanese-style toilet, all we can think is, "Gee, Toto, we aren't in Kansas anymore."

▼ *Depatos* may have a grocery store in them and almost always have a gourmet-food floor—where cooked foods, fresh fruits, and international exotics (such as David's Cookies) are sold. Samples are given happily, and you can make a meal from browsing on this floor. Toward the end of the day, prices on perishables in the grocery areas are cut. Who said there are no bargains in Tokyo?

▼ All *depatos* have a floor guide published separately in Japanese and in English. Usually it is at the information desk, as you enter. Although we include many of the floor plans in this book, and floor designations do not change substantially over the years, you should have the complete floor guide in your hand. This is also very important in stores that have many parts, such as Marui or Isetan.

▼ There are people in the store who speak English. If you are having a problem, demand (very nicely, of course) that someone who speaks English be brought to the counter.

▼ Your receipt will be given to you in an envelope and placed in your hand. It will not automatically be put in your shopping bag.

▼ Bowing is customary in Japan. You'll soon get the hang of it and enjoy it. Bowing seems very appropriate when doing business. It also expresses thanks when you may not have the vocabulary to do so.

▼ Sales help is aggressively friendly rather than aggressive in trying to sell you something. As you walk by, the salespeople will shout "Hello!" to you. Many will bow. It can get noisy. Americans like to sail around and pretend they are invisible when they shop, until they want help. In Japan, it is rude to be invisible. Get into the spirit of things, say "Hello!" to everyone, bow, smile, wave. Pretend you are Queen Elizabeth.

▼ Shoplifting is unheard of in Japan. It is considered a terrible offense and will not be treated lightly.

Specialty Stores

There are only a few specialty stores in Tokyo, and they are as large as a department store in some American cities. Sometimes guidebooks lump the specialty stores in with the department stores, but we have separated them out because they have a different purpose.

A Japanese department store is a one-stop trading post that can provide every item you need from the day you are born until the day you die. Families often hand down their credit cards and the tradition of patronage. Specialty stores offer high-fashion merchandise and/or gifts without the cultural or gourmet services.

The most famous stores are in popular neighborhoods and will be part of your walking tours:

▼

PARCO: Parco is more a specialty store than a department store, but because it is so large, we listed it among *depatos* (see page 212).

▼

WAKO: Wako is perhaps the most famous specialty store—it is like the fanciest store in your hometown where you always wished you could afford to shop but never went because you thought it was too expensive—sort of like Nan Duskin in Philadelphia. Then you walk in one day and discover that you can afford a lot of the merchandise and that it's just so much fun to shop there that you can't imagine why you were ever so shy. That's Wako for you. It's right on the main intersection of Ginza—at the point where more pedestrians converge as they cross streets than probably anyplace else in the world. By floor: B1, tableware; 1, handbags/jewelry; 2, ladies' wear; 3, men's wear; 4, jewelry/crafts.

▼

LA FORET: La Foret is the center of the Harajuku trend-spotting world (see page 143) and is a must-see in Tokyo. It has six floors of designer merchandise, including a first-floor, drugstorelike cosmetics department. There are also scads of television monitors playing fashion videotapes, and naturally there's a fortune teller.

TOKYU HANDS: There are several of these mini department stores in all the right neighborhoods. They are devoted to crafts, art supplies, and do-it-yourselfing and are nothing short of amazing. Do each floor—usually there are eight or nine floors. (See page 165.)

▼

GINZA WASHINGTON: Some people call Ginza Washington a department store; we call it a specialty store. The idea is up for grabs. They only sell shoes. It's the kind of store you think looks very ordinary and might not be worth your time and then you discover it's the agent for Andrea Pfister shoes. They pride themselves on being a little bit different, and in having something for everyone. You will undoubtedly pass right by as you stroll along the 5 Chome of Ginza.

▼

HABITAT: It looks just like London! While it's unlikely you'll be looking for furniture or even table settings while in Japan—and Lord knows, if you are buying these items you probably want traditional Japanese ones—there is a large department store named Habitat right across the street from Seibu in Ikebukuro. It's very red-tubing-and-glass and open space and Conransy.

Cherry-Blossom Retailing

C herry-blossom fever is a national epidemic that sweeps Japan in mid-April as people anxiously await word of the arrival of the blossoms on the cherry trees. Newspapers announce where the first sightings are; newscasters report the score during the weather report. Gossip about where the first sighting is spreads as everyone becomes anxious to go out to the countryside and see the breathtaking blossoms. During this season, souvenir shops in the various southern communities where blossom gawkers come to gawk pull out all the stops and sell gift items to commemorate the event.

In fact, all festivals and shrines have their shopping stalls. Here you will find some of the best souvenir-type items offered anywhere in the world. If you are not leaving the Tokyo area but want to partake in this souvenir shopping, be sure to visit the stalls at the Senso-ji Shrine in Asakusa.

The TIC will provide you with a list of the festivals for the month. Most festivals have some fun-type of souvenir item. In December there's Hagoita-Ichi, the Battledore Fair, during which time these badmintonlike rackets with geishas on them are sold; they're fabulous. We also fell in love with—and schlepped home—several rakes from Torino-Ichi. They're charming on the front door. We hang them up each year for the fall season even though they probably have little to do with harvests. (Actually, the *kumade,* or rake, is a symbol of good luck.)

At any shrine, you can buy wooden placards on which you write a message. We've done this and prayed to return to Japan for more shopping, but also have brought them home for Christmas ornaments. We let each member of the family inscribe a wish for the year, then sign and date it. Over the years it makes a meaningful collection.

Some other festivals that offer some cute retailing gimmicks are:

January—Dezomeshiki/Grand Parade of the Fire Brigades

February—Tako-Ichi/Kite Fair

March—Daruma-Ichi/Daruma Doll Fair

April—Ohanami/cherry blossom viewing (also azalea and wisteria)

May—Ofujisan Ueki-Ichi/Mount Fuji Potted Plant Fair

June—Sanno Sai/an Edo festival

July—Suijo Matsuri/Water Festival

August—Omen Kaburi/held every three years; next, 1987 and 1990

September—Dara Dara Matsuri/ginger market; major event every other year; next, 1988 and 1990

October—Furusato Tokyo Matsuri/Hometown Tokyo Festival

November—Tori-no-Ichi/Cock Day (may fall in December according to lunar calendar)

December—Hagoita-Ichi/Battledore Fair

Souvenir Shopping

I f you are looking for out-and-out souvenirs and if the festivals have not provided you with what you want, try any of the major department stores. Several of them are famous for their souvenir departments. By far the best souvenir neighborhood is the two-sided lane of shops in Asakusa leading to the Senso-ji Temple. But if you don't happen to get there and if a *depato* is convenient, you'll find everything you need.

The souvenirs are marketed to visiting Japanese from out of town who subscribe to the old custom (*omiyage*) of bringing back a gift from their travels to their friends and family members. American tourists can take advantage of this tradition by shopping the well-stocked souvenir shops. Among the more famous: Matsuya Ginza (fifth floor), which is a *depato*; and in the New Otani Hotel, New Moh Long, which is a well-stocked hotel-type souvenir shop. The selection at the airport is not great, even though there are several minishops there.

If you are a businessperson looking for quick gifts, the airport will provide what you need— although we hate to see you overpay and your loved ones get such standard items. (See page 99 for suggestions.)

Pharmacy

AMERICAN PHARMACY: This is right off the Ginza. They sell products with labels you can read and will fill an American prescription. The prices are high here, but this is your best place to know what you are getting. The pharmacy is two blocks from the TIC, so if you need something, you can combine the two visits. The American Pharmacy is not such a great retail center that you have to stop there just to see what they've got, but if you need trust during a medical crisis or minicrisis, or if you simply lost your most valued prescription, this is your place. Hours: 9:00 A.M. to 7:00 P.M.; closed Sunday.

AMERICAN PHARMACY, Hibiya Park Building, 1-8-1 Yurakucho, Chiyoda-ku

4 ▼ BUSINESS AND MONEY MATTERS

Paying Up

Whether you use cash, travelers check, or credit card, you probably are paying for your purchase in a currency different from American dollars. You may not even be aware of exactly what an item costs.

For the most part, we recommend using a credit card—especially in fancy stores. Plastic is the safest to use, provides you with a record of your purchases (for Customs as well as for your books), and makes returns a lot easier. By all means, please take the time to write on the credit-card slip what you have purchased. In Japan the entire credit-card slip will be in *kanji*—you will not be able to read one word of it. When you go through your receipts, you will have no idea what you bought and how much you paid for it. Although your bill will have the name of the shop in English, this will be meaningless to you.

Even if you spend money as if it were water and don't care to tally your records, you will have trouble getting ready to pay your duties at your port of entry to the United States if you can't read your receipts!

We are big believers in credit cards for travel and own one (or more) cards from every bank or service. But the best bargains in Tokyo go to those prepared to pay cash for them.

Travelers checks are a must—for safety's sake. Shop around a bit, compare the various companies that issue checks, and make sure your checks are insured against theft or loss.

While we like and use American Express travelers checks, they are not the only safe game in town; don't be swayed by their clever advertising. Ask around. With check competition what it is currently, you should be able to get your checks without charge. Ask the bank you do business with to extend this service to you. Thomas Cook provides travelers checks free and in foreign currencies; Bank America has a kiosk in most U.S. airports for last minute help. American Express checks also come in foreign denominations. This is a big plus when changing checks at hotels or shops, because you will have a guaranteed rate of exchange. *However,* foreign denomination checks must be bought through a bank, Deak Perera, or another currency broker, who may not give you the same rate of exchange as a credit card company.

In our hotel in Tokyo where we changed our money, we noticed that we got more money back for changing travelers checks to yen than for cash to yen. It was only a few cents' difference, but it was surprising. There was also a small machine at the cashier's that tested U.S. bills for authenticity. Save greenbacks for wholesale shops; travelers checks are best in Japan.

Envelope Etiquette

When you pay for your purchase, the clerk will take your money or credit card and go to a desk to process the sale, just as in the United States. When your purchase is returned to you, you will also be given a small—possibly even chic—envelope. Inside the envelope is your receipt. The clerk will bow when you are given the envelope. As you accept it, you bow back.

It is possible that you will be given your

purchase without the envelope, and not expecting it, or not being conscious of needing a receipt, you will start to leave. The clerk then will stop you from leaving and you will wonder what is going on. Then comes presentation of the envelope.

The envelope provides plenty of space for you to write what your purchase is—to remind yourself later on. Remember, there won't be any Roman letters on the receipt, and later you will have no idea what you spent all that money on if you didn't write it down.

If you don't happen to write down the purchases and you do have a pile of receipts and a complete panic, we suggest you go to the concierge of your hotel to get it straightened out. Or you may look at the department-store logos and learn to recognize them, so that once you realize what store you were in, you may recall just what you bought.

Cash and Carry

If you must carry cash with you, use a money belt or some safety device. Even though Japan is one of the safest countries in the world, don't be foolish about large amounts of cash. We use Sport Sac zipper bags, which are large enough to hold passport, travelers checks, and cash. We won't tell you where we secure them, but our valuables are not in our handbags, which can be rather easily stolen, or around our waists—since this can be uncomfortable. We've heard of extra-large brassieres, under-the-arm contraptions, and all sorts of more personal and private inventions. You're on your own here—but do remember to take care.

We also find Tokyo bargains are best bought in cash—most wholesale resources don't do plastic. As you figure your cash allowance for this trip, allow for more cash and promise to cut back on credit.

Currency Exchange

As we've already mentioned, currency exchange rates vary tremendously. The rate announced in the paper (it's in the *Herald Tribune* every day, if you're abroad and want to know about your net worth) is the official bank exchange rate and does not particularly apply to tourists. Even by trading your money at a bank you will not get the same rate of exchange that's announced in the papers.

▼ You will get a better rate of exchange for a travelers check than for cash because there is less paperwork involved for banks, hotels, etc.

▼ The rate of exchange you get is usually not negotiable with that establishment. Hotels do not give a more favorable exchange rate to regular patrons, etc. If you have a letter of introduction to a banker, or have zillions in a sister bank, you may get a better rate—but it's unlikely and would take some personal arranging. While you can shop for the best rate available, you cannot haggle for a better rate from a certain source.

▼ Hotels generally give the least favorable rate of exchange, but we find some flexibility here. Hilton and Sheraton hotels have been giving the bank rate lately, without a service charge, to their guests. Each Inter•Continental Hotel makes its own rules, so ask at these hotels. Since we stay at the Inter•Continental in Tokyo, we change our money there—they pay almost the bank rate, and the lines are shorter.

▼ Do not expect a bank to give you any better rate than your hotel, although they may. We've generally found the best rate of exchange at the American Express office but the Keio Plaza was so competitive, we didn't care. They usually give as close to the bank rate as is humanly possible.

▼ Don't change money (or a lot of it, anyway) at airport vendors because they will have the worst rates in town; yes, higher than your hotel.

▼ If you want to change money back to dollars when you leave a country, remember that you will pay a higher rate for them. You are now "buying" dollars rather than "selling" them. Therefore, never change more money than you think you will need, unless you stockpile for another trip.

▼ Have some foreign currency on hand for arrivals. After a lengthy transpacific flight, you will not want to stand in line at some airport booth to get your cab fare. You'll pay a very high rate of exchange and be wasting your precious bathtub time. Your home bank or local currency exchange office can sell you small amounts of foreign currency. No matter how much of a premium you pay for this money, the convenience will be worth it. We ask for $50 worth of currency for each country we are visiting. This will pay for the bus to the hotel, tips, and the immediate necessities until you decide where to change the rest of your money. Happy announcement: If your hotel picks you up at the airport, they will charge your room for this service, so you won't need money changed.

▼ On the other end, when you leave, save money for the departure tax, which must be paid in yen, not American dollars. The departure tax—2,300 yen—is very high. If you have several members of your family traveling with you, be sure you have enough money to cover this expense. They do not take credit cards. (Figure you need $13 per person, in yen though.)

▼ Keep track of what you pay for your currency. If you are going to several countries, or you must make several money-changing trips to the cashier, write down the sums. When you get home and wonder what you did with all the money you used to have, it'll be easier to trace your cash. When you are budgeting, adjust to the rate you paid for the money, not the rate you read in the newspaper. *Do not* be embarrassed if you are confused by rates and various denominations. Learn as much as you can, and ask for help. Take time to count your change, and understand what has been placed in your hand. The people you are dealing with already know you are an American (for the most part, they can tell just from looking at you), so feel satisfied that you understand each financial transaction. In some cases, the numbers you will be dealing with are so astronomical that it will be hard for you to adjust to the mathematical gymnastics you will have to perform to know how much you have paid for an item in U.S. terms and to count your change.

▼ Be prepared to make mathematical errors; translate a price twice before you decide to buy something. We bought a handbag that we thought was a steal for $35 only to discover much later that it cost $350. We got confused with the zeroes!

▼ Make mental comparative rates for quick price reactions. Know the conversion rate for $50 and $100 so within an instant you can make a judgment. If you're still interested in an item, slow down and figure out the accurate price. Otherwise you may be sorry later— and poorer.

▼ Changing money can be quite a rigamarole. We went to one bank in the Ginza area but left when we saw the sign, in English, that said "changing money—allow two hours." We changed at another bank but spent forty-five minutes waiting. Your hotel may charge a few cents more for changing money; but if there isn't a line, take advantage of the situation.

▾ Don't forget to bow after the exchange takes place.

How to Get Cash Overseas

We've run out of cash on more international trips than we like to admit (to ourselves or to our husbands, who happen to think that only women run out of cash). This happens to us not so much due to our inability to budget properly but because of our patriotic feelings in wanting to rescue a sagging economy by buying more and more goods. Besides, men run out of money, too.

If you do run out of money, know where to turn so you can do so during business hours. Holidays, weekends, and late nights are not good times to be without funds. If you think you can sail into your deluxe hotel and present your credit card at the cashier for an instant injection of cash or the redemption of a personal check from your U.S. bank, think again. Despite misleading ads to the contrary, American Express gold cards do not bring the respect you want when you are in this ticklish situation. The people who are most anxious to see your American Express card (be it gold, platinum, or plain old adorable green) are the people at American Express. Go there for quick cash. Green-card members may draw up to $1,000; gold cards can get $2,000; platinum cards, $5,000. You may also cash a check there. *(Never travel without your checkbook.)*

It's all a relatively simple transaction—you write a personal check at a special desk and show your card; it is approved; you go to another desk and get the money in the currency you request. Allow about a half hour for the whole process, unless there are long lines. Usually you get the credit advance on your card at the same desk.

Bank cash machines are extremely popular in Tokyo and are used by the population to perform all sorts of tasks. Many retailers do not understand your reluctance (or inability) to place your bank card in their machines for an infusion of cash. If you think you may want to try this, ask your banker if your card can be used in a Japanese cash-back machine. (It's unlikely, unless you use a Japanese-American bank.)

But you may be able to use your bank card at a bank. Bank cards usually allow you to withdraw the rest of your credit line through their participating banks. (If you are able, pay off your balance on your bank cards before you leave home, giving you maximum purchase and rescue power on the trip.)

It's unlikely that your hotel will take your personal check, unless they know you very, very, very well and you are (a) famous, or (b) rich, rich, rich, or (c) *both*. Be prepared to cry, whine, or go to extraordinary lengths to get your hotel to provide this service.

Many hotel and frequent-flier clubs offer check-cashing privileges; you need to be a member of this club (such as Six Continents Club, a division of Inter•Continental Hotels) to cash a personal check. Having flown a specific carrier or having booked a room in a certain hotel chain may not be enough.

You can have money sent to you from home, a process that usually takes about two days. Money can be wired through Western Union (someone brings them the cash or a certified check, and Western Union does the rest—this may take up to a week) or through an international money order, which is cleared by telex through the bank where you cash it. Money can be wired from bank to bank, but this is only a simple process with major banks from big cities that have Japanese branches or sister banks. Banks usually charge a nice fat fee for doing you this favor. If you have a letter of credit, however, and a corresponding bank that is expecting you, you will have little difficulty getting your hands on some extra green . . . or pink or blue or orange.

In an emergency, the U.S. embassy may lend you money. You must repay this money. (There's no such thing as a free lunch.)

Banking Abroad

As ridiculous as it sounds at first, it just may be very convenient for you to have a foreign bank account. We are not talking about a secret Swiss account for stashing cash so you don't have to pay taxes on it or commingle it with your husband's money. If you travel to a specific city (or even a country) often, it may make life easier to have a checking account there. Ask your own bank about making these arrangements. There are also Japanese banks that do business in the United States and Japan and allow you to open accounts in both countries—it's a new twist on being bicoastal.

Foreign bank accounts must be reported to the IRS.

Living Expenses

Tokyo got its reputation as an expensive place to visit because the cost of living is so high there. The things that are expensive, however, are food and taxis. Take public transportation (you can buy a "one-day, free-ride" card, which enables you to use the subway for an unlimited number of stops in a one-day period—but you cannot use the card on the JNR). If you are staying in Shinjuku you may not find the free-ride card a bargain because you probably will take the train more than the subway. Avoid high-priced restaurants and snacks. Investigate a coffee shop near your hotel—breakfast may be half the price your hotel charges. Numerous food stands all over town offer less expensive meals. Going to a noodle restaurant is an inexpensive way of eating a sit-down meal. We try to live modestly in Tokyo so we can spend our money on clothes. If you are not careful about living expenses, you may indeed find your shopping budget is literally being eaten away.

Keeping Track

We have found keeping track of finances more difficult in Japan than in almost any other country we have ever lived in. This is partially because we can't read anything, and also because of all the zeroes in the bills and a little bit because the touchstone of figuring money seems to be the 500-yen piece. We went through a hell of a lot of 500-yen pieces before we realized we were buying things for an amount we would consider *cher* in the United States. The 500-yen piece looks and feels like a 50-cent piece, and if you find yourself spending it with the same abandon, you'll be broke in no time at all. Five hundred yen are approximately $4—and when you start tossing this amount around as if it were potato chips, you'll have spent a lot of money in silly ways without knowing how, when, why, or where.

We started using notebooks to write down all our expenses—from taxis and Cokes, which are very expensive, to gifts and finds, which were not particularly expensive. Scrutinize your under-1,000-yen expenditures. Not only does this help you figure out how you spent your money and what to pay duty on, but it also provides an instant outline of the bargains of Tokyo. You'll cut back on meals and gewgaws in favor of buying shoes in no time at all.

One More Calculating Thought

Unless you have a Ph.D. in mathematics from M.I.T., we suggest you keep a calculator in your purse at all times. Furthermore, it should be the kind that uses batteries. Solar-run calculators are very cute, but your purse is dark inside, and many shops are, too. There's nothing worse than trying to do a hard bit of negotiating when your calculator won't calculate. If you use your calculator frequently, or your children like to play with it as a toy, buy new batteries before you leave on the trip.

If you've left your calculator at home, not to fret. You've come to the right place. You can buy a new one for about $10.

Tokyo on Business

A large number of Tokyo's visitors are businesspeople who arrive at Narita Airport—bus into Tokyo, hole up in a hotel, and do little except go to meetings, be entertained at night, bus back to Narita, and fly home. Usually they beg off an hour or two to go shopping.

While this scenario happens all over the world, it is especially prevalent in Tokyo because businesspeople are so wary of getting lost, wasting time, or being stranded and feeling foolish. Many businesspeople who could get out more, don't—merely because they are afraid.

Sadly, most businesspeople shop at the airport. Or at *depatos*. *Depatos* are perfect for this customer, of course, but they offer little of the true Japan. For the businessperson who has an hour or two—even a lunch break—we have an alternate suggestion, and it's foolproof. Take the JNR to Ueno and go to the area fondly referred to as "under the train tracks." See page 181 for details and tour information, but trust us—this market area is the least expensive place to shop in Tokyo and offers much the same merchandise as the *depatos* with a lot of local color thrown in. Don't leave Tokyo without trying it.

If you are buying gifts, you'll find everything you need right here; although it's not one of our better sources for quality pearls, you can buy just about everything else. Cameras, film, videotape, electronic toys are at Yodabashi Camera—the largest discount chain in Tokyo. Ready-to-wear for children and teens is sold from almost every booth. Branded and unbranded toys are available. A street salesman roamed up and down hawking watches—the ones that say "Rolex" on the front and "Made in Taiwan" on the back (rather good fakes—$50!). You can grab a bite at a noodle shop or a coffee shop, even buy an extra suitcase to haul everything home in.

If you've got the time, you may want to cross the street and walk through Ueno Park—the Tokyo version of the Tuileries. There's a zoo and several fine museums, or you can just walk and enjoy the trees, the fountains, and the singing of birds—something you don't hear from your hotel window. The stores here are open until about 8:00 to 9:00 P.M., so you can visit after work, which is what the locals do. It gets crowded, but that's part of the fun.

The Ueno station is also filled with souvenir shops that sell traditional curios; other train stations do not have all these souvenir booths.

Business Gifts

Those going to Tokyo for business are well aware of the custom of gift-giving and usually pack gifts with them. We heard of one American man who actually brought a suitcase with a hundred individually wrapped small presents, since he expected to call on approximately fifty different accounts. He wanted a gift for his contact and a gift in case he was introduced to a higher-up.

The gift you bring to a businessperson, especially one you do not know, should be nicely wrapped (wrapping is more important than content) and should represent your hometown or home state in some way. Souvenir items are perfectly acceptable. Food items are very much appreciated. Brands are particularly important, and well-known famous names are appreciated. Even if the gift is mundane (a jar of jam from Knott's Berry Farm, for example)—if it's from a well-known place, it has more status and value. (A&P is not considered a well-known place.)

If your trip to Japan is planned well in advance and you need a large number of gifts, you may want to investigate buying wholesale by the dozen. A minimum order may be three or four dozen, but that's still under fifty gifts, and the saving can be 50%. Make sure you will get delivery before you plan to leave. Even status stores such as Tiffany's offer discounts on large corporate orders.

Should you get to Tokyo and discover that you need business gifts, you will have no problem finding them—*depatos* offer a wide range of items. Unfortunately, American-made items will be the most costly. You have the option of buying an American brand, paying an arm and a leg for it, and eating the loss while you claim to have brought the gift from the United States, or you can buy a local product. One of the most common business gifts is fresh fruit—there are stores that sell giftable edibles, many at outrageous prices ($20 for a melon), but many at reasonable prices. Liquor also is considered a suitable gift.

The gift you bring does not have to be as expensive as it should be well presented and thoughtful. We always give calendars when we visit Tokyo in the fall; we give jam jars in baskets in spring. We spend about $6 per gift and almost fifteen minutes of wrapping time per gift.

Business Cards

Yes, you will need business cards in Tokyo. You may even want to have some made in Japanese. (Some of the airlines do this as a promotional sideline.) One of the newest things in American business cards is the card with your photo on it—this is quite a novelty to Japanese businesspeople.

Gift Items

Businessmen and women visiting Tokyo invariably decide to buy pearls for their wives and sweethearts (sometimes both) or themselves. There's no question that you will get better-quality pearls in Japan than in the United States. There's also no question that you have a better chance of not getting ripped off if you buy in Japan rather than in Hong Kong. (See page 263 for our complete primer on pearls.) One tip: We buy divine faux pearls from Giorgio, Beverly Hills—$100 for 10mm, matinee length.

We think the best buys in women's gift items are in shoes and leathergoods, so if you're not buying pearls and don't trust yourself to buy high fashion, check out the handbags in any of the boutiques or department stores. Stunning choices begin at $30—and we're talking bags that look like they would retail for $150 to $200 in the United States. Shoes are a more difficult gift choice.

Children usually want toys—they can be found "under the tracks" or in *depatos*. Don't forget to check out the hobby floor of a department store—the products for sale there are nothing short of amazing. (See page 223 for "Children and Toys.") Teen fashion is readily available "under the tracks" at discount prices. Teens are the easiest to buy for because young Japanese fashion is very fad-oriented, so you'll find scads of choices of whatever is hip and you don't have to be tuned in to the teen culture to know what you want—you'll see it parading by on the streets and in the subways.

If electronics are a must-see, must-do (don't,

if you ask us), see page 243 for the lowdown.

Kimonos are available in many types of stores, but we remind you that what you probably want as a gift item is a *hakata*—a cotton kimono that makes a great bathrobe. A real kimono, made of silk, costs $150 and up. Please stay away from tourist kimonos; they make us sad (not *happi*). *Happi* coats also are good gifts. Cotton *hakata* or *happi* coats cost about $20. If you do indeed want a fine kimono, we suggest a used wedding kimono. You may find one for the startlingly low price of $25. Good-quality kimonos cost about $150 (used, that is). See page 235 for more information.

Should you not find the gift of your dreams, you may want to drive directly from the airport to your local discount electronics store to find an American version of an Oriental bargain you will enjoy more than a Japanese nonbargain. *Ahsodeskah.*

5 ▾ WHOLESALE IN TOKYO

Wholesale Is Wholesome

F or all those naysayers who pooh-pooh the cost of living in Tokyo, we have one word to say: *bashi.*

Bashi, when used in an address, is the word for bridge in Japanese. For obvious reasons, all the wholesale markets are located near bridges (like water brings boats, boats bring trade—elementary, dear Watson), and the names of the districts very often end with the suffix *bashi*. We have even come to call the multitude of Tokyo wholesale districts the *bashis,* even though no one else knows what we are talking about.

Just as there are wholesale districts in every large city, there are various areas of Tokyo that specialize in selling to the trade. Many of them are open on weekends. They do a brisk weekend business during the gift-giving seasons. They do not have a large tourist business.

Remember:

▾ Carry cash. Few wholesale resources take credit cards. Most prefer yen to travelers checks. (Convert at your hotel before your *Bashi*-day.)

▾ If you have some kind of professional identification, be prepared to use it—business cards, badges, certifications, business licenses, etc., all will help impress the guard at the door.

▾ Very few people will speak English.

▾ Dress simply; the richer you look, the less sympathetic people will be. On the other hand, always dress properly. Tokyo is the single most fashionable city in the world. Don't wear blue

THE "BASHIS"

● STORE
▢ STATION

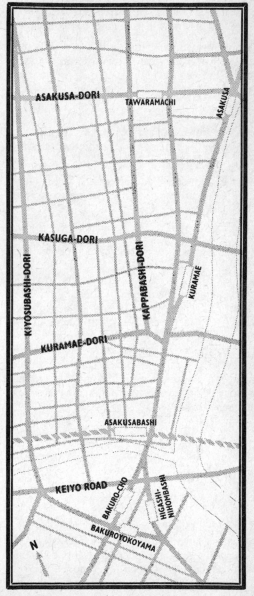

ASAKUSA-DORI   TAWARAMACHI   ASAKUSA

KASUGA-DORI

KIYOSUBASHI-DORI

KAPPABASHI-DORI

KURAMAE

KURAMAE-DORI

ASAKUSABASHI

KEIYO ROAD   BAKURO-CHO

HIGASHI-NIHOMBASHI

BAKUROYOKOYAMA

N

jeans and expect to get into a fashion house. Look the part.

▼ Consider taking an interpreter with you, especially if you tend to be a big spender.

▼ Consider hiring a car and driver, because all the *bashis* are near each other, and after a while you won't be able to carry your bargains. A taxi back to your hotel can easily cost $20.

▼ Sizes may not be true to the tags.

▼ Make sure you are buying something you can legally bring back to the States (see page 33).

▼ In a wholesale mart, prices are fixed. However, you can bargain in street markets or at flea markets.

The free-ride ticket may not pay for your normal use as a tourist in Tokyo, but you will put it to good use on the day you roam the *bashis.* You will be hopping on and off subways going one or two stops in many different directions. We use the JNR a lot because we always stay at the Keio Plaza in Shinjuku and the JNR is exempt from the free-ride card— but all the stops you need for this area are available by subway. Note: A train station and a subway station may be in the same terminal or may be in two separate stations that are close to each other.

Kappabashi

Kappabashi is the wholesale kitchen district and recently has become somewhat of a tourist attraction. In Kappabashi one can buy the plastic food models used in restaurants. Both CBS News and *The New*

York Times have done stories on this area; many tour groups include it in their itinerary. And for good reason. Kappabashi is wonderfully Japanese while still offering some of the best bargains and gift items anyplace in Tokyo. This adventure is at the heart of the reasons why we came to Japan—it's unique, it's visually stimulating, it combines art and retailing, and a few of the shops even take credit cards.

And while we don't want to offend you with our perversity, we must tell you that kimonos may be great gift items but they take up a lot of space in your suitcase; a plate of plastic spaghetti with fork posed in midair, or a cup of coffee with cream streaming from the creamer invisibly balanced above makes one of the most amusing gifts you'll ever bring back. More to the point, plastic food can be easy to pack (this depends on what you get, of course), won't break, and is reasonably priced; $15 to $20 will buy you something handsome. Whether you are friendly with Andy Warhol or are a practical joker, consider the shopping possibilities in this area. Our friend René keeps a fried egg on her carpet just because she loves to see the reaction of strangers who come into her home and are taken aback that anyone would have a fried egg perched on the living-room floor. We have another friend who glued her fried egg to a sweatshirt and wrote SUNNY SIDE UP across the shirt with a paint pen.

Now that we've got you eggs-cited about Kappabashi, here goes. On the Ginza (orange) line, get off the train at Tawaramachi station. This is a small station and has only two exits, so you can't come out in the wrong place. We will give you the names of two streets, but don't worry about them or spend time looking for signs. This is a simple adventure and it is all but impossible to get lost.

As you emerge from the stairwell of the station and stand on the sidewalk, you will see nothing that helps you feel like you are in the

right place. You will be on Asakusa-dori, and
you need to walk about two blocks to Kappabashi-dori Avenue, but you are in a panic
since you have no idea which way that is. Stay
cool. When you come out of the steps, walk
forward. With these two exits, the differential
factor is which side of the street you are on.
This doesn't much matter. Just go straight.
Further to ensure that you are going in the
right direction, look for the giant head of a
chef. He looks somewhat like Chef Boy-ar-dee
and is the size of Mount Rushmore. We're
talking big. We're talking impossible to miss.
We're even talking impossible to stop laughing. Walk toward Chef Boy-ar-dee.

The chef is on top of the Nimi Building.
You may need to cross the street, but the chef
direction is your starting point. There's nothing exciting in the other direction, anyway;
you'll know without doubt (and possibly for
the only time while in Tokyo) which way to
go. The area of interest is about three or four
blocks long on Kappabashi-dori. Both sides of
the street are interesting. Expect to find kitchen
supplies, restaurant supplies, tableware, linens,
aprons, food-related papergoods, knives, woks,
kettles, chopsticks, china, and the infamous
plastic food. A few, but not many, of the stores
will take credit cards.

One of our most recommended plastic-food
dealers is named SAMPLE TOKYO BIKEN.
We did the most business with them for several reasons: Their prices are competitive (prices
for this stuff vary by as much as 20%), their
shopping bags came in second in our traditional-
shopping-bag award, they speak some English,
and they take credit cards.

The fanciest showroom in the area is MAIZ-
URU FOOD SAMPLE, which has a rather
couture look to it. They have a bigger selection than Biken but do not take plastic. Maizuru
is onto the notion that food samples make
great gifts and prints a brochure in English
that suggests that the "single best Japanese

souvenir is neither a camera, nor an electrical product . . . but a food sample." They also boast that food samples are the single most favorite tourist gift.

A single piece of sushi costs about $2.50 (much like a real piece of sushi). A large tempura shrimp is $7.50. A cocktail—they are gorgeous—costs almost $20 but is extraordinarily heavy, unfortunately. Fruits are sold by the slice; food items can be bought by the piece or by a grouping. A plate of something usually is $15 to $20; a large arrangement of seafood is $150.

Asakusabashi

There are several wholesale districts piggyback fashion here; expect to find a string of wholesale papergoods, party goods, jewelry, and toy dealers as you continue along the main drag. We do the area by walking from the Asakusabashi station to the Kuramae station. If you happen to have bought papergoods at our resource in Bakuro-cho (see page 114), you might want to save your energy and skip the papergoods here—the merchandise is 95% the same.

To get to the main drag, which is Edodori Avenue, try to exit the station at the front of the train. Please check the map (see page 105); otherwise you may wander around this rather unstimulating residential neighborhood and wonder why we sent you here. We got off at the back of the train, followed the tracks to what we thought was a main street, but were headed in the Akihabra direction and were lost for about an hour—we had a great time visiting several small factories, the police station, and a few jobbers. It wasn't boring, but it was frustrating because we knew we weren't where we were supposed to be. If you head in the right direction when you leave the train, you should be almost immediately on Eto-dori Avenue, which, whether you can read the signs or not (there are some in Roman letters), obviously is the right place because of the many showrooms and places of business.

The average papergoods store will have a wide selection of gift wrapping and paper bags. We are not talking about paper bags like from the grocery store, but designer bags that are supplied to the retail stores. All sizes are sold, from teeny-tiny to gigantic; many fabrications are used, including various types of plastics. We stocked up on lunch bags, which our husbands thought was about the stupidest thing they'd ever seen. (What do men know?) We bought white glossy bags with red hearts; with multicolor new-wave squiggles; with silver bows; clear plastic lunch bags with blue stars; opaque plastic lunch bags with red zigzag lines. We're talking about the most fashionable lunch bags any child has ever brought to a public or private school this side of the Pacific Ocean. The bags also are good for gift-giving. Most bags are sold by the gross, some by 50s. Expect to pay $6 for a gross of delightful lunch bags. Don't forget to look at the silver foil bags . . . the epitome of lunch bag elegance.

Wrapping paper is in cut sheets, European style, and also is sold by the gross. It is very, very heavy to carry around all day, especially when you start buying several patterns. Price varies by the quality of the paper and of the design, but you can get something appropriate for any occasion for about $7 a package.

Mingling with the papergoods wholesalers are the seasonal decoration wholesalers. Because so much of the manufacturing for this business is done in the Orient, you will see merchandise for just about any international holiday, be it Christmas or Boys' Day. Christmas decorations are an excellent buy—you can get anything from the inexpensive stuff you associate with a "Made in Taiwan" label to ornaments that would retail for $10 apiece in an American department store. Goods cost from 50 cents to $4 each. Many of these shops sell floral supplies as well.

One of the biggest and most popular in the field is SAIGA, whose storefront is blessedly written in Roman letters. We also liked OH-NISHI, a big, green four-story building that does a sizable international business.

As you walk, the neighborhood will change—from papergoods to seasonal goods to jewelry to toys and, get this, police supplies. You'll find five different styles of origami paper (about $1 a pack); those wonderful kites in all different sizes; dolls, masks, feathers, belt buckles, jewelry fastenings, Chanel-like buttons, and much, much more. Some of the stores would quote prices only by the dozen; others were happy for off-the-street business. We bought a boxed set of three "Transformers" for $7.50. Just as you finish with the toys and think you've done the neighborhood, you'll see that the Kuramae subway stop is right there at a doorway. The street will have branched into Kuramaebashi-dori Avenue and Edodori Avenue. You should have stayed on Edodori for the toy stores, then gone into the subway. You're only a stop or two away from any number of other wholesale districts.

Bakuro-cho

Bakuro-cho is the wholesale clothing district of Tokyo. It feels more like the Lower East Side than Seventh Avenue and is far from elegant, but if you like street fairs, junk shops, seconds stores, and showrooms, you will find many things to make your heart (and pocketbook) sing.

Much of the merchandise you see here is familiar in style to what you have seen in department stores, but rarely is there any direct matchup. The Japanese are style junkies, so for the most part, the street resources that are open to the public sell style rather than big names. The bigger showrooms, which may not be open to you, sell higher-quality merchandise. If you like "now" fashions or have teens to dress, this is the place to come. Also, several outlets sell children's clothing, much of it in the Mikki House vein. As to the Moscow Rule of Shopping, buy it here because you won't find better prices elsewhere. You may find fancier merchandise elsewhere, but not with better prices.

To get there, take the JNR (Sobo line) to Bakuro-cho, 1 Chome, which is clearly marked in Japanese at street level. In case you can't read Japanese, look for a sign that says "SARA-ZEN" (in Roman letters) in red and yellow. Next to Sarazen is the Nakadori of Bakuro-cho; this is the main street, but every village has a main street and you won't be able to read the sign anyway, so don't worry. You can't miss Sarazen, so head for it. But if you tell a taxi driver where to bring you, mention the main street and the fact that it is in Bakuro-cho. Say, "Nakadori Bakuro-cho."

We went to Sarazen with an interpreter; we mention this only because we asked her to translate the announcement that was being made incessantly on the public-address system. We figured it would be something like, "Attention, all K-Mart shoppers. . . ." But instead it was a warning to make sure your wallet and handbag were safe. We find this extraordinary because Tokyo has so little crime. Let the buyer beware.

Sarazen has several floors and sells overruns. We don't find the upper floors to be worth the walk, but the main floor has stylish and worth-having fashions, jackets, and sweats. Good woolen blazers cost $25; men's designer neckties were $5. We absolutely adore it here, but it is more like a Turkish bazaar than anything else you may find in Tokyo. This is not elegant; there is no big-name designer merchandise here. (Who cares?)

The main shopping area here is H-shaped. Wander at your own will. You'll find some wholesale-only jewelry and accessory showrooms where you can easily meet the $500 minimum order because the goods are fun, fashionable, inexpensive, and make wonderful gifts. We went nuts at MASUAMASU. We were admitted after showing a business card, having our translator accept that we would purchase at least $500 worth of goods, and their issuance to us of a special buying card. We could not have managed without a translator. There are five floors of goodies and then two additional annex shops.

In the same area you'll find handbags you'll swear are identical to the ones you saw at Hanae Mori. At KATAYAMA we found Gucci, Valentino, Celine, and Fendi copies for $6 to $7. In many outlets, $15 will buy you a fabulous fashion sweater; $30 buys a baseball-style jacket. There are yarn shops and kids' shops. *Happi* coats identical to the ones we saw at the Oriental Bazaar were $2 cheaper here. In fact, these were the cheapest *happi* coats and *hakatas* in town. We have a more glamorous *hakata* resource on the Ginza, but you'll pay $2 to $3 more per robe there (see page 123).

On the primary main drag, where you came out of the subway, you'll note many showrooms. ÉTOILE is one of the most famous; this is a wholesale mart to which it is unlikely that you can gain admittance (we couldn't). Others may let you in. We found very handsome wool blazers we had seen for $400 in some of the Tokyo department stores for $65 at one of the showrooms that let us in. The "biggest" name in the area is SANYO, and you may or may not get in. Sanyo is the maker for Burberry, Bill Blass, and many other famous designers, as well as a big brand name on its own (not to be confused with electronics goods). Your success seems to depend on the day, the traffic, and the guard. There's also a great papergoods wholesaler on the same side of the street as Étoile, about a block up: SHIMOJIMA. They don't have anything you won't find in the wholesale papergoods neighborhood, but if you want to hit two birds with one stone, you'll be very happy here. Buy an extra gross of lunch bags and think of us.

When buying wholesale clothes in this neighborhood, be sure to check for damages. Ask if you can try items on—a few places may let you. Don't pay attention to the sizes. Ninety percent of the merchandise we saw in Tokyo was marked "size 9"; various pieces, obviously cut differently, fit anywhere from size 6 to size 12. Always remember that all clothing is proportioned for the Japanese body—shorter and smaller in frame than the typical American body. Do not expect pantyhose to fit you; shoes run wide. Shoes stop at size 9 for (American) women, but women should try men's shoes for sporty styles. The wholesale markets are mobbed with locals who know what fits them; you will be at a slight disadvantage, especially if you are tall or large.

6 ▼ TOKYO NEIGHBORHOODS

The Village System

Tokyo, like many other large international cities, was not originally a large international city. Many villages grew around the palace, villages that eventually were incorporated into one giant traffic-jammed city. Just as the *arrondissements* of Paris each have a different feel and distinct flavor to them, so the individual neighborhoods of Tokyo—once the primary villages—also are different. Some are known for certain things—either the location of specific buildings or the type of people who haunt the area. Thus Shibuya is known to be young and kicky and Akasaka is known for its restaurants.

Any guidebook or map system you use has the neighborhoods clearly marked. You will soon learn them so well that you'll be able to look at a subway map in *kanji* and figure your fare just by knowing where you are going.

Ginza

Ginza is the most famous neighborhood in Tokyo and has come to be nothing short of a shopping legend. For some reason, tourists have come to associate Ginza as a one-street shopping street, much like the Champs-Élysées or Rodeo Drive, when in fact Ginza is a neighborhood (it means silver mint), and the main shopping street is not Ginza-dori! While there

GINZA

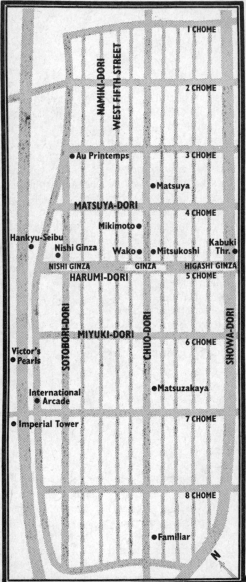

● STORE
□ STATION

1 CHOME

NAMIKI-DORI
WEST FIFTH STREET

2 CHOME

● Au Printemps

3 CHOME

● Matsuya

MATSUYA-DORI

4 CHOME

Mikimoto ●

Hankyu-Seibu ●

Nishi Ginza

Wako ● ● Mitsukoshi

Kabuki Thr. ●

NISHI GINZA

GINZA

HIGASHI GINZA

HARUMI-DORI

5 CHOME

SOTOBORI-DORI

MIYUKI-DORI

CHUO-DORI

SHOWA-DORI

6 CHOME

Victor's
● Pearls

● Matsuzakaya

International
● Arcade

● Imperial Tower

7 CHOME

8 CHOME

● Familiar

N

is a Ginza-dori, the main drag is called Chuo-dori.

The first time we went to Ginza, we walked all around and saw a few of the sights and found ourselves moderately impressed but not knocked out. "Overrated," we said to each other. The next time we went to Ginza, we walked in the other direction and found a whole new world. The 5-Chome area of Ginza (we were previously in 1–4 Chome) is like being in Europe—fabulous big stores on the main street, and alleys and back streets filled with other wonderful little shops. Even though the 5-Chome area is so well marked that it has huge arches and overhead electric banners (in English), we were so lost that we never even walked in that direction. It's not that 1–4 Chome is boring or un-Western, it's just that you shouldn't miss this other area. Look for the silver arches.

If you have the time, the best way to see Ginza is to divide it into two different days. The areas 1–4 Chome and the Yurakucho area north of the TIC can be done on one day; the 5-Chome area and up can be done with the area around the Imperial Hotel at another time. If you just want to get the idea of it all, take the subway exit for 1 Chome and walk toward 9 Chome. Don't spend a lot of time looking in 1–4; concentrate efforts in 5–7, perhaps combing some of the back streets in this area.

If you are especially a big-name-designer shopper and don't care that these items are overpriced in Tokyo, you may want to begin getting your own look of Ginza at the Imperial Tower, a modern high-rise adjacent to the Imperial Hotel that houses almost all the big European designers. You won't be getting much of the flavor of the city here. We think the Imperial Tower is very, very nice—but not what we are looking for, so we do Ginza in our own way.

We begin underground, having arrived at the Ginza station on the Ginza (orange) line. There, in the station you will see several yellow signs with arrows that point to various stairwells and directions, each labeled by a chome, or block. Ginzaitchome, which is how the stop is marked on a few subway maps, means first chome—Ginza. We walk to a lower-number chome and use that exit since we don't want to do too much cutting back and forth. Ginza is too long for you to stroll down one side and up the other, unless you are a marathon walker or don't plan to go into some of the shops. Also remember that on weekends, part of the area is closed to vehicular traffic and the whole area always is crowded. You do not want to be in the subway at Ginza during rush hour.

We will not walk you through each and every store in Ginza; our best advice is to roam the area and try it on for size. It's a great first day in Tokyo. Use the maps and remember the *koban* if you get lost. When asking for directions, mention the name of a big retailer, such as Wako, Mikimoto, or Melsa Ginza. The TIC also is in the neighborhood, and they will help you get unlost. See page 304 for our Ginza tour, or create your own. Here are some interesting stops along the way:

▼

AU PRINTEMPS: The Tokyo branch of the French department store. The costume jewelry selection alone is enough to put you in debt. (See page 213 for more.)

▼

ITOYA: Our first trip to Ginza, the day we missed part of the action, we labeled Itoya as the best store in Ginza. Even after we found all the other great places, we still think

we were right. This is *it* for office-supply fre
Buy postcards here; find $5 presents to brin
back to your fellow office workers or kids.

▼

GINZA MATSUYA: Another department
store (see page 209). We like it here. Very
young, and great for kids and teen fashions.

▼

KANEBO: An eight-story boutique or specialty
store that sells ready-to-wear and fabric and is
très chic for browsing (we don't buy). Prices
are not out of bounds; there are good working-
women type fashions here. But if you are going
on to Hong Kong, you will see much of this
merchandise there.

▼

MIKIMOTO: We think you'll be spending
too much if you buy your pearls here, but you
may want the prestige of the name and the
simplicity of one-stop shopping. Mikimoto sells
other jewelry items as well. It is the Tiffany of
the pearl business.

▼

TAMAYA: A good resource for the less expensive lines of major designers, such as Tricot
from YSL.

▼

O: The single fanciest specialty store in
yo, Wako isn't young and crazy but cer-
nly is nice. It's also easy to spot when you
get out of the subway and a good place for
meeting people, or finding yourself if you happen to get lost.

▼

TOKYO KYUKYODO: One of our favorite
places in Tokyo, this old and tony shop doesn't
just feel expensive. It is expensive. The shop
has been here for more than a hundred years
and is a lovely place to buy gift items to bring
home, especially Japanese-style papergoods.

▼

WASHINGTON: While it looks a bit cheap
from the outside, once you're inside you'll
come to love Washington and the fact that
they carry American-size shoes. In fact, this
whole department store is devoted to shoes.
Andrea Pfister fans, here you go.

▼

GINZA KOMATSU: Not as vast as some of
the department stores and a little more like
Lerner's, but there's reasonably priced fashion
here.

▼

LOVE SKIRT MANUFACTURING: We just
loved the name! The boutique is small but

very nice, sort of like a showroom. We saw the world's most stunning trench coat here—lined with sweater knit ($350).

▼

GINZA LIZA: Perhaps Liza Minnelli and Princess Diana have teamed up to open their own stores on Ginza. We think you'll like both. Liza is known for its classy boutiques and original items. They're closed on Monday.

▼

GINZA DIANA: Yet another of the many shoe shops in Ginza, but Diana carries all the big names. There's another Diana near La Foret in Harajuku; both are well stocked and filled with designer shoes from Magli to Jourdan.

▼

GINZA MAGGY: Here's where you get your Chanel copy or your glittery Italian sweater. A Louis Ferard silk blouse costs $150 (not bad!), while Italian sweaters may cost $300. There's a Maggy outlet in the alley behind the store, where sale merchandise is available.

▼

TENCHIDO: Luggage, bags, and leathergoods from various designers are in ready abundance—many at affordable prices. For about $100, you can find any number of handsome choices. You'll also find some nice leather backpacks here.

KUNOYA: A very fancy and expensive kimono accessory shop that doesn't see too many tourists, Kunoya is exactly the kind of place we so enjoy in Tokyo. We bought telephone pillows here for all our friends. The pillows cost $10 apiece and made the perfect gift for the person who has everything. Same-day delivery to the hotel cost $3 but was far better than schlepping all over town carrying six telephone pillows. Okay, so you want to know what a telephone pillow is—well, it's a square pillow about 12 by 12 inches with a doily attached to it. You snip off the doily, place the phone on top of the pillow, and then cover it with the doily. How have you ever lived without one? For some terrible reason, Kunoya does not take credit cards. So have plenty of cash on hand for your telephone pillows. You'll want a dozen.

▼

GINZA KANEMATSU: The Ginza branch of a famous shoe store that sells all the big designers like Jourdan and Magli. Signs are in English and French. We found sale shoes for as little as $30. The store goes all the way through and offers a good way to get into the alley in back that has even more wonderful stores (including the Ginza branch of our favorite makeup man, Shu Uemura).

▼

If you go to the Kabuki (which is on Harumi-dori, not Chuo-dori), the fancy stores begin to peter out along the way, but there are some interesting boutiques on Harumi-dori. We're hoping you'll see some Kabuki while you're in Tokyo, so afterward cross the street to the other side of Harumi-dori in front of the Kabuki and begin to walk back toward Wako. In the first block after you've crossed the street, on the far corner of Showa-dori Avenue, you will come to a shop we affectionately call LIBBY's HAKATA SHOP. (Named after our friend Libby who told us it was the best one in Tokyo). After checking out all the others, we've come to agree with her. If it has a real name—we don't know what it is or how to find out. The shop is very, very Japanese. They do not take credit cards or speak English. The saleswomen sit on their knees on tatami mats and bow at customers who stare into the windows. But the *hakatas* are the best in town, and the color selection (pink on white!) is sublime. *Hakatas* are almost always white with block pattern printing, but the printing usually is blue. There's nothing wrong with this, but after you've seen thousands of them, you long for something different. You can get less expensive *hakatas* in the *bashis*, but we love this store and think it's a retailing experience you won't forget.

▼

SUZUNOYA DOLL: A few doors away is Suzunoya Doll, a branch of the famous Suzunoya Kimono (see page 242). They make a unique and attractive doll that is a must-have for doll-collectors or indulgent moms.

▼

When you get to the streets between 6 Chome and 5 Chome, and assuming you are still on the side of the street opposite from the Kabuki, turn left and duck into the alleys and small streets behind the 5-Chome stores. This entire area is dense with stores and finds and even a few bargains. Mostly you will find boutiques you have never heard of who carry designers you have never heard of, but this shouldn't stop you from having a wonderful time.

The areas 4 Chome and 5 Chome are separated by a big street called Harumi-dori Avenue. If you go in one direction, you'll get to Maxim's (as in famous French eatery) and eventually the Kabuki; if you go in the other direction, you'll see the train tracks and the twin white tile towers of the Yurakucho Center, which houses Seibu and the new Hankyu. Nishi-Ginza is right here, between the *koban* and the white twin towers. (Nishi-Ginza is a minimall of shops—very young.) Sukiyabashi Shopping Arcade is across the street, between the old Hankyu and the railroad tracks; the TIC is one block away, on the Sukiyabashi side of the street but just beyond the railroad tracks.

The area directly behind the TIC, running along 6 Chome, is where you'll find the Imperial Tower and the International Arcade. The International Arcade has the famous Hayashi Kimono, where you can buy used or new kimonos (see page 240). The International Arcade was created during the 1964 Tokyo Olympics basically as a tourist trap but has survived nicely because it provides an important function in Tokyo: There's a lot that visitors want to buy located under one roof convenient to Ginza, and the salespeople are experienced in dealing with *gaijin,* speaking English, and even mailing packages. (See page 72 for more on the International Arcade.) While in Ginza, this is a must-do.

Some Ginza tips:

▼ There are tons of department stores in Ginza. We don't suggest you go into all of them or you will face mental meltdown, or at least brain damage, by sunset. We think you can easily pass up Sogo, Hankyu (at least the old Hankyu on Ginza), Mitsokoshi, and New Melsa.

▼ Some stores should be sampled in a limited manner—maybe just a floor or two. While you probably would enjoy exploring every inch of Seibu and may want to do a quick top-to bottom of the new Hankyu, you could do fine with a few floors of Matsuya and an in-and-out approach to Nishi-Ginza. Try not to overlook Au Printemps, even if you have to walk an extra block just to get to it. Of course, you do not want a case of Tokyo Overdose, especially on your first day. Remember, if you have the time, do Ginza on two different days.

▼ Whatever you do, don't miss the yakatori stands under the railroad tracks, where you can buy chicken kabobs for a snack.

▼ Because you think there is a street named Ginza that is the main shopping street, you will be more inclined to get lost. The two main streets, which intersect, are Chuo-dori and Harumi-dori. Forget anything else. You can divide 1–4 Chome into the area north of Harumi-dori, and 5–8 Chome as South Ginza, if this makes it easier for you (or you can divide into two separate days).

▼ The immediate area around the white tile twin towers is called Yurakucho. Do not let this confuse you because it is very much in the Ginza area you want to visit.

▼ If you have only an hour or two and are in the Ginza area but don't know what to do, go to Seibu first, then the International Arcade. If you have time left over, try Nishi-Ginza just to see the scene, if not to buy anything.

Shinjuku

Shinju means new accommodations in Japanese (*ku* means ward or neighborhood), which is why all the big hotels have now built in this area. Lots of new accommodations. It is a pearl of a neighborhood if you are looking for great shopping. Hordes of office workers form a passing parade of the latest fashions and tell you—without ever speaking—everything you

SHINJUKU

● STORE
▢ STATION

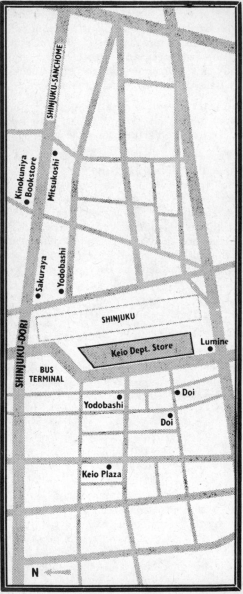

SHINJUKU-SANCHOME

● Kinokuniya Bookstore

● Mitsukoshi

● Sakuraya

● Yodobashi

SHINJUKU-DORI

SHINJUKU

Keio Dept. Store

● Lumine

BUS TERMINAL

● Yodobashi

● Doi

● Doi

● Keio Plaza

N ←

need to buy while in Tokyo. Some two million Japanese workers pass through the station each morning and night; the neighborhood retail outlets support their every need.

Shinjuku is a newly developed boom town sometimes likened to Century City in Los Angeles or Wall Street in New York—not that Wall Street is newly developed. The area is consumed with skyscrapers, high-rise hotels of the modern American type (the Inter• Continental Keio Plaza, the Hilton, and the Hyatt are a block from each other), and architectural wonders. If you're staying in a nearby hotel, you'll be able to look out your window and see an office building with gigantic, movable koi ponds and rainbow-painted elevators— alongside Mount Fuji. There is a large and complicated train station, and the area is a bit out of the central hub near Ginza. When we told Libby we were staying at the Keio, she said, "Oh, good, then you'll get to see Shinjuku; otherwise you might not take the time to go over there."

Indeed, Shinjuku is best experienced by living there as a hotel resident. It's filled with incredible skyscrapers and a plethora of trendy hanging-out spots. We chose to stay there because we wanted the Keio for a home base, but if you are not staying in the neighborhood, your reaction to it will be very different. We love Shinjuku because it's alive and bustling and crowded and exciting. If this is too much for you, you may want to skip this neighborhood, just as Libby said you might. You can find almost all the same shops in other parts of town (except Isetan), and certainly Ikebukuro is more civilized on weekends—but you just may love the liveliness of it all. And if you really have shopping in your blood, you won't give up the chance to shop at Isetan and Marui.

What you are about to read about Shinjuku may sound confusing and may make you shrug your shoulders and say to yourself, "Who needs it?" Shinjuku is by far the most difficult train

ation, but you can get to Isetan and Marui easily by using the small, local subway station Shinjuku San Chome and never have to contend with the intricacies of the main Shinjuku station. Also, just because we have written a lot about the confusion doesn't mean we want you to give up; we want to help you over the bumps we fell on. If you have the attitude that you are going to Shinjuku for adventure and don't mind getting lost, you'll have a great time.

The part of Shinjuku which is most exciting is East Shinjuku. You can get off at the Shinjuku station and follow the English (!!!) signs to the east exits, or you can get off at San-chome, which is the third block and is the central part of this minidowntown area where the big *depatos* are—Isetan, Marui, etc. When you get out of this subway, you'll emerge under a building which looks like a big bank—ask someone for Isetan. Don't just start wandering in stores, because you will wear yourself out before you get to the good stuff. Check the map for the major core of where you want to be. You should see the symbols of the youth culture—scads of movie theaters (with English voice tracks and Japanese subtitles, by the way), fast-food joints, record shops, gorgeous young men, and yuppies who are doing what the Japanese do best: shop.

If you use the main Shinjuku station, follow the yellow signs with black print in English. You can easily get Tokyo Overdose just by glancing around the Shinjuku station, so be forewarned. Do not attempt to do everything there is to do in Shinjuku in one day if you expect to live to see another day—unless you are into kamikaze shopping. If you are into true self-preservation, you may want to take a taxi from the Shinjuku station to either Isetan or the famous bookstore KINOKUNIYA.

You may not appreciate what we have told you about the east and west sides of this station until you get lost. Our trick: As soon a you get out of your JNR train, look for MY CITY, which is impossible to miss. My City is on the east side of the station; walk toward it or away from it depending on which direction you want. If you arrive in Shinjuku by subway rather than JNR (Yes, there's a huge difference!), you will come in from underground. When you get into the main part of the station, look for signs guiding you to east or west. We once got so lost here that we had to take a taxi from the east gate to the west gate, and it cost $4! However, Shinjuku is easy if you take the precautions of (a) knowing beforehand if you want east or west and (b) going in the right direction by following the signs.

The western side of Shinjuku is where the hotels are; also the Mitsui Building and most of the working world. There is a Yodabashi Camera on both sides (1-1-1 Nishi-Shinjuku, Shinjuku-ku) and there are several big *depatos* on the western side of the station, but this side is not as active from a retailing sense as the other side. You can live just fine if you skip Keio and Odakyu. You can also pass up My Lord, Lumine, and probably My City (which is on the eastern side). Remember, self-preservation is the name of the game. The Hilton has a Noritake showroom, and each of the big hotels has a shopping arcade, but for the most part, we think you can skip West Shinjuku for general browsing.

The best news about East Shinjuku is that you can have all five of the Marui outlets, and the giant Isetan with its two stores—which we love . . . in one happy excursion. There are many, many sporting-goods department stores here; if you are shopping with a man who hates fashion shopping, you may want to split up for a few hours. Also, the men's annex of Isetan is very worthwhile. There are also two famous discount camera shops in Shinjuku, Yodabashi, and Sakuraya. Doi, another camera outlet that gets a lot of print, is on the west side. (See page 243 for camera and electronics specifics.)

If you get lucky (first Saturday and third Sunday), there is an antiques flea market held twice a month at the Hanazono Jinja Shrine right there in East Shinjuku, about a block from Isetan and across the street from Marui Interior. It's directly catty-corner from Minami Sports, which has a can't-miss-it sign.

To see and enjoy East Shinjuku best, whether you have resident status vis-à-vis your hotel or not, begin your neighborhood exploration on neutral ground, at Kinokuniya Bookstore. Note: If you are staying in a West Shinjuku hotel, this is not a stone's throw from your hotel. Taxi there to save strength, unless you are prepared for a hike and an adventure, since you will have to get from the west side to the east side of the train station—no easy task. This place makes Grand Central Station look like child's play.

▼

KINOKUNIYA: We begin at Kinokuniya for a few reasons: It's a famous building that a taxi driver can take you to if you are feeling overwhelmed by it all; the store opens at 10:00 A.M., and many of the bigger stores don't open until 11:00 A.M. and you don't want to waste any precious shopping time; many of the books we paid a lot of money for in the United States (in Rockefeller Center) are sold on the sixth floor—in English—for a fraction of their price. Kinokuniya closes the first and third Wednesday of every month. It is also catty-corner to Marui Youth, so you can see the workers exercising together at 10:00 A.M. and then go into the bookstore. If you need English-language reading material, you can get it here. Kinokuniya is just off the main drag, which happily enough is called Shinjuku-dori.

KINOKUNIYA BOOKSTORE, 3-17-7 Shinjuku, Shinjuku-ku

From Kinokuniya just wander the neighborhood in a two-block radius. You'll see all the "oioi" (the logo of the Marui department store) signs, the gigantic Isetan, and several smaller boutiques that may interest you. There's a MIKKI HOUSE here (4-3-17 Shinjuku, Shinjuku-ku) and a SANRIO if any of your children are Hello Kitty freaks.

▼

AD HOC BUILDING: The Sanrio is in a corner inside this building which is a little more junky than we care for, but some people have told us they like the other shops in the building as good resources for gift items and souvenirs.

AD HOC BUILDING, 3-15-11 Shinjuku, Shinjuku-ku

▼

SUZUYA: One of our favorite stores in Hong Kong. Suzuya is known as one of the leading Shinjuku outlets for inexpensive but hot fashion looks and as a result is swarming with young people. Prices are very reasonable; if you have teens, bring them here.

SUZUYA, 3-26-14 Shinjuku, Shinjuku-ku

▼

MITSOKOSHI: This store is rather standard and not worth a lot of time. If you've heard about Mitsokoshi and want to see what all the fuss is about, do not even go into this store but wait for Nihombashi.

MITSOKOSHI, 329 Shinjuku, Shinjuku-ku

▼

MITSUMIME: Fashion-conscious men should be happy to find this shop next to Suzuya, which is actually a good resource for women who like the fashionable Japanese unisex look. We've bought a lot of blazers and big sweaters here for ourselves. There are other outlets of this shop that will cross your path.

MITSUMIME, Shinjuku, Shinjuku-ku

▼

TAKANO: Has great accessories although it also carries many famous designer lines. There are a few Takano outlets around town, but this is the most famous one. We have bought some of our greatest handbags here like gift handbags that cost $25, folded flat in suitcases, and looked far more expensive. Absolutely no one in Takano spoke any English or knew what we were talking about. Visa but not American Express. There's a small Takano under Keio in the Shinjuku station and a large one next to Yodabashi Camera on the east side, and across the street from My City. Next to Takano is a stairwell that leads to SUBNADE, an underground mall of cute little shops. Takano is closed the third Monday of every month.

TAKANO, 3-26-11 Shinjuku, Shinjuku-ku

If you go into Subnade, you can come out at the other end at either Pepe, a smallish department store, or the Shinjuku Prince Hotel. Under the Seibu Shinjuku station, next to Pepe and the hotel, you'll get to American Boulevard, where you'll find a shopping mall *à l'américain*. Mostly jeans are for sale; some of the cheaper merchandise looks like overruns and closeouts. There are some bargains here on things you wouldn't buy at home. Please note that the Shinjuku Seibu station is different from the Shinjuku station; they are not in the same building, thankfully.

▼

MY CITY: While we did tell you that you could live without it, it is home to a Hoya Crystal boutique. You may never have heard of Hoya Crystal, but they are the Steuben of Japan, and the prices are very reasonable. Hand-carry your purchases on the plane and you will have made a good investment. When we poll Northwest Orient, and Varig stewardesses for good buys in Tokyo, they invariably say Hoya Crystal. (Hoya has a shop in Manhattan, too.)

MY CITY, 3-38-1 Shinjuku, Shinjuku-ku

▼

MINAMI SPORT: Across the street from Marui Interior with a giant white obelisk with green and yellow letters that makes it a not-to-be-missed sign and a good landmark. There are nine floors of merchandise; don't miss the basement. Not to be outdone, Marui has its own sporting store, right across from the San Chome subway stop. And there's a Sport City near there.

MINAME SPORT, Shinjuku, Shinjuku-ku

▼

NIHOMBASHI

● STORE
☐ STATION

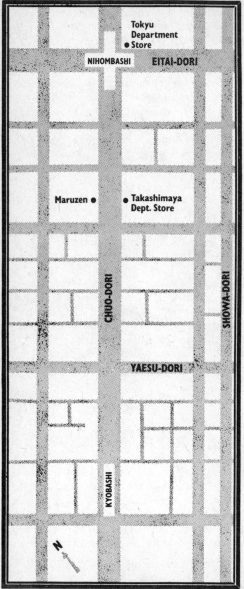

Our friend Hiro suggests that if the crowds are too much for your nerves, or if you just want to get far from the madding crowd, you can stop by Shinjuku-gyoen Garden. There is an admission charge, but it's worth it. We noticed that as wonderful as our hotel was, it did not have green grass, trees, or birds, and we really appreciated restorative trips to parks like this one.

Nihombashi

Nihombashi is part of the old Edo Tokyo and means Japan bridge. Indeed, while you are there, you will see the bridge and some of the charming architecture that survived World War II. While there are many areas of Nihombashi to explore, we devote ourselves mostly to what we call the Nihombashi Stroll; it is a short walk from point A to point B but offers a lot of looking along the way. You may begin at either point and walk to the other. You are really walking from one chome to another—as you can see from the address, should you be so brave (or ill-advised) as to look at addresses.

We begin at MITSOKOSHI NIHOMBASHI (1-7-4 Nihombashi Muromachi, Chuo-ku), because this takes a lot of strength and may be overwhelming if you don't tackle it at the top of the day. Usually we stop by every floor of the main store; we're not wild for the annex, it's too golfy. Check out kids and kimonos. (See page 210.) When you finish at Mitsokoshi, return to the first-floor cosmetics department and ask any salesgirl in your best Japanese, "Takashimaya?" You will be pointed to the proper exit. You must exit toward Takashimaya to avoid being lost. We've never been lost in this neighborhood, so if you get lost and find something wonderful, write and tell all.

The main street is Chuo-dori (which is the same main drag of the Ginza area—you are just farther downtown now), and you must cross over a bridge to complete the Nihombashi Stroll. If you don't see the bridge, ask for help. Takashimaya is a landmark, so asking anyone on the street will bring positive results. As you walk the Stroll, you'll pass TOKYU (1-4-1 Nihombashi, Chuo-ku)—another department store—and NISHIKAWA, (1-4-1 Nihombashi, Chuo-ku) a Penney's-like department store we happen to like a lot. There are also some old tea and coffee shops that package either brew in a nice tin for gift-giving purposes, and some upscale antiques shops. The Nihombashi Stroll is only three blocks long, so not too much can happen to you. As you approach TAKASHIMAYA (2-4-1 Nihombashi, Chuo-ku) you'll see Maruzen across the street. If you are looking for woodblock prints and might not get to Kanda, you must stop at Maruzen. But save some energy for Takashimaya, which is certainly one of Tokyo's leading department stores.

There is a subway under Takashimaya—it's the the Nihombashi stop. From there you can go on your merry way. You're a short distance from Ginza.

If you have the energy and like the Stroll so much, you may want to put together your own Stroll, Part Two. Try this:

▼ Continue on the main drag, Chuo-dori, for another block (big block) until you get to a large intersection; this is Yaesu-dori.

▼ Turn right on Yaesu-dori and look for stairwells that will bring you down to the Yaesu underground shopping area, which is adjacent (but all underground) to Sotobori-dori.

▼ Should you decide that you've had enough of our crazy shopping adventure for the moment, you can turn left and almost immediately be at the steps of the Bridgestone Museum of Art for some culture. Then you can go to the shopping mall.

▼ This is a T-shaped shopping complex similar to the one in and around Shinjuku station; it services all the workers in the big buildings surrounding the Tokyo station between the Imperial Palace and Nihombashi.

▼ You're not possibly this strong, but if you are, you can check out DAIMARU, an old-fashioned department store that sells virtually everything.

▼ From Daimaru you can exit the store into the Tokyo station for several lines of train or subway. You can even get the bullet train here.

▼ Don't forget to look at the architecture of the Tokyo station; it is copied from the station in Amsterdam and is a fine example of European architecture.

Ikebukuro

We know people who have lived in Tokyo for years and have never been to Ikebukuro. Like Shinjuku, it's a little bit off to the side from Ginza and gets ignored along the way. Most of our guidebooks don't even list it as a Tokyo neighborhood. It is, as the city planners say, in flux and will continue to change over the next ten years. But we've always been ahead of ourselves—we found, we conquered, we fell in love. The trip is worth it just to take in Seibu and Parco in one fell swoop. Some good things to think about Ikebukuro:

▼ If you can't pronounce it, you can think of President Eisenhower and always know where you're going.

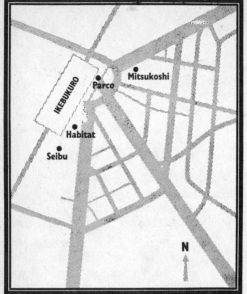

▼ If you are going to Sunshine City for business, or to the flea market at Alpha Shopping Center, your subway or train stop is Ikebukuro.

▼ If your hotel is in Shinjuku, Ikebukuro is midway between your hotel and Ueno or the *bashis* (go the top route on the JNR).

▼ It's not nearly as crowded as Shinjuku or Shibuya.

▼ And, of course, Ikebukuro houses the flagship Seibu. (Seibu, we love you.)

We arrive by JNR from Shinjuku and find ourselves right under SEIBU, so there's no problem of what to do or where to go when you get there. After working over every inch of Seibu, including the Sears inside, we go out the front door and walk to the right—into Dunkin' Donuts for a sugar-and-caffeine fix to give us strength. Seibu, we love you. While Seibu is very invigorating, after half a day in there you will need a donut. The donut shop is almost next door to Habitat and is at the tail of the area you want to work. Having consumed, return to the street or go back to Seibu and buy even more.

SEIBU, 1-28-1 Minami, Ikebukuro, Toshima-ku

▼

PARCO: Once you leave Seibu you'll see signs for this resource. In front of Parco is a traffic circle with a fountain, and there are signs for Sunshine City. This entire area is filled with shops, eateries, and chanting monks (well, a few chanting monks).

PARCO, 1-28-1 Minami, Ikebukuro, Toshima-ku

Whatever you do, don't miss the small pedestrian street by the Sunshine City sign that leads to Tokyu Hands, the hobby shop. There is a Mitsokoshi here that is okay—more with-it than the Shinjuku store, but not as much fun as Nihombashi.

Asakusa

Asakusa has only two things wrong with it:

1. The word is pronounced "A-sak-usa" and "As-ak-sa"; each pronunciation is considered correct, so you will always be confused.
2. The word looks so much like Akasaka that you might get mixed up and go to the wrong (very wrong) subway station. (We did!)

But there are several things right with it. Asakusa is a great little adventure and is conveniently near other little adventures to make your day complete. On top of that, you can combine culture and shopping. And there is a

ASAKUSA

● STORE
☐ STATION

SENSOJI SHRINE

HOZOMON GATE

Asakusa
Flea Market

Shin-Nakamise
Shopping Arcade

KAMINARIMON GATE

KAMINARIMON-DORI

NAKAMISE-DORI

EDO-DORI

ASAKUSA

ASAKUSA-DORI

N

flea market in the neighborhood. If you think you could still ask for more from a neighborhood, consider this: If you go in spring, you can see the famous cherry blossoms!

You will emerge from the Asakusa subway right where you want to be—in a shopping arcade. The arcade (see map) intersects Nakamise Street, which is lined with shops. When the shops end, the cherry blossoms begin (in season) and lead right to the Sensoji Shrine, which is not as gorgeous as Kamakura but is very nice nonetheless.

For souvenirs and knickknacks, you can't beat the stretch from the Kaminarimon Gate to the Hozomon Gate; maybe two or three blocks in length, it is door-to-door stalls that sell all kinds of good things. Surprisingly, you don't see a lot of this stuff anywhere else. Much of the merchandise here is touristy, so you may not be impressed. Or you may see just the tourist items on the surface and not realize that snuggled in among the junk stores are some of the oldest and most venerable retailers in Tokyo. While you can buy cheap ($20) polyester kimonos here, look out for some of the better kimono shops and the accouterments that go with them. Also fans, umbrellas, hair combs, religious souvenirs, toys, and, most importantly, wind-up sushi pieces that tap dance are all available. Few shops take plastic.

Study our map for a second or two so you can see where the Shin-Nakasise Shopping Arcade bisects Nakasime Street. There are also lots of little but nice shops all around the area bordered by Kaminarimon-dori Street and Kokusai-dori Avenue. The Asakusa Flea Market is mostly for locals, but it's worth a look-see on your way to Kappabashi.

You can walk from Asakusa to Kappabashi, the wholesale kitchen neighborhood, if you want; it's a nice walk unless you have small children, who may become tired, with you. Follow our map. Some of the shops along Nakamise-dori:

KAZUSAYA (kimono accessories)

MORITA (umbrellas)

BUNNY (toys)

MUSASHIYA (dolls)

ARAI-BUNSEIDO (fans)

KAWASAKIYA (toys)

SHIZUOKAYA (Japanese folk arts)

OKAYDAYA (umbrellas)

YATSUME (hair things)

NAKAYAMA (souvenirs)

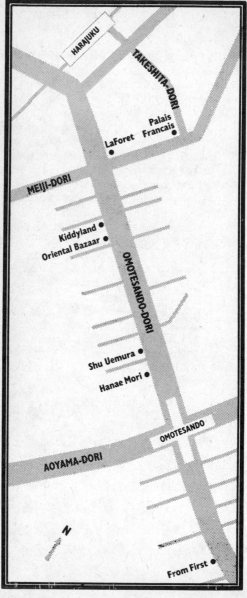

HARAJUKU

● STORE
□ STATION

HARAJUKU

TAKESHITA-DORI

Palais
Francais ●

LaForet ●

MEIJI-DORI

Kiddyland ●

Oriental Bazaar ●

OMOTESANDO-DORI

Shu Uemura ●

Hanae Mori ●

OMOTESANDO

AOYAMA-DORI

N

From First ●

HIRANO (souvenirs)

KOMONIDA (toys)

KOBAYASHI (folk arts)

Warning: Tortoiseshell cannot be legally brought into the United States. Avoid the two or three shops that specialize in tortoiseshell goods. Save the whales! Save the sea tortoises!

Harajuku

The single most must-see fashion area of To-kyo is Harajuku, which connects with Aoyama on one end of the main street, Omotesando-dori, and with the funky young fashion street Takeshita-dori on the other end. The addresses in the middle all read Shibuya, which is a *ku* (ward) that backs up against Minato-ku, where the rest of your basic Aoyama addresses fall, but never mind. Who cares about addresses, anyway?

Getting to Harajuku is easy. If you are tak-ing the JNR line, get off at Harajuku station and start with Takeshita-dori. If you are on the Chiyoda (green), Hanzomon (purple), or Ginza (orange) lines, get out at Omotesando and walk either way. If you use this method, you will come out either at Hanae Mori or across the street (at Paris), which is rather a midpoint to the area. If you want to start at the Aoyama end of Omotesando-dori, take the orange or purple lines and exit at Aoyama 1 Chome or Gaien-Mae (orange line only). You can make your subway stop choice based on where you are coming from or how much time you have. Keep in mind:

▼ You can't be in Tokyo and miss Takeshita, so be sure to come or go from this station.

▼ Aoyama is more the Beverly Hills part of

town; while Omotesando is more Paris—it's the most important stretch in Tokyo. If you have a limited amount of time, go here first.

If you just have an hour or two, opt for Omotesando and walk toward La Foret and then leave from Takeshita. If you have several hours, or the better part of a day, do the whole area.

Takeshita-dori has a life all its own. When you get off the train, you feel the energy. It is different from elsewhere in Tokyo. You will know you are in the right place because everyone else will be younger than you are. Young adults and teenagers will not want to go elsewhere once they have been here. The street has the flavor of a teeny-bopper bazaar. Each shop has its wares displayed on the sidewalk, and each shop plays its own favorite rock music—loudly. The street show is as good as the merchandise. This is definitely one of the places to spot new trends. This is also one of the best areas to get bargains. Prices in all of the stores are moderate. Some of the boutiques even carry secondhand clothing, which is not easy to find elsewhere in Tokyo. We suggest that you walk and explore. Note the cute little crepe stands. Some of the joys of Takeshita-dori:

▼ HARAJUKU LE PONT is a multistory conglomeration of shops and restaurants that stands at the entrance to the street. . . . ▼ At the other end, before you reach Meiji-dori, is another large building, PALAIS FRANÇAIS. . . . ▼ In between are a series of small boutiques set upon each other like building blocks. We enjoy visiting D'LITES PART I for watches, glasses, and accessories. . . . ▼ D'LITES PART II carries sweatshirts and leather jackets. A nice sweatshirt costs $24. . . . ▼ D'LITES PART III has great tourist buttons and backpacks, along with other wonderful junk you don't need. We put together a dinosaur backpack kit complete with buttons, soap, and crayons for under $30. . . . ▼STUDIO FLAME is a boutique catering to the more serious fashions where you can purchase sweaters, coats, and shoes that are not funky but elegant. . . . ▼ VANERA is a boutique on the second floor and caters to men only. A beautiful jacket costs $50. . . . ▼ Across the hall is BEAN STALK, which carries similarly chic and well-priced men's clothing. . . . ▼ SUN DRESS specializes in 1950s prom dresses. These are not the originals, but are in fact manufactured today. Young Japanese women consider this a high-fashion look. A beautiful pink chiffon complete with crinolines costs $50. . . . ▼ Practically next door to Sun Dress is MARCY. MARCY carries preppy clothing with a 1960s look. The shops go on and on—both sides of the street and down the side alleys.

Also don't miss: ▼ HARADA's—there are two different shops in the block, with its high-style Camp Beverly Hills look . . . ▼ MARGO for Chanel copies . . . ▼ THE SILHOUETTE for used clothes . . . ▼ GOOD DAY HOUSE for the Villager meets Kansai and all the Japanese-American preppy you could ever stand . . . ▼ HAPPY CALL . . . ▼ SOS . . . ▼CRAZY CAT . . . ▼ELEPHANT . . . ▼PIE CLUB . . . ▼ SCHEER'S . . . ▼ SPORTS VOGUE . . . all have young, trendy clothes. Then there's ▼CHICAGO-SHITEN . . . with used American clothes and vintage kimonos.

Every style, every look, every price range is available. We haven't even mentioned an eighth of what is there. It's all fun. The stores stay open until 9:00 P.M. most evenings.

After you pass Palais Français you will be at the crossroads of Takeshita-dori and Meiji-dori. You'll see an Eddie Bauer shop and Backwoods—both marked in English—as landmarks. If you are going straight to Kansai, turn left. Otherwise, turn right and continue to Omotesando-dori, where you will turn left. But don't miss some of the fun shops along the way— ▼ DIANA for great shoes and ▼ LA FORET for great so-this-is-Tokyo.

Omotesando-dori is the Champs-Élysées of Tokyo. It is not a street, but a boulevard lined with trees and street cafes. It is the place to go to ogle the fashion models as they lunch between shows at the Hanae Mori Building. It is the place to price-shop all the big-name designers. It is the place just to relax and stroll. It is a great place to shop. Sunday is the day when the park side of the street is closed to traffic and the young people dance.

Stroll and enjoy, and try not to miss:

▼

VIVRE21: This exciting building was constructed on the principle that architecture is the inspiration that will make shoppers want to come in, stay, and buy. The architects were not wrong. Vivre21 is a five-story white museum dedicated to fashion and the beautiful life. The entry and first floor are designed with rose marble floors reminiscent of Trump Tower in New York. The layout of the floors is elliptical, rotating around the dramatic center staircase, which is open to all six stories (the basement makes 6). Hanging in the center open staircase are banks of televisions displaying the latest fashion shows of the designers in the complex, and colorful banners. The building directory is a graphic tour de force, with all of the floors displayed as ellipses (they actually look more like flying saucers). Rock music plays everywhere, of course.

The individual boutiques have their own design personalities. You never feel you are in a department store. The basement contains housewares and food shops. Main-floor boutiques include Madame Nicole, Renoma, Nicole Club for Men, Takeo Kikuchi (an important find), Aujourd' hui, Yushi, and Anne Marie Beretta. Don't miss the Cafe B Haus if you are looking for a place to rest and have coffee. The second and third floors contain more designer boutiques, including Michiko Koshino (yes, this is the middle sister to Hiroko and Junko), Zelda, Junko Sagawa, Shin Hosokawa, and Norma Kamali, who is very popular in Japan. The fourth floor is a "members only" health and beauty club. The fifth floor is an Italian restaurant and professional recording studio.

VIVRE21, 5-10-1 Jingumae, Shibuya-ku

▼

KIDDYLAND: This sounds like the answer to every child's dream and every parent's nightmare. Actually, it is just that. Five floors plus basement are crammed with stuffed animals; party goods; greeting cards; hobbies; games; dolls; computers; fashion accessories for the young; and toys that walk, talk, recite stories, or just sit there being expensive. We didn't find that the prices were any great shakes; we prefer buying our toys under the tracks in Ueno. However, the selection is incredible and the prices are competitive with all the other fancies. So if you cannot get to Ueno, employ our Moscow Rule of Shopping and buy for baby, his brother, his cousin, her sister, and all those other children who are expecting toys from Japan.

KIDDYLAND, 6-1-9 Jingumae, Shibuya-ku

▼

ORIENTAL BAZAAR: This name is whispered on tour buses and in the hallways of major hotels. It is the place everyone will suggest to you, even the locals. It is a landmark in Harajuku. It is a place to see for yourself. In our opinion, you can do better elsewhere. The Oriental Bazaar has the reputation for making shopping easy if you are looking for "Japanese products." If you are shopping for only one day and must bring back some touristy items, here you go. However, if you are seriously shopping for antiques and kimonos, understand that you will not necessarily find the best selections or prices. You will find quantity, and shopping is easy. You'll also find that you are treated like a tourist and that this shop is not much different from your local Azuma or Pier One Imports. The sales help cater to Western ways, and most of the help either speak or understand English. The building is a replica of an old Japanese pagoda, complete with a big Buddha in the entry. The basement carries used Japanese kimonos in a variety of styles and price ranges. We do speak highly of the kimonos just because it is hard to find nice, used kimonos—prices here are much cheaper than at Hiyashi. You'll pay $30 for a clean used kimono, as opposed to $60 at Hiyashi. The main floor has Japanese bronze lanterns ($250), new wooden lacquer boxes (over $15), antique netsuke and carved vases (over $30), Imari plates ($300), blue and white ware lamps (over $50), and Satsumi and Kutani vases ($60 to $250). The second floor has the Mori Art Silver shop (specializing in pearls, silver, and ivory carvings), and the best collection of tourist junk—including inexpensive dolls—this side of the airport. This is *primo* tourist ground—be warned.

ORIENTAL BAZAAR, 5-9-13 Jingumae, Shibuya-ku

▼

PAUL STUART JAPAN: We consider this building to be a wonderful peek at modern Japanese architecture. The base of the building looks like a sixteenth-century fort shipped directly from London. The four-story office building above is 1950s reflective glass, cement, and glass block. The Paul Stuart boutique occupies the main floor, with a mezzanine above. The door handles to the boutique are brass with leather wraps. When you walk inside the boutique, you will think you are back in America, and we don't mean in the sixteenth century. The shop has emerald green carpet, elegant wood-paneled display cases, and a wishing fountain under the wide staircase that leads to the mezzanine. The clothing is pure Paul Stuart. Shirts cost $50. A cashmere cardigan runs $200. Wool crew necks in fabulous patterns cost $90 to $100. Ladies' clothing also is available. Formal wear is on the mezzanine.

PAUL STUART JAPAN, 5-7-20 Jingumae, Shibuya-ku

▼

ISHIZAKI FUR COMPANY: This award-winning fur company is worth a look even if you are not buying. The designers have done some beautiful things combining minks of different colors in geometric shapes. The displays in the window are for special order only, and we would hate to ask the price. More reasonable furs are available on the racks. A good-quality female skin mink jacket is $3,500, and a Fendi look-alike fur raincoat runs $900.

ISHIZAKI FUR COMPANY, 2-3 Jingumae, Shibuya-ku

▼

SHU UEMURA BEAUTY BOUTIQUE: This is the largest of the various Shu Uemura boutiques and usually is jammed with customers.

Shu Uemura began his business designing makeup for the theater. However, when he branched out to the general public, he became a sensation. The color selections are very dramatic and unusual. Many of the colors are too strong if you are trying to look like the "girl next door." But if you love fashion and design as we do, putting on a fresh lavender or aubergine shadow can make your day. The eye shadows go on smoothly and stay on well. The eye pencils are just the right consistency for good application. The brushes are very overpriced but wonderful. You can put together your own makeup boxes by combining little individual eye shadows and blushers into a bigger box. This makes a superb gift for your most up-to-the-minute fashion friend back home. You better like them a lot, however, because the makeup is not inexpensive. Each individual eye shadow runs $8. Brushes go from $2 for the teeniest to $30 for the biggies. Although we complain about the prices when buying, every time we return home we complain that we did not buy more.

SHU UEMURA, 5-1-3 Jingumae, Shibuya-ku

▼

HANAE MORI BUILDING: Hanae Mori is the unchallenged *grande dame* of Japanese fashion. Her building is a brilliant tribute to this fact. Built in 1978 by Kenzo Tange, who also designed the Akasaka Prince Hotel, the structure mirrors all that goes on around and in the center courtyard is a series of off-center stacked building blocks that look like they were put together by a talented five-year-old. In fact, achieving this look takes a lot of knowledge and talent. The center sculpture, which sits in the courtyard entry, is a silver obelisk with a moving spiral top. Watching it twist is quite hypnotic. Just inside the building on the right

is a cafe, which also has tables in the courtyard. This is our favorite place to sit and sip
cappuccino while watching the most chic of
the Tokyo fashion crowd come and go. Enter
the building and go to the right for scarves,
accessories, shoes, and handbags. These items
are the best values in the building. Wonderful
black and white pleated evening bags cost $90.
Gold and black evening slippers cost $75. The
matching handbag costs $90. If you buy a few
pairs of shoes and don't want to carry them
with you all day, they will deliver to your hotel
(free, of course). Beautiful evening scarves that
pack flat and make spectacular gifts cost $75.
Little handkerchiefs with the Hanae Mori butterfly design printed in the corner are $2. Um-
brellas using the Hanae Mori butterfly motif
cost $35.

Announcement: Not all the merchandise is
from Hanae Mori; some imported stuff is
thrown in for good measure. Shop carefully—
that gorgeous Carlos Falchi bag is no cheaper
in Tokyo than at home. It's also no more
expensive. If HM makes it, buy it; otherwise,
just sniff out the territory.

The upstairs floors house the ready-to-wear
and couture collections as well as offices and
showrooms and a very formal kimono shop.
The basement contains an interesting collection of antiques shops: ▼ETSU carries traditional Japanese goods ... ▼SOUL TRIP has
American flapper dresses and Victorian lace
collars ... ▼GOOD GIRL sells a good deal of
1950s memorabilia ... ▼JAPANESQUE is a
good place to look for quality Japanese antiques ... ▼ There is also a wonderful antique
doll shop and a shop, NANCY, that carries
Art Nouveau pieces.

HANAE MORI BUILDING, 3-6-1 Kita-Aoyama,
Minato-ku

AOYAMA

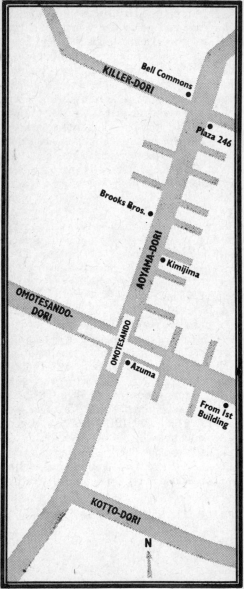

Aoyama

At one end of Harajuku's Omotesando is Aoyama-dori, the main street of the Aoyama district. Aoyama-dori does not have the high-fashion feeling of Omotesando or the young and trendy look of Takeshita-dori. It caters more to the mid-twenties, thirties, and forties working set who want quality. Aoyama has as many boutiques as any other area. Some are designer but more are "real people." One end of the main street, Aoyama-dori, connects into Roppongi's Gaien-higashi-dori. The other end dead-ends into Shibuya. Aoyama includes the far side of Omotesando, and the famous antiques street Kotto-dori.

To reach Aoyama, take the Hanzomon (purple) or Ginza (orange) line, exiting at either Gaien-Mae or Aoyama 1 Chome. We prefer to exit at Gaien-Mae because it puts us almost directly in front of Bell Commons and the street affectionately called Killer-dori by many who have gone to the limit with their credit cards. See our tour (page 302) for this street.

▼

BELL COMMONS: Built by the owners of Suzuya, Bell Commons has become a fashion center for the young. All shops are individually owned, although the building works like a department store. The eight floors plus basement carry a diverse assortment of goods. . . . ▼Start in the basement and check out MIHAMA SHOES, a brand that is very popular with young working women . . . ▼ Also in the basement, BOUTIQUE COFINTEX CAROLL carries a wonderful and colorful knit line. The main floor sells accessories, shoes, and gift items. The second through the seventh floors have the usual assortment of ready-to-wear and restaurants; the eighth floor is a full-service health club. You may want to check in.

BELL COMMONS, 2-14-6 Kita-Aoyama, Minato-ku

▼

JAPAN TRADITIONAL CRAFT CENTER: Located on the second floor of an office/retail building, this is a wonderful place to spend some time if you are interested in the arts and crafts of Japan. There are selected items for sale, as well as exhibits of items that are not. The display space is very big and is broken down into areas. The back is devoted to research and education. A videoscreen shows craftspeople at work. The voice-over narration (in English) explains what is being done. A library (Japanese-language only) has reference books that we can only imagine are wonderful. The opposite side of the floor is a permanent exhibit of the best of different craft items, including masks, lacquerware, textiles, and rice papers. In the center are items for sale.

JAPAN TRADITIONAL CRAFT CENTER, 3-1-1 Minami-Aoyama, Minato-ku

▼

BROOKS BROTHERS: We almost fell over the first time we saw the Brooks Brothers store on Aoyama-dori. There is nothing wrong with it; it's just not our image of Japanese fashion. Imagine Issey Miyake in a Brooks Brothers suit. However, if the truth be known, Brooks Brothers is more the image of the conservative businessman than Miyake. Japanese businesspeople are very conservative! The atmosphere is Madison Avenue, and a lot of the shoppers are *gaijin* who are hoping their arms aren't too long for the shirts. Warning tip: These clothes are made for the Japanese; the pattern is different from the American cut. Suits are still boxy, but the boxes are smaller.

BROOKS BROTHERS, 3-5-6 Kita-Aoyama, Minato-ku

▼

TWO: This is the shop of a young designer, Yuka Ikura, who we think is going places. She is just in her twenties but has a sense of style and fashion that is very exciting. The shop is teeny. The interior architecture is dramatic. The merchandise is wonderful. Not all of the things in the shop are designed by Ms. Ikura.

TWO, 3-12-12 Minami-Aoyama, Minato-ku

▼

KIMIJIMA: Ichiro Kimijima has been designing for the rich and famous for over twenty-five years. He is "in" with the royal families, "in" with the ambassadors' wives, and "in" with those who love *haute couture*. Every season he has a fashion show at the Imperial Hotel, where all of his fans come, buy, and applaud. Actually, there are three separate lines. One line is designed for the European market and the Paris collections (Kimijima has a boutique on Avenue Victor Hugo in Paris). One line is done for the Japanese *haute couture* buyers only. One line is a ready-to-wear line that is sold in the Japanese department stores and small boutiques, including his own, which is directly across the street from his *haute* *couture* boutique and offices on Aoyama-dori. Prices are high—a suit starts at $1,000. Evening dresses are much more.

KIMIJIMA, 3-18-19 Minami-Aoyama, Minato-ku

▼

JUN ASHIDA: This boutique is our favorite for interior design. The look is Neoclassic Memphic Milano at its finest. Theatrical klieg lights, faux marble columns, and hi-tech accessories all blend together to create a stage setting. Actually, the interiors rather overwhelm the clothes. Jun Ashida's designs are popular with wealthy middle-age ladies and their daughters. The look is simple and clean, not at all exciting. The line resembles the Villager clothing of the 1960s, done with Victorian lace collars.

JUN ASHIDA, 3-5-7 Kita-Aoyama, Minato-ku

At this point you will have reached Omotesando crossing. Since we have already covered the boutiques to the right (this is Harajuku), we suggest you turn left and head away from the Hanae Mori Building. You should be on the same side of Aoyama-dori as Azuma.

▼

AZUMA: This is a good sporting-goods store in the area for buying Fila, Munsingwear, and Grand Slam. The Japanese manufacture their own Fila under license. The quality is excellent, although the styles are scaled down to fit the smaller Japanese man. Size 44 American men need not apply. There is good stock in skiwear and tenniswear. A Fila ski jacket costs $200; ski sweater, $100; tennis skirt, $40; and shirt, $40. It is located on the corner of Aoyama-dori and Omotesando-dori.

AZUMA, Minami-Aoyama, Minato-ku

▼

PLANTATION: Farther down Omotesando is the Issey Miyake Plantation boutique for men and women. The store is long and narrow, with the men's collection upstairs and the women's downstairs. The men's store is designed so that the minimal space is used to the best advantage. On the left are shelves for sweater displays. On the right, the suits and shirts are combined in ensembles and racked on hangers. The result is a functional and colorful display of the collection. The women's shop downstairs is claustrophobic. Prices are 30% cheaper in Tokyo than in the United States—no steals here, but some savings if you've got the money for Miyake.

PLANTATION, 4-21-29 Minami-Aoyama, Minato-ku

▼

PORTOBELLO'S: Although this is also a two-level display of men's and women's clothing, it has a very different look. The men's collection is classic and stylish; the women's, glitzy. Evening sweaters in the women's boutique cost in the $400 range.

PORTOBELLO'S, 4-21-24 Minami-Aoyama, Minato-ku

▼

FROM 1ST: This is not a boutique but a building housing many boutiques. Designed by Yamashita Kazumasa to be housing, From 1st has become more famous as the location of Issey Miyake, Comme des Garçons, Alpha Cubic, Cerutti 1881, Moga, and the trendy restaurants Cafe Figaro and Le Poisson Rouge.

FROM 1ST BUILDING, 5-3-10 Minami-Aoyama, Minato-ku

▼

ISSEY MIYAKE: There is a very good selection of Miyake's latest styles in this large, open boutique in the From 1st Building. The boutique is glass-enclosed and light-filled. The decor is minimal. Miyake's clothing stands on its own and does not need any hype.

ISSEY MIYAKE, From 1st Building, 5-3-10 Minami-Aoyama, Minato-ku

▼

COMME DES GARÇONS: Rei Kawakubo designs in natural fabrics and colors. Nothing is glitzy, garish, or glamorous in her look. However, she is an international hit for just that reason. This is the largest of the women's boutiques. Buy black, white, or grey.

COMME DES GARÇONS, From 1st Building, 5-3-10 Minami-Aoyama, Minato-ku

▼

ALPHA CUBIC: Three levels of classic, well-priced sportswear, shoes, and accessory items are housed under Alpha Cubic's sign. The basement carries the Alpha Cubic and Linea lines. The top floor has a complete Guido Pasquali boutique. A tailor on the premises will shorten or lengthen hemlines. This is a very popular shop for the area's working girls. The prices are terrific, and service is great.

ALPHA CUBIC, From 1st Building, 5-3-10 Minami-Aoyama, Minato-ku

▼

CERUTTI 1881: Very expensive and very beautiful, the Cerutti clothing is hidden in the basement. The styles are direct from Paris, which is why they are so expensive. Silk shirts sell for from $150 to $600. Suits can be purchased for $300 to $1,000.

CERUTTI 1881, From 1st Building, 5-3-10 Minami-Aoyama, Minato-ku

The only other street to be concerned with in the Aoyama district is Kotto-dori, which is farther down Aoyama-dori toward Shibuya. After passing Omotesando, it will be the next large street. You want to walk left. We discuss most of the antiques shops on this street in our section on antiques (page 294), but there also are some boutiques not to miss.

▼

SHIMADA FOREIGN BOOKS: We know you can't wear books, but when you are in a city where you don't speak the language, a foreign bookstore is often a sight for sore eyes. This particular one is small and jammed with both people and books. Your tendency will be to pass it by, but if you don't know how wonderful Japanese publishing is, now is the time to learn.

SHIMADA FOREIGN BOOKS, 5-9-19 Minami-Aoyama, Minato-ku

▼

KINSHIDO: This is a tiny and elegant women's clothing shop selling Miss Carven from Paris and other French lines. It seems out of place but is a nice find in the midst of craziness.

KINSHIDO, 5-9-15 Minami-Aoyama, Minato-ku

▼

COMME DES GARÇONS—HOMMES: Rei Kawakubo's designs for men become even more spare than is almost possible to bear. The interior architecture consists of silver poles, granite flooring, and not much else.

COMME DES GARÇONS—HOMMES, 5-12-3 Minami-Aoyama, Minato-ku

▼

PAUL SMITH: This is the Tokyo branch of the London boutique that is so popular there. The styles and sizes are duplicated. The materials used are the original British.

PAUL SMITH, 6-3-11 Minami-Aoyama, Minato-ku

▼

JUNKO KOSHINO: The boutique is at the far end of Kotto-dori. You will need a transfusion by the time you get there. However, if you are determined enough to walk the distance, you won't be disappointed. Koshino's designs are well stocked and well displayed. Junko is the youngest of the three sisters.

JUNKO KOSHINO, 6-5-36 Minami-Aoyama, Minato-ku

Shibuya

Shibuya is a fashion extension of Harajuku and Aoyama. Unlike them, however, the area is dominated by a few very large fashion buildings and not many boutiques. The emphasis is on young fashion and life-style. Shibuya caters to a more conservative group of young people than Harajuku, and a less sophisticated group than Roppongi. The styles in the stores here blend trendy and everyday.

Shibuya station is the focal point of the area, being the third most traveled station in Tokyo. Five different subway and rail lines converge here. Use either the JNR (Yamanote line) or the Ginza (orange), Hanzomon (purple), Inogashira, or Shin-Tamagawa lines to reach Shibuya. As you exit the station be aware that you are under the Toyku department store. This is a great place to pick up odds and ends you might have forgotten in your travels. Like all the Tokyo department stores, Toyku has everything. Surrounding the station are many colorful buildings with banners and neon signs. Throngs of people are walking in every direction. If you don't stand aside and collect your

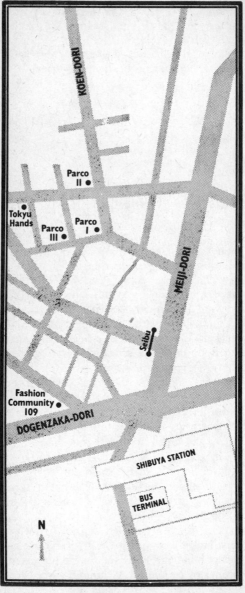

SHIBUYA

● STORE
□ STATION

KOEN-DORI

Parco II ●

Tokyu Hands ●

Parco III ●   Parco I ●

MEIJI-DORI

Seibu ●

Fashion Community 109 ●

DOGENZAKA-DORI

SHIBUYA STATION

BUS TERMINAL

N

thoughts, you will most likely end up across the street before you know whether you want to be there or not. Actually there are two directions in which you should walk to find the major fashion buildings. Left will take you to the Fashion 109 Building, and straight ahead will lead you to Parco, Seibu, and Tokyu Hands.

▼

FASHION 109: As you go left from the train station, look for a silver tower and a fork in the main drag. At this intersection you will see the high-tech Fashion 109 Building. Built by Komada Design Office, this is the gathering place for the youth who want to hang out, disco, and shop. The eight floors include teen thrills, big names, and a rock video screening room on the top floor. However, just because the merchandise is geared to the young does not mean it is cheap. Prices are mixed. Charles Jourdan shoes cost $150. However, you can buy a very chic jacket for only $75. The styles are trendy, not funky. All floors have a mixture of fashion and accessory items.

FASHION 109, 2-29-1 Dogenzaka, Shibuya-ku

▼

SEIBU: Walk back toward the Shibuya station from Fashion 109 and take a left on the second major street. You will be walking parallel to the aboveground train tracks. Look for the Max Factor sign. Seibu will be on your left and is contained in two buildings joined by bridges on every other floor. This is one of the largest and most fashionable Seibus in the chain. Don't miss the basement for used clothing— very unusual in Tokyo. The basement also contains a wonderful charcuterie and fruit market. Look on the main floor for top-notch accessories. The second and third floors have big-name designers, including Ralph Lauren, Norma Kamali, and Jean-Paul Gaultier. A Kenzo sweater costs $150, a Burberry raincoat, $400 (Japanese franchise). We have seen Burberry raincoats, imported from England, for $1,000. There is a crossover bridge to the men's store on the third floor. The fourth floor is for children, with an especially good boys' section. The fifth floor has Japanese designers, including Madame Hanai, Takeo Nishida, Yuki Torii, Yukisaburo Watanabe, and Jun Ashida. The sixth floor is Issey Miyake, kimonos, and a sleep shop. The seventh floor has Hermès, fine jewelry, and bridal, while the top floor is devoted to restaurants.

SEIBU, 21-1 Udagawa-cho, Shibuya-ku

▼

PARCO I, II, III: Walking away from Seibu and the train station, look up and to the left. You will immediately see the large Parco I building. Parco has three separate stores, each broken up into even more boutiques. Part I has nine floors, Part II six floors, and Part III seven floors. With an average of five boutiques to a floor, how many does that make? Each complex has the feel of a department store but is run more like a shopping mall. There is great variety in the individuality of each boutique. Lots of trendy fashions are represented, along with some of the big names, such as Issey Miyake. Most of the fashion lines represented are names you will not know. These will be your best bargains. Don't miss the sixth floor of Parco Part I. As you get off the escalator look at the yellow, blue, green, and pink booths. Each has a cutout of some heavenly item (star, moon, etc.), behind which sits a fortune teller. We were dying to ask one of them if we would have the good fortune to find an Issey Miyake sale. The Issey Miyake boutique is on the street level, between Parcos I and II. We did find a sale. Parcos II and III are yet more of Parco I, with a twist. Just doing Parco could easily be a two-day adventure. We enjoy coming here, especially on a Saturday, when most of the locals are shopping. Trend-spotting is the best at this time.

PARCO I, II, III, 14 Udagawa-cho, Shibuya-ku

▼

VICTORIA: Another large building in Shibuya, behind Parco II, is Victoria. This is the place to come for sports gear of any kind, shape, style, or variety. Every major brand is represented, as is every sport. Rock music blares over the loudspeakers. No one speaks English. All the prices are clearly marked. Yamaha sweatsuits are $50. Ellesse ski sweaters cost $150; sweatsuits, $40. Killy skisuits are $200. There are eight floors of outfits and equipment. This is one of a chain of such stores. They publish a great catalogue—if you read Japanese.

VICTORIA, 3-10 Udagawa-cho, Shibuya-ku

▼

TOKYU HANDS: Billing itself as a "creative life" store, Tokyu Hands is the largest hobby shop in Tokyo. There are three sections, with eight floors per section. Each floor is filled with things to do or make for your home. If you are looking for electronic equipment, stationery, jewelry crafts, ceramic supplies, hardware, knock-down furniture, paint, models, wallpaper, bathroom goods, gift items, curtains, blinds, kitchen utensils, party supplies, gardening tools, or a flower shop, don't forget to stop here. Did we leave anything out? This is an unbelievable store.

TOKYU HANDS, 12-18 Udagawa-cho, Shibuya-ku

▼

HIGHSTONE: Across the street from Tokyu Hands is another fashion building with only five floors of boutiques, restaurants, and things to do. This is a young-fashion building, with an emphasis on sports as represented by the sports boutique Highstone, which occupies three of the five floors.

HIGHSTONE, 4-7 Udagawa-cho, Shibuya-ku

▼

CABIN BUILDING: On your way back to the train station, you might want to stop at yet another fashion building, directly across from the *koban*. Our favorite boutique within this building is The Concept, which carries a wonderful line of inexpensive knit separates. All of the Japanese girls are buying these like crazy. Prices are cheap. A knit skirt costs $30; a coordinating top, $40. The eighth floor of the Cabin Building is a video screening room showing all of the latest rock videos. The young people love to gather here.

CABIN BUILDING, 30-7, Udagawa-cho, Shibuya-ku

KANDA/JIMBOCHO

● STORE
☐ STATION

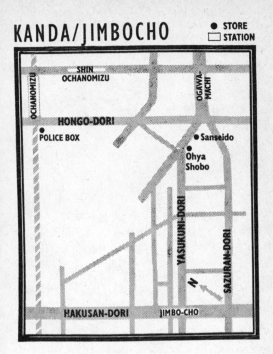

Kanda/Jimbocho

Kanda and Jimbocho are both book towns. They are side by side, and walkable, to and fro. Take the Tozai (blue) or Chiyoda (green) line to the Jimbocho station. If you want to start in Kanda first, the JNR or Ginza (orange) line will take you to the Kanda station.

Kanda and Jimbocho have an abundance of stores with used books, many of which have *ukiyo-e* prints—those fabulous hand-colored wood blocks—in the back. We have found some of our most prized prints under books hidden on the shelves of these shops. These areas cater to students and collectors alike. As a result, you will find modern textbooks on the shelves next to tattered old manuscripts. If you are allergic to dust watch out; these shops are filled with fine print and dust. Kanda also has a large number of sports shops catering to the students of the area.

We have had the best times in these two sections on days when we were not rushing anywhere and had the time to wander, get lost, and wander some more. The number of wonderful bookstores is endless. The sports shops just seem to multiply. Some of our favorite finds are the following shops (there are a hundred more):

▼

MINAMI SPORTS: This is by far the most famous of the sports shops in the area. There are several branches in Kanda alone. This one is the biggest and has many floors, each one catering to a different sport. You don't have to waste your time kicking aside soccer balls when you are really looking for golf shoes.

MINAMI SPORTS, 3-1 Kanda Ogawamachi, Chiyoda-ku

▼

VICTORIA: The Japanese have a love for big shops, and Victoria fills the bill. This is the main branch, but there are ten others you can visit in Kanda. Skiing is the specialty here, with every detail of a ski outfit available.

VICTORIA, 3-6 Kanda Ogawamachi, Chiyoda-ku

▼

SANSEIDO: This is a modern and clean book-tower in the heart of the Kanda used-book area. Eight floors of books, magazines, videotapes, and computer software are available in many languages, including English. There is a large selection of technical engineering works.

SANSEIDO, 1-1 Kanda, Jimbocho, Chiyoda-ku

▼

OYA-SHOBO: This is our favorite find in Kanda. It is practically next door to Sanseido, and it can't be missed because of the framed picture of a samurai that hangs over the door. Inside, the shop resembles something out of a Peter Lorre mystery movie. Stacks of old books and magazines are piled on the windowsill, on the floor, on the stairs, and on the counters. Rare old manuscripts are shelved lovingly in the back. Usually there are two old Japanese men poring over tattered and weatherbeaten texts, talking excitedly about whatever they have found. Old maps hang from the walls. The atmosphere is dark, dank, and dusty—just what a shop for old books should be. *Ukiyo-e* (woodblock) prints are available in many price ranges. Original ones from the Edo Period run $100 and up, depending on their condition. Good duplications, hand-colored, cost about $20 to $30. No credit cards are accepted, so come armed with *mucho* cash. You will be disappointed if you have to walk away from this find empty-handed. Not much English is spoken here.

OYA-SHOBO, 1-2 Kanda, Jimbocho, Chiyoda-ku

▼

HARA-SHOBO: This is another wonderful place to browse for old books and *ukiyo-e* prints. Don't be put off by the books you see upon entering. The good stuff is all on the second

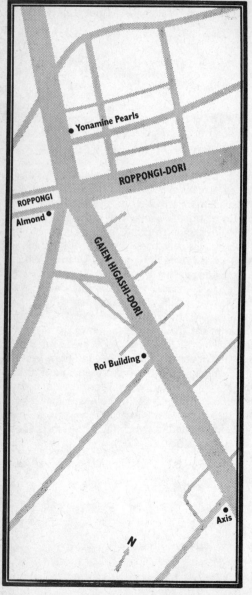

ROPPONGI

● STORE
☐ STATION

Yonamine Pearls ●

ROPPONGI-DORI

☐ ROPPONGI

Almond ●

GAIEN HIGASHI-DORI

Roi Building ●

Axis ●

N

floor. Hara-Shobo has a great section for *omiyage* (gift-giving), as well as an exceptional selection of *ukiyo-e* prints. They are one of the few stores that will mail-order. Ask to see their catalogue.

HARA-SHOBO, 2-3 Kanda, Jimbocho, Chiyoda-ku

Roppongi

Roppongi takes a little getting used to. When you step out of the subway, you may be singing, "Is that all there is?," but by the time you've been to Axis you will be thinking that this is the Tokyo version of the New York Upper East Side, or better yet, the new Upper West Side. Roppongi is the area where you will find the chic, fun, young set hanging out, dining, and shopping. Spago, Tony Roma, expensive American restaurants—here you go. The American Club, even the Soviet embassy—step this way. The famous Almond? This is the place. The area is very often grouped together with Akasaka, but we see no physical or shopping reason to do so. Roppongi has an abundance of stores catering to Japanese singles and yuppies. Good design is the emphasis in all of the stores. It is an easy area to walk and is one of the few areas where it is actually hard to get lost. Just remember: Don't judge a neighborhood by the way the street looks when you come out of the subway.

Get to Roppongi via the Hibiya subway line.

Once you hit the street, you will be in the middle of the action. The Almond Restaurant at the corner of Roppongi-dori and Gaien-higashi-dori is the focal point for the area. As the day wears on, more and more young people gather in front of the Almond to chat and discuss their evening's activities. Roppongi starts to vibrate after dark. The shops aren't open then, but hundreds of restaurants and discotheques entertain the after-work crowds. Roppongi can be an all-day, all-night adventure for the strong of pocketbook and stomach.

Although we love the night life, the shop life really is where our interest remains, especially in Roppongi. Gaien-higashi-dori is the main shopping street. If you stand in front of the Almond (it's pink, you can't miss it) and are facing the entrance, Gaien-higashi-dori will be the large street to your left that intersects Roppongi-dori. If you look carefully, you will find a street sign identifying the street. Take a right down Gaien Street and walk on the right-hand side—where the majority of boutiques are located.

▼

HOTMAN: This is a very popular shop with the locals. When we first peered through the windows, we couldn't quite understand why. The shop is teeny and usually is overcrowded with shoppers. The merchandise looks nice, but it takes a second look to see why the popularity is there. Quality is the answer. Hotman produces styles not found on every towel rack. The first floor has towels; the second, bathrobes and baby wear. Hotman is the Japanese answer to Pratesi.

HOTMAN, 5-2-1 Roppongi, Minato-ku

▼

SHU UEMURA: This is mentioned in various neighborhoods because this fabulous makeup designer's boutiques are everywhere. This one is set back slightly from the street and housed in a little building all its own. Look to the right at the McDonald's, or watch for the Spago sign. The standard wonderful colors and brushes are all there. The atmosphere is, however, more relaxed than in the department-store boutiques. We did not feel that anyone was pressuring us to buy, and we were able to spend an hour testing various colors and combinations of colors without any bother.

SHU UEMURA, Roppongi, Minato-ku

▼

ROI ROPPONGI: This is a four-story building housing many well-known designer boutiques and restaurants. The atmosphere is somewhat like an office building instead of a department store because each boutique is self-owned. Some of the designers found here include Madame Hanai (not to be confused with Hanae Mori), Christian Dior, and Jean-Louis Scherrer. There's even a furrier selling leopard coats, if you want to see the last of a dying breed. The Roi Building has a monthly sale that is famous in local as well as international buying circles.

ROI ROPPONGI, 5-5 Roppongi, Minato-ku

▼

ROPPONGI FORUM: This is just down the street from Roi Roppongi and is a wandering conglomeration of restaurants and shops. The emphasis here is on restaurants, but there is the toy shop Bandai; the boutique Arc-en-Ciel, which carries the Giorgio Armani line; and the Jelart jewelry boutique to keep you occupied between snacks.

ROPPONGI FORUM, 5-16-5 Roppongi, Minato-
ku

▼

AXIS: This is the high-style design building
that is equaled nowhere else in Tokyo. The
building was the first of its kind in the area
and is dedicated to high-style home furnishings where design takes on an art form. The
Axis quarterly journal is published on the premises and describes in detail (in Japanese, of
course) the work of the designers and stores in
the Axis compound. The architecture of the
Axis building is open, flowing, and moving. A
center courtyard opens up to Le Garage, with
its emphasis on everything you never knew
you needed for your car, motorcycle, Honda,
or bicycle, and Living Motif, a store specializing
in hi-tech, well-designed items for the home,
office, and school. The boutiques on the second through fourth floors are a combination of
art galleries (Axis Gallery—4F, Photo Gallery
Wide—4F), design studios (Tokyo Designers
Space—4F, Design Matrix—2F), clothing boutiques (Comme des Garçons—2F, Nuno—B1),
furniture and lighting shops (Arflex—B1F,
Chairs—4F, Cassina Japan—3F, Livina Yamagiwa—2F), and an assortment of other design
sources (Lapis—3F, stationery supplies; Green
Collections—3F, cards; Playthings—2F, games
and puzzles). Our very favorite boutique in
the complex is Nuno—B1, which is the fabric
and design outlet shop for Junichi Arai, former
fabric designer for Issey Miyake and Comme
des Garçons. End bolts of fabric are stacked on
pine shelving on both sides of the shop. The
middle table, Japanese height, contains baskets
of scarves made from some of the fabrics, which
sell for $15. One meter of fabric sells for $30.

AXIS BUILDING, 5-17-1 Roppongi, Minato-ku

At this point we suggest you cross the street and walk back up Gaien-higashi-dori to the intersection of Roppongi-dori. As you cross over from the Axis Building, look on your right for two very interesting antiques shops that are side by side.

▼

DAISHIN SHOKAI: Carries a good selection of porcelains, boxes, clocks, and potpourri.

DAISHIN SHOKAI, 3-15-18 Roppongi, Minato-ku

▼

NISHIDA: Next door to Daishin Shokai, this shop carries a limited selection of lacquer, bronze, and porcelain antiques. There are a few knitting shops here, which sell Australian wool at bargain prices.

NISHIDA, 3-15-18 Roppongi, Minato-ku

If you are interested in pearls and more antiques, cross Roppongi-dori and explore North Roppongi. On North Gaien-higashi-dori you will find Fuso Antiques (3-13-7 Roppongi, Minato-ku), Kurofune Gallery (7-7-4 Roppongi, Minato-ku), and Wally Yonamine Co. Pearls (11-8 Roppongi, Minato-ku) (see page 273).

▼

THE WAVE BUILDING: The only other shopping of interest in Roppongi that is also convenient is in this building located on

AKIHABARA

● STORE
☐ STATION

SUEHIROCHO

CHUO-DORI

Yamagiwa Duty Free

Yamagiwa

Laox

Laox
My Way I
My Way II

Minami

AKIHABARA STATION

SOTOBORI-DORI

N

Roppongi-dori. After you visit North Gaien-
higashi-dori and cross back over Roppongi-
dori, turn right and walk a few blocks until
you spot the sign for the Wave Building. It's
on the same side of the street as Almond.
Basically this is a massive record and video
store, the first and largest in Tokyo. Floors
one through four offer a complete selection of
records, cassettes, and videos. If you can't find
it here, don't bother looking elsewhere. Each
floor has an audiovisual booth where you can
purchase concert tickets or get information on
current artists. The basement houses a movie
theater, Cine Vivant, which often screens foreign films not available for viewing elsewhere
in Tokyo. The main floor has a cafe, and an
assortment of stationery products that are fun
and interesting. You will see some of these
same products at the Axis Building or in Itoya
on Ginza. The prices are all comparable, so if
something strikes your fancy, remember the
Moscow Rule of Shopping and buy it. Only in
the wholesale district will you get a better
price, assuming you can find the same item.
The second floor specializes in videotapes and
cassettes. The third floor has records, and the
fourth floor is where you will find the sheet
music and music books for all of the records
you have just bought.

THE WAVE BUILDING, 6-2-21 Roppongi,
Minato-ku

Akihabara

There isn't an electronics, camera, or sound
freak in America who hasn't heard of Akihabara—the famed circuit city of Tokyo. We do
not recommend that you buy electronic goods
in Tokyo, and we give you the rhymes and

reasons in "Cameras and Electronic Goods" (page 243). We figure you're either going to ignore our advice, or do some pricing on your own, so here goes. And if you find that we are right and electronics are cheaper in the United States, don't forget that we have a nice discount handbag and leathergoods resource (Kuonoike) right next door to the station.

About that station: It's petite when compared with Shinjuku or Ueno, yet is still confusing because it is so long, and if you exit the wrong way, you will get lost; we did. We found the handbag store this way, but we were very frustrated to have seen all the bustle from the train window and to have totally lost it when we got off. The beauty of elevated trains is that you see some of the country; the woe is that in Japan you can't find your way back to where you want to be. Please study the map to get yourself off to a good start. When you leave your train, you want the west exit. This exit is marked in English, but when we went that way we thought we were on another platform, so we turned around and went to the east exit. Don't panic. Follow the crowd out the exit, not to the platform you will pass on the way out. If you pay attention, you'll see what we mean and won't get lost. You may also exit through Akihabara Department Store, a K-Mart type of a place.

Let's just say you go out the east exit. It's the wrong way, but here's what you do. First of all, when you hit the street, turn left for one or two shops until you see a handbag jobber named KUONOIKE, where you'll find high-fashion bags for as low as $50. Their hours are 10:00 A.M. to 6:30 P.M. Once done at Kuonoike, walk back past the train station to the first corner and turn right. You will feel totally lost and miserable. Then you'll see the Washington Hotel (English letters) and know that you've been found. Electronics shops will start popping up, but you won't be in the heart of

Akihabara until you turn right at Minami—or go through the My Way alleys. So that's the worst that can happen, and it's not so bad.

Stores in Akihabara open at 10:00 A.M. and remain open until 7:30 P.M. Usually they are open seven days a week. There is an annual sales festival at the end of the year, usually from about November 15 until January 1; if you buy something valued over $25, you probably will be presented with festival tickets. Tickets qualify you to win various prizes—like in a drawing.

We found the lowest prices in two resources on the far side of the station, off the main drag but near the Washington Hotel—one at ECCS, with its six attractive floors, and the other at SHINTOKU, not as modern or spic and span as ECCS but certainly the exact kind of discount warehouse you are looking for. Look at the multitude of TV tubes at the entrance with the stools set into the ground. There's also a full screening room inside so you can rest your weary body and watch a movie—in English!

Shintoku is easy to shop. There's a huge English sign that says "Welcome to Shintoku." We always take signs in English as a good sign, especially in Tokyo. The duty-free shop is on the second floor. The screening room is on the third floor. The toilets are okay.

Before we go any farther in telling you about Akihabara, a warning word about prices and comparison shopping. Obviously, when we began this adventure, we planned to compare prices, stock, availability, and everything in the neighborhood to give you all the details. But lo and behold, there are very few matchups. One guy sells the Sharp WD200 and the next guy has the WD50 but no 200. On top of that, the marked price—even the marked discount price—may not be the price you pay if you are willing to buy a lot or do some time-consuming, heavy-duty, show-them-your-cash bargaining. In the end, you pretty much have to pick a store and buy all at once to get the best price. While we think Shintoku offers the easiest shopping, that doesn't mean you can't get a good deal at any of the many similar shops here. Besides, we do our serious buying from Leo's in L.A.—his prices are far cheaper than those in Akihabara—or at Forty-seventh Street Photo in Manhattan.

But we digress.

Okay, from Shintoku, walk up the street a few yards and enter either the two arcadelike alleys called MY WAY 1 and MY WAY 2; you'll get to "1" first. They are crammed with electronics and tapes and electronic toys and telephones and people eager to help you. Some of them speak English. You do not need that much English here, just a calculator and some cash. You'll make the best deal with cash. In My Way, while looking to price both the Sharp WD200 and Sharp WD50, we found that they carried only the WD100. Welcome to Tokyo. Don't miss the electronic mah-jong game ($85) if your Aunt Helen has a birthday coming up. CD's were consistently in the $200 to $250 range; they can cost $150 in the United States.

As you walk around, hawkers will note your *gaijin* appearance and speak to you in English, saying things like, "Export here, madame," or "Tax free on second floor, please."

If you think you want to give your business to LAOX—a well-publicized chain of stores—be advised that there are several outlets in the neighborhood. This is where we ran right into the refrigerators because we didn't know any better. Before you make the investment of your time to go upstairs into a shop, ask someone "Tax free?" and motion upward.

Once you turn to the right on the main drag, you see the area you saw from the train and it is an amazing sight. There are three or four blocks of solid electronics shops (some sell electrical goods for contractors), and more neon than you ever will again see in your life.

Many *gaijin* walk around with dazed expressions on their faces.

If you need emotional sustenance, there's a Mister Donut along the way. There are three YAMAGIWA shops, another popular outlet. We like Yamagiwa Hobby for kids' toys, robots, and videogames. Expect to pay $30 for a small electronic game.

After you've seen all and are on your way back to the station, you can walk through the Kanda Fruit and Vegetable Market, which is signed in English. It's not that quaint, but it's kind of fun. The best time is from 6:00 to 9:00 A.M., but if you're there before lunchtime you can buy some fresh fruit or snacks. This is also a good place to buy inexpensive baskets.

LAOX, 1-2-9 Sotokanda, Chiyoda-ku (Akihabara main store)

LAOX, Shinjuku, B-1 Duty Free, 15-16 Shinjuku, 3-Chome, Shinjuku-ku

YAMAGIWA, 3-13-10 Sotokanda, Chiyoda-ku

MINAMI DENKI, 1-15-2 Sotokanda, Chiyoda-ku

SHINTOKU, 1-16-9 Sotokanda, Chiyoda-ku

Ueno

Just in case you were missing our little slogans and nicknames for Japanese places of the heart, here goes: *Ueno is bueno.* If Spanish isn't your language, either, then you'll just have to take our word for it that Ueno is a very good place.

You can "do" Ueno in a variety of ways:

▼ Quick one or two hours in Ameya-Yokocho Shopping Street, the famed "under the railroad tracks" discount area that was home to the black market in World War II.

UENO

● STORE
□ STATION

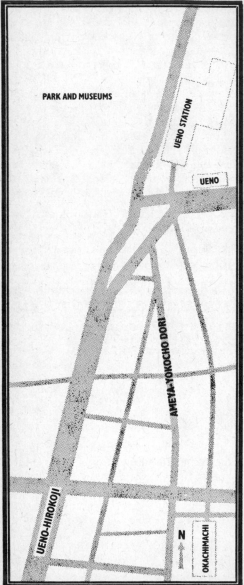

PARK AND MUSEUMS

UENO STATION

UENO

AMEYA-YOKOCHO DORI

UENO-HIROKOJI

N

OKACHIMACHI

▼ You can make an entire day of it and take in the park, the pandas, the art museums, the natural science and natural history museums, the pond (you can rent a boat); you can even see the cherry blossoms in April.

▼ You can make a whole day of shopping by doing a half-day bargain day and another half-day nonbargain day in the streets that surround Ameya-Yokocho; after all, "under the tracks" is not the only place you can shop in this delicious area.

▼ You can make a half-day shopping adventure by beginning at Ueno station and walking to Okachimachi station, a walk of probably not much more than a mile but one dense with shops and bargains and people and fun.

▼ If you just want to do the bargain end, begin at Okachimachi station and work the surrounding area (see map), then enter into Ameya-Yokocho Shopping Street and walk toward Ueno station. You cannot miss the area because there is a huge archway with neon letters that say "Shopping" (in English). It's our favorite word. The Okachimachi end is more bargain- and junk-oriented than the Ueno end; here you'll find many small department stores selling American and European closeouts and discontinued Japanese merchandise.

Since by now you love Ueno, you are smiling and nodding and drooling but don't know where to begin. We'll start you off; just reverse it if you begin at Okachimachi.

The Ueno train station is a large combination train and subway station, but it's light and bright and relatively easy to find your way here. It is not nearly as confusing as Shinjuku. Ueno is a very friendly place. Inside the train station you will see some souvenir shops selling lanterns and junk that you haven't seen sold in other train stations. Don't miss the gigantic (fake) stuffed panda in the glass case in the front portion of the station. This is a good place to meet people or to take family pictures. Although there are several exits from the station, don't worry about getting lost here. Attached to the station on the outside are many vendors and minimalls selling more tourist items; they lead all the way to the steps into the park. Between the elevated railroad tracks and the steps to the park you will see an arch with dark letters that say *Ueno* on the top, then *kanji, kanji, kanji* (the *kanji* part is in red), and then *Ameyayokocho* on the bottom; there are also little picturegrams on the sign of people shopping. You can't miss it.

There are a couple of department stores in the area: Keisei, AbAb, and the more well-known Matsuzakaya. We love the sights and the bargain prices of a street market, so we stay in the flow where the average shop has seven feet of frontage space. Fresh fish and foods are sold, as well as everything from real guns to toy guns. We have mentioned "under the tracks" repeatedly throughout the text of this book; this is it. Everything you want, except pearls, is here at the best prices in Japan. Some of the things we bought:

Men's high-fashion flannel blazer, fully lined, $60.00
Kids' running shoes, high-fashion design, $7.00
Preppy button-down shirts, $15.00
Transformer toy, $2.50
Teen high-fashion baseball jacket with chenille letters, $50.00
Boys' Popeye baseball-style jacket, $40.00
Chanel handbag (the real thing), $385.00
Imitation (very) Rolex watch, $50.00
Alligator logo men's socks, $2.50 a pair
Luggage carts, $10.00
Backpacks, $20.00

At Okachimachi, the quality of the merchandise dwindles. While everything sold "under the tracks" is new and just discounted, the stores that cluster around the Okachimachi station sell Korean-made fakes, factory overruns, old merchandise, and discontinued junk. We found many European-designer goods here for a fraction of their cost—shoes by Madras, Bally, Yves Saint Laurent, etc. Lots of Roberta DiCamerino merchandise, as well as shirts and sweats with a little alligator on them.

Now then, a few words of directions. If you go directly to Okachimachi by JNR, you will exit the train station across from the arch that says "Shopping." This is the far end of the Ameya. If you take the Hibaya subway line to the Naka-Okachimachi station, you will exit right in the middle of junk heaven. There is only one block between these two stations, but we mention this because you may get confused otherwise. The train station and the subway station are not one and the same. If nothing makes you happier than prowling around imitation and junk merchandise, take the Hibaya line—exit for the junk—then waltz under the "Shopping" arch and into the Ameya strip, walking toward Ueno. You have to like down and dirty (or fun and funky), but if you do, this just may be the highlight of your trip to Tokyo.

If you still are interested in the Ueno area, check the map to see that there's indeed more here than the park, the museums, and the bargain area "under the tracks." Away from the park, you'll see a large Matsuzakaya, sort of a neighborhood Sears department store. There is a triangular shopping area bordered by Shinobazu Park on one side (that's the pond where you can rent a boat) and Kasuga-dori Street on the other; Kasuga-dori Street will cross Ueno-Hirokoji Street at Matsuzakaya, just about two blocks short of the Okachimachi station. This whole area is dense with shops, many of them the oldest shops in Tokyo, since this is the old downtown area. If you want the exact subway station (remember that subway stations often are different from train stations), use Ueno-Hirokoji on the Ginza line.

If you want to start at the farthest-away point and then work your way toward Okachi-machi and Ayema, get off at Yushima on the Toei–Shinjuku line. Warning: This is a hell of a schlep, but some of the retailers here represent the old Japan you have been looking for; it's a nice adventure. Walk the area marked in the map, or go off on your own. If you want to take a stab at reading addresses, you'll note that the higher chomes are the ones closer to Ueno (Ueno station is in 7 Chome); the lower numbers are closer to Yashima. Follow chomes, understanding that Yashima is toward Yashima and Ueno is toward Ueno when reading the street address; don't worry about the *ku*, since that is the ward, and it is far bigger than the area you will be surveying.

▼

TOKYO TOY: A shop that mostly features old Japanese toys and that is rather unique, since there aren't many of these things in traditional antiques shops. It's also a unique folk art resource. The shop is open only from 2:00 to 7:00 P.M.

TOKYO TOY, 2-31-18 Yashima, Bunkyo-ku

▼

SHINRISE OHSAWA: Although there's a nice old-fashioned tea shop in Nihombashi, if you didn't get there, you may want to go out of your way for this one.

SHINRISE OHSAWA, 3-36-5 Yashima, Bunkyo-ku

▼

JUSNAYA: Old-fashioned, traditional hair ornaments and boxwood combs.

JUSNAYA, 2-12-21 Ueno, Taito-ku

▼

KYOYA SHIKKITEN: Fine-furnitureholics unite; this one's for you. Traditional furniture, newly made, from styles of the Edo Period.

KYOYA SHIKKITEN, 2-12-10 Ueno, Taito-ku

▼

DOMYO: Cords, belts, and braids made the old-fashioned way; royal warrant.

DOMYO, 2-11-1 Ueno, Taito-ku

▼

KOBIKEYA: Mostly made-to-order kimonos for members of the Kabuki; fabulous accessories.

KOBIKEYA, 2-12-1 Ueno, Taito-ku

▼

SHINASEIDO: Artists' supplies, old Japanese style. Closed Monday.

SHINASEIDO, 2-12-4 Ueno, Taito-ku

7 ▼ BORN TO SHOP TOKYO

Announcement

We're on to you, we know all about it! We know that some of our readers don't like to read the front of the book. Or they read a few sections here and there, mostly to see if they can get by U.S. Customs, and don't read the rest. The lists are all they care about. It's okay. We understand. That's why we have this announcement.

Tokyo is very hard to get around in. In any other city, it is perfectly acceptable to look up a listing and plan to go to a specific address. In Tokyo, this may not work for you. We have lost precious time trying to find addresses. We don't want this to happen to you. In fact, we even considered writing this book without any addresses. We didn't do that, but we want you to understand, right up front, that having an address or even a telephone number, may do you absolutely no good.

If you must go to a certain shop, get the name and address written in *kanji* and go directly there. Otherwise, please try to be flexible. You will find other places just as wonderful as the ones you wanted when you get lost. We have done more tours and neighborhood walks in this book for a very good reason. It is hard to find specific addresses. So please use these listings with a grain of salt. Or soy sauce.

The Big Names

Every big name in the world sells in Tokyo, and it is impossible to list them all.
While we have never attempted to list
every big name in our other books, there
was always a reason to list some. In Tokyo, no
one street houses big-name boutiques, and many
of the big-name designers do not have free-
standing boutiques. Some designers have free-
standing boutiques but also have shops in the
depatos. Our big-name listing, therefore, is more
to give you an idea of who is where rather
than to tell you what's available. The Japanese
big names are handled on page 198. There are
few bargains on international big names unless
we have so noted in our listing; we are not
impressed by prices. This is for your reference
more than for your tour planning. If you hit a
sale, great; otherwise, we'd like you to buy
Japanese while in Tokyo.

But here goes; you decide:

▼

ARMANI: Seibu's got him, all locations. The
boutiques are surprisingly similar to the Milan
flagship store, although on a smaller scale.
Armani luggage and accessories are in Isetan.
Prices are outrageously high.

▼

LAURA ASHLEY: Right there smack in the
middle of Tokyo you're going to find a Laura
Ashley that looks just like every other Laura
Ashley anyplace in the world. It's almost comi-

cal. But then, it does make sense. Laura Ashley just wouldn't look right next to a *torii*. The very pretty shop has Ashley merchandise, but we have never seen this merchandise in Europe or the United States. The items are not licensed, but are imported all the way from Wales. Children's dresses are about $100; women's dresses are $150 and up. Wallpaper and accessories are on the second floor. The freestanding shop is in a blue and burgundy granite building with the classic green lacquer trim. The address is 10–12, 6 Chome, Ginza. But you'll have to turn off Chuo-dori when you get to the side street that separates the chome and turn toward the Kabuki.

▼

BACCARAT: The free-standing boutique in the Imperial Tower is elegant and friendly. You will be given a gorgeous brochure and urged to use their price lists to compare prices. While prices are not as low as in France, they are not outrageously high. They will ship.

▼

BENETTON: There's one in Nishi-Ginza, there's a free-standing shop in the Ginza 5-Chome area, and there are two in Seibu Ikebukuro—a 0–12 for the kids' line, and a separate Benetton for grown-up sizes. We vote for Seibu for the best selection. Prices are comparable to those in the United States.

▼

BOTEGGA VENETA: Your favorite woven

leather handbag begins at $250 and goes up, up, and away. We're not interested; if you are, *depatos* carry them.

▼

BURBERRY: Original Burberry coats are available at Hankyu for $1,400, while licensed coats that seem to be identical are $400 at Seibu. We buy in London.

▼

CARTIER: There is a free-standing Cartier in the Imperial Tower as well as many self-sufficient boutiques in various department stores, including Mitsokoshi and Seibu. The watch is 40% higher than the U.S. price.

▼

CELINE: Mitsokoshi; Seibu. Prices are high; an ostrich handbag is $2,500; shoes are $200.

▼

CHANEL: The boutique in the Imperial Tower looks just like many of the international boutiques, but you'll be handed free samples of cologne. It's not the only game in town—there's a Chanel boutique in almost every major *depato* in Tokyo. Prices are high. The best buy we ever found on Chanel was on quilted leather handbags in a shop in the Ameyoko ("under the tracks"). Currently Tokyo is Chanel-crazy, so you'll have no difficulty finding faux in any resource you shop.

▼

COURRÈGES: André Courrèges is quite the rage in Tokyo, if not in clothing then in licensed goods. Check out the towels and bathgoods in the linen department of any major department store. We bought an off-to-college friend a cute bath set from Takashimaya that was $30 and looked very expensive. The Courrèges logo is affixed to many items.

▼

ROBERTA DI CAMERINO: When Roberta closed the New York store we thought it was the end, but the Japanese don't seem to agree. You'll see those famous "R's" everywhere—in all department stores and often in discount outlets.

▼

CHRISTIAN DIOR: A shop is in the Roi Building in Roppongi on the main floor, but there are boutiques in all the department stores. *Très cher.*

▼

DUNHILL: Free-standing shop in the Imperial Tower for the usual preppy British look. While reaching for a business card in the shop, we were slapped across the hand by an aggressive saleswoman.

▼

FENDI: Isetan has a nice boutique, replete with furs. No bargains here.

▼

VALENTINO GARAVANI: We don't know the real reason, but we assume Valentino could not get the use of his first name in Japan, so he uses his entire name here. Or to differentiate his Japanese-made merchandise from his Italian-made line, he uses his whole name. Whatever, this is our pal Valentino. (Joan Collins likes him, too.) Seibu Ikebukuro has a small boutique. ITF Japan is the agent for local goods, and they are plentiful; accessories are available even in wholesale markets.

▼

GUCCI: Almost all department stores sell Gucci; Sogo has a wide selection. Prices are high. There is a small, free-standing Gucci boutique in the Imperial Tower. The Gucci agent in Tokyo is Sun Motoyama; you will see this name displayed prominently in the shop and may be confused. Wait for Italy.

▼

HARRODS: Yup, there's a Harrods inside

Mitsokoshi, Nihombashi. But it's not worth a special trip.

▼

HERMÈS: The boutique in Seibu Ikebukuro is as large as a free-standing shop and is quite impressive, but you'll faint when you discover that the scarf costs twice the European price; the Kelley clutch is almost $2,000.

▼

NORMA KAMALI: The Japanese have gone bonkers for Kamali. We saw a marvelous selection at Matsuya Ginza as well as other *depatos*. Prices are slightly cheaper than in the United States. Sizes are cut for the Japanese body. Fabulous for your teens.

▼

CALVIN KLEIN: Klein's clothes are traditional Klein styles but looked unfamiliar to us—we think they are made for the Japanese market. A sweater is $200; prices are comparable to those in the United States. Matsuya Ginza has a nice selection.

▼

KRIZIA: Wait for Hong Kong.

▼

RALPH LAUREN: Seibu has a boutique; prices are equal to those in the United States. We think these goods are made in Hong Kong, but they could be locally made.

▼

LOEWE: Say it "lou-vay," and stop by while you're in the Imperial Tower. Prices are as high as in the United States, but the leather-goods are sublime.

▼

BRUNO MAGLI: We always check for our friend Laurie Grad—the queen of the Magli. Most *depatos* sell Magli, but Ginza Kanematsu is the official agent. Pumps are about $150. Charles Jourdan is also sold here. Signs are in French and Japanese but not English.

▼

MARIMEKKO: Nishikawa isn't a big, fancy *depato*—in fact, it's kind of like a Penney's—but here you'll find the Marimekko boutique. If you walk from Mitsokoshi to Takashimaya in Nihombashi, you'll pass by.

▼

MISSONI: The Missoni boutique in the Seibu Ikebukuro is large and more luxe than the Missoni boutique in Milan. Prices are almost double those in the United States—socks that sell for $7.50 in Rome and $15 in the United

States are $25 in Tokyo. This is a must-see if you adore Missoni and aren't on your way to Europe. But you have to be King Midas to buy this stuff.

▼

PRADA: So what's Prada? you're asking. Prada is the hottest handbag among *garmentos*. It's a Chanel look-alike and costs $98 in Milan, $150 in New York, and $300 in Isetan in Tokyo. We mention it to make the basic point about merchandise in Tokyo: Everything in the world you might want is indeed here, but if it's imported to Japan, it is extraordinarily expensive. Prada will soon open U.S. stores, by the way.

▼

SONIA RYKIEL: Across the floor from Missoni at Seibu Ikebukuro, this is a well-stocked boutique with the latest from France at twice the price. Wait for the U.S. sale if you must have it.

▼

YVES SAINT LAURENT: It's the same old problem with YSL: There's so much licensed junk out there that it's hard to know whom to trust. Trust your eyes, or walk into Rive Gauche boutiques in *depatos,* which are different from the YSL counters in *depatos.*

▼

JEAN-LOUIS SCHERRER: Free-standing boutique opposite Dior in the Roi Building; also boutiques in many *depatos*.

▼

SOULEIADO: Pierre Deux to us Americans, Souleiado has a small but very country French boutique in Seibu Ikebukuro. No bargains, but not outrageous.

▼

TIFFANY: Maybe you don't shock as easily as we do, but we almost fell over when we saw the Tiffany store inside the main Mitsokoshi in Nihombashi. The store is larger than the old store in Beverly Hills and has exactly the same wallpaper. Absolutely amazing. The large Peretti heart, in gold, is $620; gold bean earrings are $900. Ouch.

▼

JOSEPH TRICOT: One of our favorite names from London, Tricot has a Tokyo branch that is to die for, as they say in the fashion biz. Check out the in-store boutique at Isetan in Shinjuku. Sweaters are about $50—a saving of $100 or more.

▼

UNGARO: Seibu Ikebukuro. Outrageously expensive. But—get this—we found some Ungaro pajamas for $35 at Nishikawa, an inexpensive *depato* that has scads of licensed merchandise. We didn't happen to like the pj's, but you might. And they had very statusy Ungaro labels. Robes, too.

Japanese Big Names

Most Americans have a hard time with Japanese names, mostly because they don't take the time to learn how to pronounce them. If you can't say a name, at least learn to recognize it when written out, since all these names are well represented in *depatos* and definitely are worth remembering. These are the big names of Japan that will make your trip worthwhile and your bargains true finds.

▼

BIGI: Not to be confused with an inexpensive line from Bergdorf Goodman, Bigi is the name of a ready-to-wear collection—men's and women's. The designer is Yoshie Inaba. The clothes are everywhere. Au Printemps has a nice boutique. The styles are slightly retro but wearable. Also check out Parco. Moderate prices.

▼

COMME DES GARÇONS: There are two lines that hang together; one is less expensive. In the cheapie line, you can get a whole outfit for about $100. Designed by Rei Kawakubo, the line is very Euro-Japanese and makes the statement that you have just been to Tokyo.

Buy in black, which is the predominant color in each collection, anyway. Best choices: Marui in Shinjuku and Sogo in Yokohama.

▼

KANSAI INTERNATIONAL: We love the Kansai appliqué sweaters and find a lot of the other pieces fun but slightly wild. A sweater that was $200 in the United States was $150 in Tokyo. There's a free-standing, two-story Kansai boutique in Harajuku, and a selection of goods at La Foret and Au Printemps. All three stores have different merchandise! There's also Kansai at Isetan in Shinjuku and Marui—where we bought a sample for full retail price (no bargain there!). Kansai International, at 3-28-7 Jungumae, Shibuya-ku

▼

TAKEO KIKUCHI: Our single favorite find with boutiques in Vivre21 in Harajuku and a few *depatos*. This is the rich Japanese chic unisex look at its best. We'll take Takeo any day-o.

▼

HIROKO KOSHINO: It was Carolyn who flipped for Hiroko Koshino back in Milan and at Alma in New York. Hiroko is the eldest of three designing sisters. The most beautiful dress in the world was $500. On sale you can find a smart knit dress for $150 to $300. Marui; Sogo.

▼

JUNKO KOSHINO: Try Seibu Ikebukuro to look at a younger sister, who is sportier in design and less expensive. Also very hot if you're into dropping Japanese names.

▼

TOKIO KUMAGI: If you thought Maud Frizon was fun, get a load of Tokio Kumagi, who is now the rage of Paris and New York. We have never seen more creative shoes in our lives. If you've got $200 for artwork for the feet, plunk down your money and dazzle your friends. Isetan Shinjuku.

▼

JURGEN LEHL: Okay, he's German. But he's been such a hit in Tokyo, and Tokyo is his home base, so we call him a Japanese designer. He has his own boutique in the trendy Aoyama area at 1-13-18 Jingumae, Shibuya-ku, not far from Issey Miyake's free-standing shop.

▼

MITSUHIRO MATSUDA: It's Matsuda in the United States and Nicole or Matsuda for Nicole in Tokyo and Hong Kong, and we love it—but it is pricey Japanese elegance. You'll pay about $200 for anything. The clothes are Western with a touch of Japan; boutiques are in every *depato*—we like Sogo in Yokohama and Marui in Shinjuku, also Hankyu's new store on Ginza. Robinson's in California has the best prices; other United States department stores also must carry this line. Ask around.

MILK: We thought this was part of Milk Mary—a Hong Kong maker of fun kids' clothes—but it turns out it's the line of Hitomi Okawa and is one of the best known of the teeny-bopper high-fashion lines. There is a free-standing Milk boutique at 4-30-10 Jingumae, Shibuya-ku.

▼

ISSEY MIYAKE: The clothes are the most exciting in Japan, and if you can buy only one outfit, consider a Miyake. The construction is unbelievable—as is the comfort factor. There are two or three lines; the least expensive is about $100 to $120 for an outfit. That's considerably cheaper than in the United States. If you have $200 to spend on a jacket or top, you'll walk away with something very sensational. For $500 you can look like a million. Miyake in Sogo, Seibu, Marui, etc.

▼

HANAE MORI: Step right up to heaven as you enter the Hanae Mori Building. Prices also are divine—about 40% less expensive than in the United States. We found shoes and handbags for $90 to $125 that were sensational. There's also more than HM merchandise here—there's also a Carlos Falchi area, where prices are exactly the same—to the penny—as in the United States. Be sure to have a coffee in the cafe and watch the street show—models and geeks parade by, and you will adore it.

▼

PINK HOUSE: A few years ago, when 1950s-style fashion was the newest thing, Pink House became internationally famous. Now the look is so knocked off that the novelty is thin. Kaneko Isao is the designer; try Marui for a look at the line; other *depatos* as well.

▼

Y: Yohji Yamamoto is called "Y" by his friends, and that is the name of his line. He is very exclusive, very elegant, and quite "in." Many *depatos* carry the line. He's even got his own L.A. shop on Melrose Avenue.

▼

YUYA: Suzy Joseloff turned us on to Yuya. Yuya sells old kimonos and makes new clothing from them. The boutique seemingly is unfindable in Roppongi: You turn down an unnamed street alongside the Axis Building and walk to the on-ramp of a highway. You'll pass apartments and an old mansion on your right. Then you'll get to the modern boutique—which is brand new. It's worth the walk—which really is only two blocks from the main drag. Expect to pay $200 for something wonderful—maybe more if you go nuts. This find is worth the quest.

Hot Young Japanese Designers

These names aren't as established as those in the preceding list, but are considered up and coming by the Tokyo Fashion Watch and *Women's Wear Daily* for Japan:

At Off

Ca et la Cacher

Cascade Blanche

Cielun

Civ

Civisk

Cremona

Diva et Diva

Elfan

Eva Louise

Favorite

Fore & More

From Nil

Haff Duff

Hermana

Idée Milano

Jil Sport

J. McLaughlin

MB

Neanmoins

Parisienne Part I

Popacoco

Ian Revell

Rouge Loup

Sab Street

Zaza Sandiford

Sun Rose

Tricot e Alfa

Depatos

Many department stores began as kimono shops or small trading posts at major crossroads and date back hundreds of years. Invariably they are near train stations and in busy sections of town. Be it in a commercial zone or a suburb, usually there's a "shopping zone" that hosts several *depatos*. Remember, the *depatos* don't expect to make their money on the merchandise they sell but on the range of life-style services they can provide. As a result, anything you may need—from birth to death—can be arranged through a department store. This includes your wedding and your funeral. (We had always intended to have our ashes dropped over Neiman-Marcus but now are considering something appropriate at the Sogo in Yokohama.) While the merchandise is totally diversified, think of each department store as a one-stop-meets-all-needs home away from home. There are movie theaters, live theaters, cultural events, markets, opticians, and playgrounds. One department store even has a minicircus on its roof.

To get into the proper mood, arrive at a department store about a half hour before they open, and look in the windows. You may see the staff do exercises together! As the doors open, the doorkeepers will bow to the oncoming crowds. Each store dresses its personnel in a different uniform—all very chic. There is a winter uniform and a spring uniform, and they change with the times. We'd sign up to work at Takashimaya if we could get one of those cute suits to fit us. (Actually, we love the hat!)

Department stores have street addresses, but you don't need them to find a store. You can spot the store rather easily—because each is the size of a smaller American city—or ask anyone on the street. We are talking about buildings that in many cases are larger than Macy's in Manhattan, rise into the sky as many as twelve stories, and take up at least one city block. The names of all big stores are written in Roman letters someplace. The stores also sport their logos quite prominently. You shouldn't have any trouble finding a store; we have noted in the listing anything we found confusing. Remember that most stores are closed one day a week.

▼

DAIMARU: Daimaru is one of the older, more traditional Japanese department stores. Located at Tokyo station above the Yaesu Central exit (which is marked in English), the rather modern building is stocked full of merchandise that reminds us of the kind of goods sold in the leading department store in an All-American city in the days when you went downtown on Saturday with your mother. This was before there were malls. This isn't a very young store in terms of wild fashions, and its location may not be in your path if you are in town for three days only. You'll survive without it. Hours: 10:00 A.M. to 6:00 P.M.; closed Wednesday.

▼

HANKYU: There is only one thing that is confusing about Hankyu: There are two of them, and they are across the street from each other! But wait! They are dramatically different from each other, so it's okay. The old Hankyu is very nice in the Western traditional department-store mode; it's kind of like Saks. It's also kind of boring. The new Hankyu, which is in a white tile twin tower (Yurakucho Center Building), is connected on the ground floor to the new Seibu, in the other twin tower. This Hankyu is younger and likes to think it's the Bloomingdale's type. Every new store in Tokyo likes to say it's the Bloomingdale's type, and this comparison will only make you nuts, so let's leave American store comparisons behind—but you get the idea. We think you will like the new Hankyu better (if you are over sixty, maybe we're wrong).

The departments at the Hankyu in the Yurakucho Center Building are as follows: B2–4, parking; B1, food; 1, accessories; 2, women's wear and shoes; 3, women's casual; 4, Japanese fashion designers; 5, men's; 6, children's—home furnishings; 7, restaurants and community.

Hours: 10:00 A.M. to 6:00 P.M.; 10:00 A.M. to 7:00 P.M. Friday and Saturday; closed Thursday.

▼

ISETAN: Isetan is now famous as the young, hip, with-it store frequented by the Tokyo yuppies. Kind of like Bloomingdale's. Oops, sorry. Just a joke. Isetan is mobbed on weekends and may make you claustrophobic, but otherwise it is one of the largest, more complete stores in the world. Don't miss the Joseph Tricot boutique; if you want to overpay on a Prada bag, you can do so here. Adrienne Vittadini has a boutique here; so does every other designer you can think of. We were quite shocked to find that the American designers are priced within a few dollars of their U.S. prices. The Vittadini selection was excellent and we would have bought tons if we didn't feel silly buying from a U.S. designer while in Tokyo. Displays are creative; merchandise is well bought and well hung. The men's store also is marvelous, and we suggest that women shop here as well (for themselves). We don't think the traditional Japanese floor (7) is much to write home about, but on the whole this store is one of the best in Shinjuku and one of the best in Tokyo.

There are several restaurants; a beauty and barber shop; and even a consumer consultant, who is open from noon to 5:00 P.M. A repair shop is on 4; a dentist is on 6. Calvin Klein and other designers are on 3. The main building and the annex are connected in the basement, and on the third and sixth floors by bridges. (This is where we got lost.)

In the main store: B, foods and restaurants; 1, fashion accessories; 2, young sportswear; 3, women's wear; 4, housewares; 5, furniture; 6, children's; 7, kimonos; R, pet shop, Kiddy Land, and potted plants (bonsai).

In the annex: B–4, men's; 5 and 6, sporting goods; 7, arts and crafts and restaurants; 8, Isetan Museum; R, tennis machine and putter course.

Hours: 10:00 A.M. to 6:00 P.M.; 10:00 A.M. to 6:30 P.M. Saturday, Sunday, and holidays; closed Wednesday.

▼

KEIO: Keio is right over the Shinjuku station and essentially is an average department store offering convenience to the flocks of office workers in the immediate area. We went nuts for the ski clothes and also got quite lost in the store. If you go in from one entrance you must take an elevator up to get into the store; if you go out on the street, you'll find it's not the street you thought it was. We don't know if it's worth the trouble, but the shops in the Shinjuku station immediately *below* Keio are worth a visit. Surprisingly, they are not part of the Keio *depato*. We bought from Takano—sort of a specialty shop—and thought we were in Keio. Oh, well.

The departments: B1, train, food, and fauchon; MB, book promenade, food, and restaurants; 1, accessories; 2, ladies' wear; 3, ladies' wear (Ralph Lauren); 4, men's sporting goods; 5, home furnishings, and hobbies; 6, kimonos and souvenirs; 7, children's; 8, gift center and restaurants; R, Kiddy Playland.

Hours: 10:00 A.M. to 6:00 P.M.; 10:00 A.M. to 6:30 P.M. Friday, Saturday, Sunday, and holidays; closed Thursday.

▼

MARUI: Marui is known to many *gaijin* as Oioi because the store says "oioi" all over it. Well, it turns out that these letters are the symbol of circle, which is the store logo. *The name of the store is not Oioi, but you will think it is.* (Often we call it Oyoy.) Marui has five different parts, and while you may get worn out visiting all five (they're bunched together in Shinjuku), you certainly will have a good time. The electronics store (called Techno) is connected to the main fashion store. Big-name designers abound in the main store; younger, less expensive fashions are in a different store, called Young. There're also interiors and sports. For just a sample of what's available at Marui, here's the lineup for the sports store alone: 1, dance and sports casual; 2, training stadium; 3, playing stadium; 4, out tour and touring; 5, fairway; 6, tennis court; 7, skiwear; 8, ski and credit.

You get the general idea. Techno has seven floors and two subfloors. Fashion has eight floors and one subfloor. Interior has eight floors, as does Young. Marui (fashion) is across the street from Isetan. These two stores (or seven stores, if you count separate buildings) can put a dent in your budget and holes in your shoes—but you'll leave with a smile on your face.

Hours: 10:30 A.M. to 7:30 P.M.; closed on second and third Wednesdays.

▼

MATSUYA: We've only been in the Matsuya Ginza (and Hong Kong, of course), but we loved it. It's very youth-oriented, not that well displayed, and the merchandise seems to be crowded into every nook and cranny—but there are tons of things to look at. We also found merchandise here we had never seen anywhere else. The weekend crush can be upsetting, but it's worth a try. Hours: 10:00 A.M. to 6:00 P.M.; 10:00 A.M. to 6:30 P.M. Saturday, Sunday, and holidays; closed Thursday.

▼

MATSUZKAYA: Matsuzkaya is over 350 years old. The Ginza shop is all reflective glass and modern exterior over a conservative, very basic store. There is another shop, in Ueno. Too conservative for our taste, but serviceable nonetheless. Hours: 10:00 A.M. to 6:00 P.M.; 10:00 A.M. to 6:30 P.M. Sunday and holidays; closed Wednesday.

▼

MELSA: Known as the new Melsa—as opposed to the old Melsa, which is actually called Meitetsu Melsa—this newest addition to Ginza 5 Chome is a quite stunning piece of modern architecture and zigzag escalators. Although it looks just like many other *depatos* (after a few, they will all look alike to you), there are a few special reasons to go in—there is a nice selection of some Japanese designers and boutiques that you can see here without then having to revisit their boutiques. We like Boutique Maggy (who has two shops on Ginza), Ginza Kanematsu (a great shoe store), and the outlet for Suzunoya Kimono—one of the most famous kimono shops in Tokyo. We think that Melsa is one of those department stores that leases the space to individual boutiques—it's unlikely that their buyers compiled all this merchandise.

The departments: B1, ladies' fashions; 1, ladies' fashions, George Jensen, and imported bags and sundries; 2, Charles Jourdan and accessories; 3, shoes and men's and ladies' fashions; 4, ladies' fashions; 5, ladies' fashions and men's fashions; 6, Japanese traditional items; 7, restaurants and an art gallery; 8, restaurants.

Hours: B1 to 8, 11:00 A.M. to 8:00 P.M.; 7 to 8F, 11:00 A.M. to 9:30 P.M.

▼

MITSUKOSHI: Mitsukoshi is perhaps the single most famous department store in Tokyo, possibly because it is one of the oldest (it was founded in 1673). Also, the BBC did a documentary on it. The flagship store is in Nihombashi and is worthy of a visit, but many of the other branches are disappointing. (The Hong Kong store is fabulous.) We suggest you pass on Mitsukoshi Shinjuku and Ikebukuro—there's nothing wrong with them, they're just rather standard. The main store, however, has a three-story cloisonné goddess in the middle of the front hall and one of the most amazing collections of merchandise you'll see anywhere. Don't forget there is an annex in the back— across the driveway. There's also a Mitsukoshi in ten foreign cities, including London, Paris, Rome, and New York. You can use your charge in any of the stores. English-speaking sales clerks wear tags that say "I speak English." Speakers of French, German, and Chinese also are available. Among the big names featured here are Anne Klein, Oscar de la Renta, Lanvin, Claude Montana, Loewe, Chanel, Tiffany, Dunhill, Kilgour, French & Stanbury, and Harrods.

In the main building: B1, food; 1, boutiques; 2, men's and ladies' designer goods; 3, ladies' wear (more designer goods); 4, kimonos and children's; 5, home furnishings; 6, art and jewelry; 7, exhibitions and bargain counter; R, pets and garden.

In the new building: 1, sports fashions; 2, sports goods and service center; 3, special services (travel agency, etc.); 4 to 9, car parking; 9, book gallery.

Hours: 10:00 A.M. to 6:00 P.M.; 10:00 A.M. to 6:30 P.M. Saturday, Sunday, and holidays; closed Monday.

▼

ODAKYU: Odakyu stands opposite Keio but on the same side of the Shinjuku station. Odakyu is a bit younger and more hip than Keio. There's the Ace arcade, which is at train level, and then two different buildings above the train station—a bit confusing. The children's department is one of the best in Tokyo. The annex is named HALC and specializes in interior design on the upper floors.

In the main building: B2, foodstuffs; B1, train; 1, cosmetics and sundries; 2, accessories; 3, men's; 4, women's wear; 5, children's goods and prêt-à-porter salon; 6, kimonos; 7, household goods; 8, toys/stationery; 9, Playland and restaurants (open until 10:00 P.M.); 10, restaurants; 11, Grand Gallery; 12, books, dental clinic, and barber; 13, beer garden; 14, restaurants.

In HALC (the annex): B3, restaurants; B2, sweets; B1, foodstuffs; 1, accessories; 2, women's wear; 3, sporting goods; 4–6, home furnishings; 7, Japanese furnishings; 8, Chinese restaurant; R, beer garden and golf driving range.

Hours: 10:00 A.M. to 6:00 P.M.; 10:00 A.M. to 6:30 P.M. Friday and Saturday; closed Thursday.

▼

PARCO: Parco has a reputation for being a must-see kind of place, so we checked out two Parcos and found them very different. Both are conveniently located next to a Seibu because—you guessed it—Seibu owns the store. The one in Ikebukuro is a bit tame; although we found some great merchandise there, it was dark, cramped, and not that easy to enjoy. The good news: It was not very crowded on either of the two Saturdays we went there. In Shibuya, however, there are three different buildings; they're all fun—and full of people. Concentrate on Part One, which is modern, spacious, and the absolute must place to be seen if you are under twenty-one; concentrate on Part Two if you are into designers. Also note that it's a bit hard to find Part Two and Part Three, but Part One is next to Seibu. Use our map, or ask people to help you. Here are the layouts for the Shibuya stores:

Part One: B1, ladies'; 1, fashion variety; 2, ladies'; 3, designers and kimonos; 4, ladies'; 5, men's; 6–8, Restaurant City. Part Two: B1, designers; 1, ladies' and variety; 2–6, designers.

Part Three: B1, ladies'; 1, fashion variety and children's; 2, men's campus; 3, interior; 4, interior and living goods; 5–6, sports; 7, interior.
Hours: 10:00 A.M. to 8:00 P.M.

▼

AU PRINTEMPS: Au Printemps is indeed the big-time Paris department store, which in Tokyo is owned by a supermarket chain and looks very little like its Paris counterpart. But lots of signs are in French, the *tricouleur* is flaunted, and the store is plain old fun. It's not nearly as big as the monster department stores (even though there are two buildings—the second is interiors) and feels more like a specialty store. You may find the manageability of it a refreshing change after wandering around the other gigantic complexes. Special announcements are made on a public-address system in French, and we found it a boost to go somewhere where we understood what people were saying—even if it was just a reminder to visit the market in the basement level. About 25% of the merchandise is French; Dim pantyhose is $5 (it's $4 in the United States; $13 in Paris). We found more never-seen-before choices here than in almost any other *depato*. Au Printemps is truly one of our favorite haunts.

The departments: B2, *marché* (market); B1, *épicure* (epicure); 1, *vivant* (accessories); 2, *dépêche* (contemporary); 3, *contemporain* (contemporary); 4, *carrier* (women's); 5, *raffiné* (women's); 6, *lousir* (stationery and Musée du Louvre); 7, *physique* (sporting goods).

We found it wonderfully refreshing to find signs in French that we could sort of understand. No signs are in English—just French and Japanese. So we put our own translation of the floors in parentheses. *Pardonnez.* Among our favorites at Au Printemps are Bigi, Kansai, Half Moon, Persons, the children's selection,

the fashion backpacks, and costume jewelry.
Hours: 10:00 A.M. to 6:00 P.M.; closed
Wednesday.

▼

SEIBU: Every time we walk into a Seibu, one
sentence comes to mind and heart: *Seibu, we
love you!* To paraphrase Will Rogers, we never
met a Seibu we didn't like. If you have time to
pick only one *depato* to visit and you are in the
Ginza area—as, of course, you will be—choose
Seibu Yurakucho Center—it's in the twin white
towers matched up with Hankyu.

At Seibu Yurakucho: B1, food; 1, delica; 2,
designers; 3, ladies' and sports; 4, men's and
ladies'; 5, interior goods; 6, Creators' World;
7, arts and crafts; 8, Saison Square.

The main Seibu, however, is in Ikebukuro,
and it was—until the recent opening of the
Sogo in Yokohama—the largest store in the
world. The Ikebukuro store is older, and it's a
bit hard to shop because it is so incredibly
large—it is, indeed, bigger than Macy's in New
York—but it is almost as exciting as Sogo in
Yokohama. We adore Ikebukuro; but if you
go to Shibuya, you may end up bypassing
Ikebukuro. Shibuya is more exciting—as in
young and with-it—but Ikebukuro also hosts
the Sunshine City Trade Center, which will
entertain many business visitors. Fashion mavens also flock to Sunshine City twice a year.
When other neighborhoods have terrible crowds,
Ikebukuro is not so crowded—and the flagship Seibu store is worth it. If we sound like
we're pushing Ikebukuro, we are. This Seibu
should be seen.

The main store is built over the train station. The Seibu Sports Center is next door,
where the car parking is, but the main building runs something like this: B2, hot delica
fresh-food market; B1, Okazu market; 1,

cosmetics, accessories, and women's shoes; 2, teenage wear and children's wear; 3, women's fashion; 4, men's fashion; 5, furniture and household goods; 6, art, jewelry, and kimonos; 7, toys and appliances; 8, stationery, hobbies, and restaurants; 9, Children's Play Center; 10, Book Center II; 11, Book Center I; 12, the Seibu Museum of Art.

Every designer we've ever heard of has a boutique in this Seibu—including Turnbull & Asser, Louis Ferraud, Giorgio Armani, Liberty of London, Soulieado, Ralph Lauren, and Yves Saint Laurent. You can buy Wedgwood china, or Noritake, or many others; shipping is on the sixth floor, right near the bridal salon. There's even a Sears in the store! Be sure to check out the knitting, hobby, and stationery areas.

The escalators sometimes are hard to find, but this gives you an opportunity to explore the entire store. (It's not that they are really hard to find, but the ups and downs are not together, so if you don't go all the way up and then cross over the store and go all the way down, you may get lost.) Plan to spend a whole day exploring the area, and all your savings.

Hours: 10:00 A.M. to 6:00 P.M.; 10:00 A.M. to 7:00 P.M. weekends and holidays; 10:00 A.M. to 6:00 P.M. in January, February, and August; basement food sections open weekdays until 7:00 P.M.; eighth-floor restaurants open until 8:30 P.M.

▼

SOGO: Sogo is one of our favorite department stores in Hong Kong, so we were expecting great things in Tokyo. We had two shocks: We were disappointed with the Tokyo store and flabbergasted with delight in Yokohama. First things first.

The Tokyo Sogo is near the Ginza train station, across from the JNR tracks, and near everything else in Yurakucho. The new Hankyu and Seibu so overpower this area, however, that everything else pales; the Sogo is an older store that just seems boring compared to its new neighbors. Perhaps no one knew this better than management, who probably thought that competition in Tokyo was so steep that they decided to blaze new trails, get out of town, and open in Yokohama. See page 309 for more about Yokohama, but you'll just have to take our word as experts that Sogo in Yokohama is without question the best department store in the world.

We wouldn't be brokenhearted if you skipped Sogo in Tokyo, but if you decide to try it, this may help: B2, fruits, foods, and kitchen; B1, food; 1, money exchange and accessories; 2, ladies'; 3, ladies'; 4, men's; 5, kimonos, pearls, and sporting goods; 6, toys, children's, and stationery; 7, restaurants; 8, Audiovisual Library Hall.

Hours: 10 A.M. to 6 P.M.; closed Thursday.

▼

TAKASHIMAYA: Takashimaya is also several centuries old—and holds an imperial warrant, to boot. We don't think that Emperor Hirohito is quite the shopper that Princess Di is, but an imperial warrant is an imperial warrant. How much do we love Takashimaya? Let us count the ways. Hmmm, we can't count that high. We do think, however, that American GI's must have loved this store—because they didn't bomb it in 1945. Takashimaya is more old-fashioned than many of the others. It's large, the outside looks like the finest hotel in Paris, and it's conveniently located in Nihombashi across from Marazen and down the street from the big Mitsukoshi.

The store is modern inside, with two completely different sets of up-and-down escalators—which are side by side. Bathrooms are quite nice; tax-free counters are on the first floor in ladies' jewelry and on the sixth floor (Mikimoto pearls and jewelry). Our favorite quote from their brochure: "English speaking guide being available here." Oh, well, no one's perfect. But Takashimaya is nearly perfect.

In the main store: B2, restaurants; B1, food floor; 1, accessories; 2, men's; 3, kimonos and ladies'; 4, ladies'; 5, children's; 6, furniture; 7, living floor; 8, exhibition and special-sale floor; R, roof garden and pet shop.

In the annex: B2–3, parking; 4, special dining rooms; 5, beauty salon and photo studio; 6, restaurant; 7–9, offices.

Cosmetics

We've heard those glorious rumors about Japanese cosmetics; we've seen pictures of the Kabuki—we know that Japan makes the best cosmetics and makeups in the world. At least that's what we thought we knew. We were almost disappointed, however, with selection and prices. There weren't nearly as many young, kicky things to try as we anticipated. But we did find one source in Tokyo that is so outstanding it's worth a trip just to shop there. But on the whole, we did not find the face-paint glory we'd hoped for. Also, we were surprised that we couldn't find places we'd heard of and that there wasn't more of a knockout nature. If you are expecting makeup nirvana, you may be disenchanted.

We had one tip from the States—POLA—that didn't pan out for us. We use a Japanese line that has an American branch called I.S.

The line is made by Pola in Japan, one of the biggest brands there. Pola is not carried in any of the department stores, though. We did see a free-standing boutique while we were in a taxi whizzing through the darkness of the midnight hour, but we never found another one. This rather epitomizes the entire shopping experience in Tokyo: Very often you know there is something you want out there, but you just can't get to it. So if you happen to bump into a Pola while you are out there—lost—one day, please try it. Their crayon eye colors are superb.

SHISEIDO, a Japanese brand with international distribution, is just as expensive in Tokyo as anyplace else. We paid $15 for one type of Shiseido lipstick and $25 for their top-of-the-line lipstick. Shiseido has its own boutiques (actually they are minifranchises that also sell other things; the selection of cosmetics and beauty products depends on the shop you go into) and is well represented in major department stores. There is a Shiseido on Ginza, 8-Chome.

Other brands are also found in the department stores. Not all department stores have extensive first-floor cosmetics departments like American stores do. The Isetan in Shinjuku has a rather generous makeup department (first floor)—American, French, and Japanese brands are available. Mitsokoshi in Nihombashi also has an excellent first floor. The prices are so high that you will laugh out loud. The Lancôme mascara that we buy in Paris for $6.50 costs $10.50 in the United States and $20 in Tokyo. Honest Injun! If you are a Mary Kay dealer or an Avon lady, we suggest you pack up your stock and make office visits to the skyscrapers of Tokyo. You could make a fortune. We don't know how working women can keep themselves in mascara. Of course, spending $20 for a mascara makes it a big status move in Tokyo. It is quite a thing to wear Lancôme there.

We don't want to be catty, but we think

you'll be amused to know how the cosmetic system works—although it is much like any other international fashion business. Many of the "foreign" makeup products are made in Japan by subsidiary companies. Thus Chanel is made by Chanel K.K., a company in the French quarter of the Mitsui Building in Shinjuku. (That's where the offices are, not the factories.) Cosmair, which owns Lancôme and L'Oreal, has offices and factories in Japan. Just as the FDA is strict about what goes into American cosmetics, the Japanese are even more strict. Many health and beauty aids have to be produced in Japan to meet quality requirements. While prices could be less expensive for many items, the trading companies that are responsible for placing products in the stores sometimes insist on higher price tags for these items to keep up cachet. There are, of course, some imported goods . . . and they also are pricey!

You can also buy fragrance and cosmetics "under the tracks" (see page 181), but prices here are just as steep as stores. Chanel lipstick is $20. But don't despair. Shu is there.

We don't know why anyone would want French (or American) cosmetics when SHU UEMURA is handily available in every good neighborhood in a free-standing boutique and at makeup counters in some department stores. Shu Uemura is a Japanese makeup artist who spent his first career in Hollywood making the best kind of magic. He has since returned to Japan and made himself into the fashion sensation of town. We go into every boutique of his we can find, but the Harajuku one is the best. Also please note that Shu Uemura is the first-place winner of our traditional shopping-bag contest (silver foil!). Before we start running at the mouth about the wonders of Shu Uemura, a bargain tip: Ask for a Members Club card at the time of your first purchase. It's free. Each time you buy something, the amount is punched into the card. When you have filled up the boxes, you get a free gift. If you run in and buy more items every time you see a Shu Uemura boutique, you will fill up your card in a week. (We did!)

Okay, now for the details. Each Shu Uemura boutique is designed in what the Milanese design mavens call soft-tech—a combination of high-tech and Japanese modern. There's a lot of shiny black trim; a lot of glass; and a lot of clean, open space, even in the teeny-tiny shops. The biggest shop is on Omotesando in Harajuku—just a few stops away from Hanae Mori and on the same side of the street. This shop has a salon where you can have a makeup done (weddings are their specialty), a manicure, or any other number of beauty services for about the same price as you would pay at Georgette Klinger or Elizabeth Arden. (Wedding makeup is $200; a makeup lesson is $15; a facial is $20 to $40, depending on the type; a manicure is $10 to $25, depending on the type. No tipping; lots of bowing.) While the help may not speak English, you point to the part of your body you want made over and you can work things out. We went for a manicure at Roppongi, only to find out there were no salon facilities there.

In the Harajuku shop, the windowsill is filled with colored face brushes and all sorts of makeup-applying devices. The right-hand wall is mirrored and has testers; the left-hand wall is a panoply of wild color that turns out to be the product. There must be two hundred shades here, all arranged in a chromatic rainbow. In the back of the shop—behind a partial wall—is the receptionist to make salon appointments, and all the professional equipment you might need—shiny black lacquer plastic cases and big Hollywood-style black leatherette boxes with drawers. The largest-size black plastic box—which could house a selection to delight the entire cast of *Dallas*—costs $30. Each eye shadow costs $8.00; loose face powder is $30.

We could drool on and on here, but we'd

probably just get the makeup soggy and bore you to death. If you are a makeup freak, plan to drop $150 here and be smug for the next year of your life. If we had to tell anyone the single best place for fashion and excitement in Japan, Shu Uemura is it. Hours: 11:30 A.M. to 8:30 P.M.

SHU UEMURA

Ginza—5 Chome (5-6-12 Ginza, Chuo-ku)

Roppongi (look for the sign to Spago and Tony Roma; as you turn to the sign, you'll see the boutique)

Omoteosando-dori (5-1-3 Jingumae, Shibuya-ku)

Cars

Okay, now you know a lot of people—or have at least heard of some people—who fly to Europe on vacation, buy a car that they pick up at the factory, drive all around Europe, and then ship back while they brag for at least a year about how much money they saved. Well, if it works for a BMW, a Volvo, or a Mercedes-Benz, would it work for a Honda, a Datsun, or a Toyota?

In a word: no.

First of all, few street signs in Japan are in English. So you would have one hell of a time driving anywhere. Second of all, Japanese specifications are different from American specifications: It is against the law in Japan to drive on their roads with an export car, and conversely your Japanese specifications would not do in the United States, and you would not need just a few modifications on your car— you would need to rebuild it. And, of course, the Japanese drive on the same side of the road as the British, so your steering wheel is not going to be conveniently situated once back in the States. If we're beginning to make the point clear, good. You would also be amused to know that the Japanese pay the sticker price for their cars—there's no bargaining—and the car salesperson comes to your home or office to discuss it with you. While there are car showrooms, they sell the snazzy dream cars rather than the family wagon for car pool.

But there's more than meets the eye in this situation. You can buy an American export model and have it shipped to you in the States and save a good hunk of money. You cannot drive this car in Tokyo—naturally—but since the car will never even be on Japanese soil, you won't have that temptation to deal with.

If you are interested in saving $1,500 to $5,000 off the U.S. price on a Japanese car, you might want to have a meeting with someone from Jackson Motors. Its Tokyo sales office is run out of an apartment. If you get an answering service, leave a message. In the evening, your call will be returned. Mr. Jackson and his partner Mac Cookson are Americans in the car business as a sideline. They deal in legal export models that come from Guam or Saipan; these are not gray-market cars, they stress. "We just cut out the middleman," says Cookson. "There's nothing illegal about it at all."

Payment can be in dollars or yen and is worked out in Tokyo. No personal checks are accepted; money can be telexed from the United States. You can look at several brochures or tell them what you want. No cars meet California standards. Most Americans want Hondas, but other cars are available. According to Jackson, you get:

▼ a U.S. export model Japanese car with a worldwide reputation for quality, reliability, and mpg

▼ a full warranty

▼ a car that meets all U.S. federal motor vehicle safety standards and EPA air-pollution-control regulations

▼ your choice of any major make—sedan, hatchback, sports car, station wagon, or pickup

▼ a wide range of colors and options

▼ wholesale prices from U.S. $5,990.

Mr. Jackson has been in business in Tokyo since 1952. We did not buy a car from him simply because we didn't need a new car. But if anyone wants to send us a birthday gift, we'd like the Samurai Jeep, please. They have no address; call (03) 583-0739 for information or an appointment.

Children and Toys

When our friend David said he was thinking of taking his kids (ages six and seven) to Tokyo, we began a forty-minute monologue on all the wonderful things to do with children in Tokyo— a life-size brontosaurus, the pandas in the zoo, the kiddy parks on top of all the *depatos,* the robot toys sold cheaply under the tracks, etc.

Whether you bring your kids or not, you can't be in Tokyo without thinking about them because there is so much available in terms of entertainment and ready-to-wear. If you've left your kids at home, you'll be missing them more than ever but enjoying the Japanese children and enjoying all the toys and clothes that fill the stores.

While all the department stores have excellent toy selections, we find the prices in *depatos* a bit too high for us. We have seen much of the same toy merchandise for 20% less when we shop "under the tracks" (see page 181). If you are looking for toys to bring back for your kids, don't buy in a *depato* unless you have only one hour to shop and will not be in Ueno. If you are looking to buy in a *depato,* check out the hobby floor as well as the toy floor—there are fabulous craft kits for sale, all demonstrated leisurely in the store. Tip: If you buy a kit, make sure you understand exactly how it works before you leave the store. Chances are excellent that the instructions in the box are in Japanese only. One of the best gifts we bought our kids was a set of crayons that look like eyeshadow pencils; we've never seen them anywhere else in the world, although we think they are German. They came from the art-hobby department in Sogo and we saw them in only one other store—an art supply resource in the Axis Building. Seek and ye shall . . .

Toys are cheaper in Macao, but you can find a few $2 to $5 robots and whatnots under the train tracks. When you shop the *bashis,* you will also find discounted toys. While there are several large toy stores that are famous, we mostly found them so expensive as not to be amusing. We considered buying some Godzilla masks for three seven-year-old boys we know. Each mask cost $10 and looked like the kind of thing people would laugh at and say, "Oh, look at that cute three-dollar present they bought in Japan." It was hard to find value for the money. American toys are twice the price, even though they often are made in Hong Kong. A GI Joe figure—$2.77 at Toys-R-Us—is over $5 in Tokyo. While the selection in Tokyo may be immense, this is no place for U.S. toy bargains.

But let's say a few wonderful things about the children's department at your typical *depato*: Not only is the selection huge, but also there usually is a play area where the kids are encouraged to use the toys (not the one you are planning to buy—there are tester models). The Japanese thoughtfully believe that you can't buy a toy unless you've tried it out—it's like test-driving a car. You can leave your children in one of these play areas and come back for them after you've done all your shopping.

You may also find items you've never seen in the United States. The selections of Mickey Mouse, Snoopy, Betty Boop, and other characters are much more elaborate than in the United States. Felix the Cat is big in Japan. You pay for this selection, but it is more fun than going to F.A.O. Schwarz.

If you are a doll fanatic, prepare to lose your mind.

Our rules of thumb on toys:

▼ American-made toys: Do not buy in Japan.

▼ Japanese junk toys: Buy on the street.

▼ electronic toys: Buy in Akihabara.

▼ hobby items: Buy in *depatos* or Tokyu Hands.

▼ fine Japanese dolls: Buy in specialty stores; see page 282.

Aside from the department stores, a few stores are virtually department stores devoted to kids. Mostly they sell toys, but Familar sells clothes as well as maternity items.

▼

FAMILAR: A teddy bear clock on a blue and white sign beckons the shopper into the wonderful world of Familar, a children's department store in the 6 Chome of Ginza. The entire store is decorated in blue and white and an overabundance of teddy bears. It's all to guarantee that you, or your kids, leave behind your life's savings and college money as well. There aren't any bargains here—a Florence Eiseman dress costs $100! If you are rich or brave, here's the blow-by-blow: 1, toddler clothing; 2, larger-size clothing; 3, infants; 4, toys.

There's a video screening room on the fourth floor so you can park your kids here and do your shopping unhampered. Most of the merchandise here is very preppy, very American, and very much available to you at home for less money. This is the status shop for locals. Hours: 11:00 A.M. to 6:30 P.M.; 11:00 A.M. to 7:00 P.M. Saturday and Sunday.

FAMILIAR, 6 Chome, Ginza

▼

HAKUHINKAN TOY PARK: Conveniently located as you wind down your Ginza stroll (it's in the 8 Chome), Hakuhinkan Toy Park is exactly where you need to go to get revitalized. And if the largest toy store in Japan doesn't perk you up, nothing will. On the other hand, if you think you'll be too exhausted from your hike around Ginza to enjoy a toy store, or if your kids are driving you crazy, you may want to start your Ginza adventure here and walk toward 1 Chome. Everything you could possibly be looking for—and many things you never thought of—are nestled in this store. Just to give you an idea: B1, dental clinic; 1, variety; 2, games and hobbies; 3, toys; 4, dolls; 5–7 restaurants; 8, theater.

Prices are high, as at all the fancy toy stores, but you just may want to pay these prices as part of the fun of being in Japan. A radio-operated Porsche twin-turbo car is $35; a large robot called Dancougar (similar to Voltron) is $30; Monopoly is $35; Zoids are $15 to $20; Legoland airport is $45; Barbie is $17; Koeda-Chan's House (this is a really cute doll house from a popular local character) is only $15. Japanese toys are a much better value than American ones! Hours: 11:00 A.M. to 8:00 P.M.

HAKUHINKAN TOY PARK, 8-8-11 Ginza, Chuo-ku

▼

KIDDYLAND: If you've heard the hype about Kiddyland, you may be disappointed; if you haven't heard a word, you may go wild here. This store is not as big as Toys-R-Us but does have several floors devoted to toys, and a basement as well. We liked the first floor with its Christmas stocking-stuffer-type of selection but found the prices on most of the upstairs toys so high that we lost our appetite. You can find a kimono for your Cabbage Patch doll, but do you want to pay $25 for it? There is an excellent selection of Japanese-style robot toys—and this is where we found the expensive Godzilla masks. Since you will walk right by Kiddyland while you are in Harajuku, you may want to pop in. Hours: 10:00 A.M. to 7:00 P.M.; 10:00 A.M. to 8:00 P.M. Saturday and Sunday; closed on third Tuesday.

KIDDYLAND, 6-1-9 Jingumae, Shibuya-ku

▼

MIKKI HOUSE: One of the most striking things you will notice when shopping for kids' clothes in Japan is that everything looks alike. The prevailing look currently is designed by Mikki House; Mikki House and Mikki House knock-offs are everywhere. While a small amount of American and French merchandise is available, the Japanese do not believe in freedom of expression when it comes to dressing their kids. It's imperative to them that everyone look alike—this is a very homogeneous society, and without giving you a gigantic lecture of a political—and boring—nature, we think you should know that the kids' clothing is adorable—but cloying. While clothes are no more expensive than they are in the United States—for example, $25 for a shirt or pair of trousers—there are no moderately priced or moderately designed lines like we have. There is no Health-tex or Carter's or Sears or Penney's for clothes that will be outgrown before they are worn out. While there are cheaper versions of Mikki House—and you can buy clothes for kids under the tracks and in the *bashis*— there's no such thing as a simple pair of pull-on corduroy trousers with a cotton knit striped shirt. Everything is very fashionable and very "in."

There is a free-standing Mikki House in Shinjuku, but the line is available in every *depato*. Everything is color-coordinated, prematched, and drop-dead kids-chic. A baseball jacket of the latest fashion for a two-year-old costs $110. Some items are more reasonable, but remember that the Japanese like to overpay! We like a French line—not available in the United States—called Mike & Son, which is a little more European than Mikki House. Mike & Son is in most department stores— Sogo in Yokohama has a nice selection, as does Odakyu in Shinjuku. A fashionable baseball jacket for a six-year-old boy is $50. There's lots of Snoopy (intarsia sweaters, $15 to $20) merchandise in all the stores—it's of high quality, and Snoopy is quite acceptable to the Japanese; Daniel Hechter shirts like we buy in Paris are $20; the Popeye line—very similar to Mikki House—is in stores and "under the tracks." Shirley Temple is a popular line for little girls.

One of the best things about children's stores is the selection of shoes—lavish choices of every fashion from traditional to un are available. We did find a rainbow selection of running shoes on sale at Sogo, but for the most part, the cheapest shoes—for kids, anyway—are "under the tracks." Remember, Japanese shoe sizes are different from American and European. We now trace the foot of each child we are shopping for before we leave town and carry the pattern in our passport case. We also aim to buy large rather than small. We also have a closetful of mistakes if you want to buy any of them.

For preteen clothes, there are many more choices than in the United States. If you have kids who love fashion, you can outfit them easily by carefully shopping wholesale, "under the tracks," and in the *depatos*. Don't forget the teeny-bopper outlets in Harajuku and the *bashis*.

MIKKI HOUSE, Remina Building, first floor, 4-3-17 Shinjuku, Shinjuku-ku

Stationery

I f you adore office-supply stores in the United States (we do), you will go stark, raving hysterical when you check out the stationery and office- and art-supply possibilities in Tokyo. The visual arts are extremely important to the Japanese—presentations, be they business proposals or birthday gifts, always are sensational to look at. Great care and expense are put into paper communications—so you will find marvelous pens, markers, gift wrapping, portfolios, etc. You owe it to yourself to browse through the stationery department in any department store. Among *depatos* with wonderful stationery departments are Sogo in Yokohama, Seibu in Ikebukuro, and Mitsokoshi in Nihombashi.

▼

MARUZEN: And speaking of Nihombashi, we would like to discuss Maruzen. Our friend Libby, who lived in Tokyo, raved about Maruzen as a great resource for books and office supplies. When we got there to check it out, however, we discovered it was also a mini department store devoted to the preppy look and not unlike Brooks Brothers. For more on Maruzen see page 136, but don't overlook the stationery department, woodblock prints, and English-language books. The store is conveniently located directly across the street from the front entrance of Takashimaya. Hours: 10:00 A.M. to 5:30 P.M.; closed Sunday.

MARUZEN, 2-3-10 Nihombashi, Chuo-ku

▼

ITOYA: When you are shopping in Ginza, be sure to visit Itoya. In fact, do not leave town without having been to Itoya, the nationally acknowledged best stationery-goods specialty store in Japan. Itoya welcomes you with its racks of postcards on the sidewalk—yes, they have regular postcards, but they also have woodblock-style postcards that are divine. There are two subfloors, sort of a mini half-floor down and then another down—one has gift wrapping and Hallmark-type items, but the basement floor is better—traditional Japanese gift wrapping, all kinds of bags, invitations, paper-goods, hole punches (in shapes), etc. Upstairs there are all sorts of office supplies. Colored marking pens are a bargain in Japan—they are half the U.S. price. But the Team Demi mini-office, although made in Japan by Plus, is cheaper in the United States. (If you insist on a Team Demi office kit, the least expensive price is at Yodabashi Camera in the tax-free department.) Itoya has colored staplers and paperclips and gewgaws for the desk, and all kinds of fun things. Bargain tip: When you pay for your purchase, you will get discount coupons with a yen value to use for your next purchase. Save the coupons and spend them another day—we bought so much we had enough coupons to buy a whole set of marking pens. The rebate from the coupons equals about a 20% discount.

At Itoya in Ginza: B1, social stationery; G, Hallmark gallery and information desk; M, gift garden; 2, office supplies; 3, home stationery; 4, materials for hobbyists and designers; 5, paper and letters; 6, designers' tools; 7, artists' materials and Japanese papers; 8, frames; 9, tea lounge and gallery. Hours: 9:30 A.M. to 6:00 P.M.

ITOYA, 2-7-15 Ginza, Chuo-ku

▼

TOKYO KYUKYODO: This is another shop in Ginza that sells some of the same merchandise, but it has the feeling of Gumps rather than an office-supply store. It is the fanciest tourist souvenir shop we've ever been to. The store is very old, very famous, and very nice. You'll know it by the gold-embossed double doves over the front doorway. There are many marvelous gift items here as well as pens and the like; prices are topnotch to go with the decor, but it's such a pleasure to shop here that it may be worth the extra markup. This is also a good place for postcards and Christmas cards. Hours: 10:00 A.M. to 8:00 P.M.

TOKYO KYUKYODO, Ginza 4 Chome, Chuo-ku

▼

KUROSAWA: And if you think a stationery store should be like the Hallmark shop in your local mall, be sure to stop by Kurosawa, also in Ginza. Hallmark may even own this company, or be its agent. They have adorable cards (in English) and the most wonderful Christmas cards, if you happen to be in season. There's an upper mezzanine also; the wholesale showroom is down the stairs in the back. This may strike you as ridiculous, but if you happen to need photocopy services (as in use of a Xerox machine), they have copy service in this store; also, typewriter repair. You never know. Hours: 10:30 A.M. to 7:00 P.M.

KUROSAWA, 9-2 Ginza, 6 Chome, Chuo-ku

▼

LAPIS: In the Axis Building in Roppongi, Lapis is a small art-supply shop, but they did have the crayons we loved at Sogo and couldn't find anyplace else. Don't make a special trip here, but since you probably will be in the Axis Building, anyway, poke your head in. *Depatos* have larger selections, but there are some unique things here. Hours: 9:30 A.M. to 8:00 P.M.; 10:30 A.M. to 7:00 P.M. Sunday and holidays.

LAPIS, Axis Building, third floor, Roppongi

Shoes and Leathergoods

We have a confession to make. We planned to tell you that the best buys in Tokyo were in shoes and leathergoods. Then we realized that what we were claiming were leathergoods actually are plastic goods. As in fake leather. But if you trust us, you won't care. In the $30 price range we found in Tokyo handbags that are made of various varieties of stamped, tooled, colored, and quilted vinyl that were so stunning that we wouldn't want real leather. Vinyl (or whatever it is—possibly a polymer) is inexpensive, indestructible by children, great for travel, and supremely lightweight. Maybe it wouldn't work at Bottega Veneta, but it sure is great in Japan, where the technology and the creative mind merge to produce fun handbags for not much money. We saw many exact styles we had priced in the United States for $100 to $125 for no more than $30 in Tokyo. Tokyo is the place where you buy a purple handbag because it costs only $25 and really is fun—an expression you don't latch on a $150 purple handbag. (That's a seeeerious handbag.)

You'll find handbags everyplace. Make sure the ones you buy are made in Japan, as these will be the cheapest. Don't let fancy French (or Italian) names fool you. Our favorite Japanese maker is called *Saint Surplice*. Go figure. Law requires a country-of-origin label, so look for "Made in Japan." Don't forget to look at backpacks—everyone in your family should have one (except maybe Brandy the dog). Status handbags will be pricey, but they are also available. Our opinion: Who needs them?

Check all the department stores, especially ISETAN, TAKASHIMAYA, and MAURI, as well as AU PRINTEMPS. Don't forget specialty stores such as WAKO (famous for its handbags) and TAKANO; we did major damage at Takano.

We also went nuts for shoes. Several stores that specialize in shoes on Chuo-dori in Ginza 5 and 6 Chome also sell bags, and one or two shops that specialize in handbags are fabulous. In fact, these few blocks of Chuo-dori offer so many choices you'll wish you had two more sets of feet and arms.

If you are a couture shoe freak, your whole

trip to Tokyo will be rewarded with the discovery of Tokio Kumagi, the Maud Frizon of Japan. Isetan carries the shoes in a first-floor boutique. There are shops also in Paris and New York; this guy is the rage of the *garmentos* and the only person who could make us covet a pair of white witch shoes with gold paint drips on them.

If you need cheap luggage, go "under the tracks." There are also numerous handbag sellers there. We bought a beautiful Chanel bag there, with papers. Shoes also are available "under the tracks" and in many train stations. The Japanese coordinate their clothes to perfection, so matching shoes are very important to them. You've never seen cuter shoes in your life. Shoes are small and wide (see our size chart, page 314), so if you have Cinderella feet, you may be out of luck. Stepsisters, unite: Short, wide, peasant feet will find Perry Ellis for $60, YSL for $90, and no-name bargains for as low as $30 a pair. ODAKYU in Shinjuku has an excellent shoe department. Big-name-designer shoes are, of course, available. But the prices are equal to those in the United States—about $120 to $150 for a pair of Magli or Jourdan. The last may be different.

Don't forget that there are scads of cute children's shoes as well. You may pay as little as $6 a pair (at Sogo) for running shoes in fashion colors not available in the United States. We bought more for kids at Odakyu and "under the tracks."

Remember that Japanese sizes are different from American and European, so use the chart in the back of this book and keep tracings of your children's feet if you buy for them. Measure on the back of the shoe.

Kimonos

I t was Barbara Cohen who first taught us the beauties of the kimono. She sailed through her Park Avenue apartment with a layer of hand-painted silk wafting about her ankles—first a pale blue number with beige branches and white cherry blossoms; it was replaced years later by something in peach. We thought she was elegance personified, so when we got to Tokyo, one of the first things we did was rush to the kimono department of a well-known department store. After touching several dozen, we found just what we wanted. Then we looked at the price tag: $180! Surely there was some mistake. Hadn't Barbara been waltzing around in some *schmateh* of undetermined origin? Quick call to New York. Oh, no, Bobbi assured us: A good silk kimono costs at least $150 and possibly twice that—and then she reminded us that she has hers altered to make them the right length for wearing around the house; a kimono is by definition very long and becomes the proper length for walking once it is wrapped and bundled beneath an *obi*. If you plan to wear your kimono bathrobe-style, *sans* belt or without *obi,* you must take up the hem. Do not choose a kimono whose pattern is mostly at the hem. Yeeks, this is more expensive than we ever imagined—but thanks, Bobbi.

Our shock at the expense of kimonos didn't stop us from looking and learning. Eventually we bought a few used kimonos. But we had a lot of fun looking. Whether you are looking or buying, you might want to remember:

▼ New kimonos are sold in all *depatos*—some of the more famous departments in specif stores are Mitsokoshi (Nihombashi), Ise

(Shinjuku), and Takashimaya (Nihombashi). Takashimaya sells used kimonos in the basement.

▼ There are specialty stores that sell only kimonos. You can see several, almost next door to each other, in Ginza off Chuo-dori in the 5 and 6 chomes. There also are several in Asakusa.

▼ A kimono, like a dress, may be bought in ready-to-wear form or can be made to order. The fabric is sold in kimono length, which is all that is on the bolt.

▼ When you look at a ready-made kimono, you will note large white basting threads and little white cotton patches at integral spots on the gown. You may think this means you have a used or defective gown. Actually, it means that the gown is clean (white basting threads signify that the garment has just been cleaned) and brand-new—the white patches cover the circles where the *mon,* or family crest, will be painted. A kimono may have one *mon* in the center of the shoulder blades on the back, three *mon* (back and arms), or five *mon* (back, both arms, and both breasts). The number of *mon* on a garment signifies its formality; five *mon* are the most formal. There may also be protective fabric patches along the hem.

▼ To be properly cleaned, a kimono must be taken apart (totally) and each piece must be cleaned separately, since there will be some shrinkage. Then the garment is stitched back together again; hence the white basting thread and the large expense of cleaning a kimono. In the United States, you can just send your kimono to the dry cleaner's (unless it is a collector's piece).

▼ If you are planning to wear your kimono in an informal or nontraditional way (for example, over a turtleneck and trousers), do not do so while in Japan. The Japanese know that all *gaijin* are crazy, but this is an affront. If you n to appear in a kimono in Japan, have help getting dressed and make sure you do everything properly. If you want to use your own personal style to add some flair to the gown, please wait until you are somewhere else.

▼ If you need help in wearing your kimono properly, ask your hotel maid to help you. While you cannot tip for this service, you should give a small gift. Be sure to bow your thanks.

▼ Because the Japanese do not like used kimonos, most of these are sold in bulk to American brokers who specialize in this. A perfectly nice silk kimono may be sold as cheaply as $10 in an American flea market. Collector's items, of course, are very expensive and rare. (Fine pieces tend to stay in families or go to museums.) You can buy used rental kimonos from the department stores, or try one of few—but excellent—resources for used kimonos in Tokyo. The rental sales are held once a year, so you just have to get lucky.

▼ There are tourist kimonos made of polyester that are sold in souvenir shops; we are offended by them and hope that anyone with any decent respect for fashion and fabric will not buy them.

▼ If you thought you could get a kimono for $20 and are disappointed that $200 is more the going price, consider a *hakata,* which is a cotton kimono. They come lined or unlined and make better bathrobes than silk, anyway. The least expensive *hakata* costs $15 in the wholesale market; $20 will buy you one at the Oriental Bazaar or any *depato.* Don't forget Libby's Hakata Shop, one of our favorites (see page 123).

▼ When wandering around a kimono department, look for tatami matting. If you see tatami, take off your shoes!

▼ Check out men's wedding trousers that go

with kimonos—they are giant pleated culottes and are stunning. They're in the $200 range, so they are no bargain, but if you love a high-fashion look, you may want some of these. (Don't wear them in Japan!) They're very Perry Ellis.

▼ Kimono accessories mix nicely with Western clothes, but be prepared for some steep prices. Our friend Lynne decided she needed an *obi* belt (not an *obi*, but the belt that goes over the *obi*) to go with her mink coat and spent almost a week tracking one down. Many of the hand-braided ones she looked at cost over $100. Finally she found a beauty for $40 at Sogo in Yokohama. Kimono accessories offer you the opportunity to put a touch of Japan on an existing outfit and come out with something very unique for not too much of an investment.

▼ If you want to know what it all feels like, you can rent at any of the big department stores. They will dress you and do the whole number, makeup and all. Prices vary; ask first. Top of the line for everything can be about $200.

▼ The *obi* always costs more than the kimono: Figure $200 to $400 for a fancy one that is new, $20 for a used one that is a simple print on plain silk.

▼ Kimono underwear (very interesting) can be bought in *depatos* or, more cheaply, from street vendors on market days in some neighborhoods. We gave some kimono undergarments to a friend who was getting married; this particularly inventive style was something Frederick's of Hollywood had not yet come up with.

▼ Bargain shopper of the year award goes to Suzy J., who paid $1 for a kimono at the Roi Building sale. Check it out.

▼ Idea of the year: Buy $1 kimonos and use the fabric to make your own clothes, accessories, or whatever. We cover notebooks and datebooks with kimono fabric. Nice gifts.

▼ Prices vary tremendously for merchandise that seems very similar. Some of this is related to the retailer, but also check the age of the garment, the wear, and the quality of the embroidery. You should automatically be paying for silk with hand stitching. Machine-made kimonos should be very inexpensive. Kimonos for collecting and for wearing are two different ball games; prices will reflect this. For collecting, see page 285. Collectors can really get taken if they don't know what they are looking for, because kimonos are very hard to date, especially brocades.

▼

AYAHATA: Our friend Suzy J. brought us here since Ayahata is in her neighborhood but is a little off the beaten track for tourists. If you are interested in antique or used kimonos, this is worth your time and trouble. Prices aren't as inexpensive as at flea markets and temple sales, or even the Oriental Bazaar, but the goods are lovingly cared for and you will enjoy your visit. They are closed on Sunday and don't open until 11:00 A.M.—but, good news, they are open until 8:00 P.M., and since Akasaka is such a fabulous restaurant neighborhood, you just might want to take advantage of the otherwise not-on-our-schedule difficult neighborhood. If you are staying at the Akasaka Prince, we take it all back. The street address is 2-21-2 Akasaka, Minato-ku. You may want to ask for better instructions, since you have to zig around beside the exit from the subway, pass the local "love hotel" that loc like a castle from Disneyland, and go up one block. Love hotels have nothing to do with shopping.

▼

HIYASHI KIMONO: About the most famous kimono resource for tourists is Hiyashi, located in the International Arcade, which is a tourist haunt because of its good location and the availability of the items tourists want most. The open-area boutique has two parts: One sells used kimonos; the other, new. The kimonos mostly are folded and must be opened to be seen, which makes you feel very guilty after you've looked at a few. Browsing isn't discouraged, but you feel obligated to buy after you've tried on a dozen. A used kimono from the 1940s in good condition costs $60; a wedding kimono is $175. The least expensive piece in the house is $40. The selection of used kimonos is one of the best in Tokyo, but if you feel the prices are high, don't give up. You can find used kimonos (maybe not as nice or in as good condition) for as little as $6.

Hiyashi has this business quite tucked in its *obi* and even publishes two free little booklets that give you tips on their basic wares (much of it touristy) and their antique used kimonos. They sell children's-size kimonos and do a big mail-order and international-mail business.

▼

HANAE MORI: There is a very couture, so-expensive-looking-you-dare-not-set-foot-in-it salon for kimonos in the Hanae Mori Building.

Prices are *cher,* but so is the quality. New and custom only.

▼

ORIENTAL BAZAAR: While we really aren't crazy about the Oriental Bazaar, there are a few things going for it that we can't ignore. The location is supreme, as you cannot leave Tokyo without a visit to Omotesando; the collection of used kimonōs is rather good and definitely is well priced. They have some used wedding kimonos in the $50 to $100 price range and a whole display of stacked used kimonos, all freshly cleaned but without white threads in them. We bought two kimonos here for $15 each. You can buy similarly used kimonos at temple sales for about $6, but then you must have them cleaned. Oriental Bazaar prices are approximately half those at Hayashi. If you are serious about a wedding kimono, spend a lot of time looking before you buy. We found the stitching and embroidery on several models at Oriental Bazaar to be inferior to those at Takashimaya. You always will get the best price and the highest quality at a department store selling its rental pieces.

▼

SHIMA KAME: Although their main store is in Kyoto, the Tokyo shop is impressive. Since 1810, Shima Kame has been making kimonos for the well-heeled; the quality is impeccable. It is open at noon on Sundays but otherwise is open from 10:00 A.M. to 7:00 P.M. This shop is a must-see if you long for a peek at the Old World elegance that Barbara Cohen and the Japanese women of wealth have long known.

In the 6 Chome of Ginza, the exact address is 6-5-15 Ginza.

▼

YUYA: If you have $200 or more for an outfit, you may want to spend it on a new design made from an old kimono. Yuya has a very sophisticated business in this field and seems to be the only one in Tokyo doing this kind of work. If you can sew, you may want to visit the boutique and get some ideas. If you pay between $1 and $6 for a kimono, you have room to experiment once you get home to your Singer. Yuya is in Roppongi on the teeny-tiny street immediately next door to the Axis Building.

▼

ICHI-FUJI KIMONO STORE: Located in the Keio Plaza Hotel and in grasping distance of thousands of tourists, this shop is very standard hotel fare. We found the prices high; the hype, higher. If you want classic tourist stuff, there is no reason to avoid the shop. If you want better prices on the good silk stuff, keep looking. Wedding kimonos start at $175.

▼

SUZUNOYA: We spent a lot of time looking for Suzunoya because it was so highly recommended and we never could find it, no matter where we prowled in the primary Ginza neighborhood. Then, one fine day, we spotted a handsome kimono shop and went it. It was gorgeous (check out the border fabric near the ceiling) and we loved it and then, on leaving, discovered we had wandered into the famous Suzunoya. Not too many people speak English here, but if you are looking for top-of-the-line couture kimonos, this is the place. Upstairs there are plush chairs where you can be the lady and make your selection in serenity. Prices match the decor. There is also another fancy shop—not owned by Suzunoya—next door. No one speaks English, so we can't tell you its name. But this definitely is kimono heaven, in the 5 Chome of Ginza, on a side street on your way to the Imperial Hotel: Suzunoya, 6-10 Ginza, 5 Chome, Chuo-ku. We think the shop next door is called Masuiwa-ya, 5-12 Ginza, 5 Chome, Chuo-ku. But we could be wrong. When we learn to read *kanji*, we'll let you know and firm this up.

Cameras and Electronic Goods

F ACT: Tokyo has a lot of cameras and electronic goods for sale.
MYTHS:

1. Tokyo has a lot of cameras and electronic goods for sale at bargain prices.

2. Japanese makers try out their new items in Tokyo first, so you can buy the latest equipment in Tokyo.

3. If you shop wisely, you will save enough money to pay for your trip.

We know you think there are great camer bargains and electronic bargains in Tokyo a that you want us to steer you to them and point out the pitfalls of being taken. Sadly, this is even simpler than you can imagine. If you buy in Japan, you are being taken.

It works this way:

▼ There is no discount business in Japan; even if a store says they are discounters, they are not.

▼ What they call the "discount" is the tax-free price for tourists.

▼ The tax-free price is less expensive than the regular Japanese citizen price, but it is not the cheapest price for the goods. It merely is the cheapest price in Japan.

▼ The cheapest price is out of Japan, possibly in Hong Kong or Taiwan, but more likely in the United States, where true discounting is a way of life.

▼ Because the trading companies supply all goods to retailers in Japan, they serve as providers *and* protectors. The trading companies make sure that no one undersells another one of their clients. Put simply, the powerful trading companies aren't going to let anyone mess up what they've had going for hundreds of years. There are no bargains in Japan in electronics or cameras.

So where are the bargains? In the United States. The two single best discount sources we have found anywhere are FORTY-SEVENTH STREET PHOTO in Manhattan and LEO'S STEREO in Southern California (there are some forty Leo's Stereo stores). At either of these places you can buy almost anything you can buy in Japan at a fraction (25% less) of the cost (no cameras at Leo's Stereo) and the stores will tell you up front what you are buying.

Treat yourself to a Sunday *New York Times* find the ad for Forty-seventh Street Photo.

One item reads "Nikon F3 with U.S.A. warranty"; another item advertises the same camera without the words "U.S.A. warranty." The U.S.A. warranty camera came directly from Nikon U.S.A., a division of Nikon in Japan. The price offered at Forty-seventh Street Photo is the cheapest you will find for U.S.A. merchandise. However, you may also buy the identical camera without the U.S.A. warranty but that was brought into the country through a different Nikon distributor—maybe one from Hong Kong, maybe one from Saudi Arabia. This camera may be 20 to 25% cheaper than its twin because it is sold without the U.S.A. warranty. But wait: You can buy a warranty for it at Forty-seventh Street Photo. (Leo's Stereo also sells warranties.) And yes, this is completely legal.

FORTY-SEVENTH STREET PHOTO, 67 West 47th Street, New York, NY 10036

LEO'S STEREO, 10915 Santa Monica Boulevard, Los Angeles, CA 90025

Since you will take the previous advice with a grain of salt, we will give you some information on the most famous camera discounters in Tokyo. For more cameras and electronic goods, see the section on Akihabara, page 177. While there are branches of several shops in different locations, you can visit just about everyplace you need to while in Shinjuku.

▼

SAKURAYA: This is one of the most famous camera shops, and we wandered into it quite by accident—it just looked like a great place to shop. Partially built against an alley (we love alleys), the store flows outward like a bazaar—tapes, games, and electronic cars are everywhere. Colorful banners, lots of *kanji*, and milling shoppers make it look like a carnival. Prices, it turns out, are identical to those in Akihabara—and merchandise is much the same. We're not sure why this is known as a camera store, since it also sells robots, videogames, telescopes, copiers, typewriters, computers, and just about everything else. There are five floors of fun here, if a Chinese fire drill is your idea of fun. As a first place to look, this is one of the best because it really does feel like fun. (After you've been in three of these shops, the glamor wears thin.) There are no bargains here, it's hard to find someone who speaks English, and it's almost impossible to find the name of the shop (written in English, it's on only one small yellow sign out front), but you might have a ball. Sakuraya is in East Shinjuku and is conveniently near Isetan and Marui.

SAKURAYA, 26-10 Shinjuku, 3 Chome, Shinjuku-ku

▼

YODABASHI CAMERA: This is closer to My City and the train station but still on the East Side of Shinjuku. There is a second Yodabashi, on the West Side, and it is slightly different and a few cents more expensive than the East Side store. Who knows why? Maybe the cost of rent. The West Side store feels a tad more elegant than the one on the East Side, but both have floors and floors of merchandise. If you want the Team-Demi miniature office in a case, this is the cheapest price in Tokyo.

YODABASHI CAMERA, 11-1 Nishi Shinjuku, 1 Chome, Shinjuku-ku

▼

DOI CAMERA: This is on the West Side, around the corner from Yodabashi West. We don't know why so many people suggest it, but it is another well-publicized and famous tourist stop. Prices are the same here as at the other outlets. It may not be quite as crowded, but it's also not quite as much fun.

DOI CAMERA, Shinjuku, Shinjuku-ku

8 ▾ LOCAL TREASURES: CRAFTS AND PEARLS

History in Art

Japan's folk art is its history. Perhaps this is because Japan always has been, and still is, an insular culture.

The Japanese value their artists, their old, and their traditions. Many of these traditions can be studied through the art. Hundreds of customs involve folk art as part of ceremony or ritual. Many of the artists who have been practicing these arts are now considered "national treasures." But many arts are dying out because the younger generation is becoming Westernized and moving out of the villages for the experience of working in an office. It is both a curse and a blessing.

To get a real feeling for Japanese folk art, head first for a museum or your local Japanese bookshop. We recommend two books especially. *Mingei: Japan's Enduring Folk Arts* by Amaury Saint-Gilles is wonderful as far as explaining what everything is and where each tradition originated. *Kites, Crackers and Craftsmen* by Camy Condon and Kimiko Nagasawa is a specific guide to shops in Tokyo that have been family-owned for several generations.

Folk art has endured through all periods of Japanese history. However, sometimes it is important to date the beginnings of a certain craft to a time frame:

. 600	Founding of Japan
–794	Asuka and Nara periods
1185	Heian Period
1333	Kamakura Period

1333–93	Nambokucho Period
1393–1573	Muromachi Period
1573–1600	Azuchi Momoyama Period
1600–1867	Edo Period
1867–1912	Meiji Period
1912–26	Taisho Period
1926–present	Showa Period

Getting Started in Folk Art

Most craft shops specialize in specific items. Some shops have been in business for centuries, selling the same thing. Usually these shops are not easy to find. You will not have time to visit lots of shops in a day. Unless you know exactly what you want to buy, the experience could be a nightmare. Here are some things to remember when shopping for folk art:

▼ If you are looking for antique folk art, make some phone calls first. Unlike antiques shops, folk-art shops don't always have the old version of what they are selling. Sometimes they do have an antique collection, but it is just for display. You might have more luck in the antiques shops (see Chapter 9).

▼ Consider how you are going to get the item you purchase home. Is it too delicate to ship? Will you have to hand-carry it on the plane?

▼ Folk art is a very personal choice. If you are buying for investment, know your market. What you "think" is valuable is not necessarily so. Ask the experts. Talk to shop owners. See page 290 for English-speaking owners of antiques shops. They can save you hours of searching in vain.

▼ If you are buying just for fun, think about what you are going to do with the item when you get it home. We have a closetful of mistakes. Are you buying for gifts? Do you have some specific use for the item? It's hard not to buy items that look wonderful in the shop . . . in Tokyo. Will they look as nice in your home . . . in the United States?

Remember, *mingei* can be any folk craft used by the people. *Ko-mingei* are those items no longer being made. *Shin-mingei* are items still being produced and used today.

▼

JAPAN TRADITIONAL CRAFT CENTER:
If you are not sure what you want to buy and need some education, we highly suggest visiting this center in Aoyama. This shop/gallery specializes in the traditional arts and crafts of Japan. One end of the large second-story space is a research library. Continuous video demonstrations show artists working in a specific art form. The demonstrations change weekly. If you are interested in a particular craft, ask if a video has been produced on that subject. Many of the videos are in English. All are beautifully filmed. The other end of the space is a gallery with the finest examples of specific crafts. Usually the exhibits are varied to appeal to a wide audience. The middle section of the space contains items for sale. The sales staff is extremely knowledgeable. Some of the staff speaks English.

JAPAN TRADITIONAL CRAFT CENTER, 3-1-1 Minami Aoyama, Minato-ku

▼

BINGO-YA: If you are interested in seeing a diversity of craft items and in simple shopping, do not pass Go, just head for this shop. Opened in 1948 as an outlet for tatami mats, Bingo-ya has grown into the most complete *mingei*—folk-art—shop in Tokyo. Its owner, Hiromu Okada, admits that when the shop first opened he had no idea what it would become. His customers encouraged him to carry more and more items. From tatami mats he went to baskets, then on to other *mingei*. Today the shop has six floors brimming with fabrics, baskets, lacquerware, furniture, dolls, fans, drums, masks, kites, and pottery. Antiques items are on the top floor. Bingo-ya is not in an area you will otherwise be wandering about in. From the Shinjuku station, take a taxi (it will cost over $10 and you will think you are being abducted before you get there), or take the No. 76 bus from the Shinjuku station, west exit, and get off at the Kawadacho stop. You'll be in front of Bingo-ya. We admit that we were chicken to take the bus, so we taxied. Then we took the bus home, and it was a delight. The bus is a pleasure (you get it going back to Shinjuku across the street from Bingo-ya) and costs only a few cents. We interviewed the mostly American shoppers in Bingo-ya, and almost all of them had come with cars and drivers. Don't be shy—this is worth it, and you'll have fun on the bus. But use a car and driver if you are making a day of hopping from one folk-art resource to another; otherwise you'll spend all your time and energy getting to places.

BINGO-YA, 69 Wakamatsu-cho, Shinjuku-ku

Folk Art by Category

T he items most popular to the collector fall into a few categories:

Abacus

We all should have an abacus in the closet. If you don't, you had a deprived childhood and should absolutely rush to our abacus source rather than admit this lack to anyone. Actually, an abacus is a practical item. Some people call it the predecessor to the calculator. Others say it is better than the calculator. If you watch a shopkeeper work with an abacus, you might tend to agree with the latter opinion. In fact, in a contest held a few years back, an abacus was put to the test against a state-of-the-art calculator. Like the tortoise and the hare, the abacus shut out the calculator. The *soroban* (abacus) comes in three sizes for different uses. The smallest is pocket-size. Materials used vary from ivory (most expensive) to boxwood and birch (common variety). If you are collecting for display, ask to see one made of ebony. The quality of the carving and the fitting of the beads on the rods are most important. We highly recommend a shop that has been in the *soroban* business for over a half century: Kinjiro Kudo (the owner) imports *soroban* from all over Japan. He has every style and price range, including a seven-foot model that stands in front of his shop.

YAMAMOTO SOROBAN-TEN, 2-35 Asakusa, Taito-ku

Books and Prints

See our chapter on antiques (page 280).

Brushes

Any artist knows the quality of Japanese brushes or *fude* is the finest in the world. Because of the Japanese emphasis on calligraphy as art, brushmaking has remained an honored *mingei*. Brushes are made from many different types of hair, including weasel, wool, cat, dog, raccoon, and horse. Any animal that sheds might find its hair at the tip of someone's brush. In fact, over two hundred different kinds of hair are used in the production of *fude*. Some brushes, like the *mizu-fude,* are so delicate it takes fifteen years to train an artisan to make them. This is a concept that the Western mind finds hard to grasp, but the art of brushmaking is just that. A variety of stores sell wonderful brushes in Tokyo.

▼

KOH-UN-DO: This is our favorite shop. It has a well-deserved reputation as the home of the best brushmakers in Tokyo. In fact, one of them is a fourth-generation brushmaker. The owner of the shop is Zensuke Ohtani.

KOH-UN-DO, 30-11 Asakusabashi, Taito-ku

▼

GYOKUSENDO: Carries a wide variety of calligraphy items, and stationery goods.

GYOKUSENDO, 3-3 Jimbocho, Kanda, Chiyoda-ku

Clothing

Articles of clothing considered under the *mingei* heading include kimonos/kimono fabrics, *obi*, *geta,* and kimono accessories.

Kimono: The kimono is a traditional garment worn by Japanese that also represents a combination of fashion and culture. At the beginning of the Edo Period the art of fabric-dying took on new importance, and the kimono designs became a way of distinguishing class. The *shōgun*'s kimono did not resemble that of his *samurai.* Women's kimonos originally were no different from men's. Later in the century, however, women's kimonos changed according to the age of the wearer and marital status. Today, kimonos also have ceremonial status. Black kimonos are considered formal, as are those with very elaborate and rich designs. Each kimono, new or old, is considered an object of folk art in Japan. You can buy new kimonos, as well as the accessories that go with them, in any department store; or you may prefer some of the specialty stores. Old kimonos are harder to find since they usually are handed down in families. See page 235 for more on buying kimonos.

Kimono accessories: These are the sashes and belts, not the *obi* worn over the kimono. *Obijime* are the cords tied over the *obi* and knotted in front. *Obiage* are the fabrics, usually silk, tucked into the top of the *obi.*

▼

KUNOYA: If you want a real treat, visit this shop where things are outrageously expensive but gorgeous beyond belief. This is where we buy our telephone pillows, by the way.

KUNOYA, 6-9-8 Ginza, Chuo-ku

Obi: The sash worn over the kimono has a history dating back to the eighth century, when it became popular as a replacement for the cord that had been used. Since that time the *obi* has become the most elaborately decorated part of the kimono. *Obi* come in various styles. *Nagoya-obi* are the least expensive, are pre-folded, and are easy to tie (our kind of *obi*). *Maru-obi* have the design running the length of the fabric and are made of the most exotic brocades. These are approximately two feet wide. They are also the most expensive. *Fukuro-obi* also are wide and long, although the design appears in only three places. *Odori-obi* are the narrowest of the *obi* and are used by children. *Kaku-obi* are the *obi* used by men. *Hakata-obi* are the striped *obi* you see worn in the summertime by both men and women.

Two shops that we particularly like have been in the *obi*-weaving business for decades.

▼

MASUDA-YA: In the Ginza district, sells silks that can be made into *obi* or kimonos. Fabrics are hand-dyed to a customer's order. (As a matter of fact, one of the shop's dyers has been declared a living national treasure.)

MASUDA-YA, 8-15 Ginza 2 Chome, Chuo-ku

▼

FUJIWARA OBIJI-TEN: In Nihombashi is a wonderful, old-fashioned shop with a lor history of *obi*-weaving. Kyoto was the origi home of Fujiwara Obiji-Ten, where the first owners sold their *obi* door to door. After moving to Tokyo, Fujiwara made *obi* for the imperial family. He has now returned to Kyoto to obtain his fabrics, which are magnificent.

FUJIWARA OBIJI-TEN, 2-8 Nihombashi, Chuo-ku

Geta: Although the *geta* is a simple clog shoe, it is considered so much part of the "tradition" of dressing as to warrant consideration as art. Originally, different constructions of *geta* were restricted to different classes of people. However, today it is possible to buy every variety and style. *Nikko-geta* have a bamboo padding between the wood and the wearer and originally were designed for priests in the temple. Two of our favorite sources for *geta* are HASETOKU, 1-18-10 Asakusa, Taito-ku, and YOITA-YA, 5-4-5 Ginza, Chuo-ku

Combs

The most beautiful collections of combs always contain a large number of Japanese *kushi,* or combs (not to be confused with *sushi,* which normally is not worn in the hair). The art of comb-making was introduced into Japan from China and gained popularity in the Edo Period. The comb has different uses, and over two hundred varieties are made. *Sashi-kushi* are the decorative combs that are most popular for collections. Don't make the mistake, however, of giving a comb to your Japanese hostess— it is considered bad luck. There are only four remaining traditional comb shops in Japan.

▼

NO-YA: Our favorite—run by Mitsumasa

Minekawa, this shop has been in its present location for over half a century and was founded in 1673.

YONO-YA, 1-37-10 Asakusa, Taito-ku

Dolls

Probably the oldest dolls were the paper dolls of the Heian Period. (See antique dolls, page 282.) Since then, the art of carving, painting, and dressing dolls has only grown in importance. Dolls represent the history of the culture, and are revered by the Japanese as in no other culture. Many different types of dolls represent different customs or traditions.

Hina dolls: The origin of the *hina* doll is attributed to the ninth-century custom of making dolls in miniature. These dolls were meant to be substitutes for the people who owned them. When the people wished to rid themselves of their sins, they would send these dolls downriver and therefore "wash away" their troubles. At about the same time, a game involving dolls representing the emperor and empress came into popularity. As generations passed on these miniature dolls, the celebration called Girls' Day evolved. Today, Girls' Day is celebrated on March 3. The *hina* doll now is reserved for this occasion. About a week before the festival, the *hina* dolls representing the emperor, empress, and members of the nobility are placed on a display stand containing several steps. On the festival day the little girls in the family gather before this display and give thanks for their good health. A similar celebration for little boys occurs on May 5. *Gogatsu* dolls representing great warriors are brought out on this day and decorated with armor. Kites are flown, and the manly arts are celebrated. *Hina* and *gogatsu* dolls still are handmade by craftspeople and represent a very important cultural tradition.

Kokeshi: A wooden doll with a round head and cylindrical body, the *kokeshi* dolls' origins are traced back to the Edo Period and religious customs. These dolls were believed to hold the spirit of a departed family member and were kept in their memory. The early *kokeshi* are not decorated and look something like a clothespin. Later *kokeshi* are decorated in patterns and are quite colorful. They are still made from a single piece of hardwood, usually dogwood.

Miharu papier-mâché dolls: Papier-mâché, or *hariku,* is used in the formation of many Japanese dolls. This doll is made by first forming a wooden model and then applying layers of papier-mâché. After it's dry, the doll is painted and glazed.

Daruma: Also a papier-mâché doll but with a personality all his own, the *daruma* doll of today has a special task—that of fulfilling wishes. The *daruma* looks like a cross between a meditating Buddha and a bad nightmare. He is legless, and his arms are painted in front of his round, fat body. No matter how often you try to push him over, he rights himself due to his weighting. Original *daruma* had their eyes painted in. Today, however, custom dictates that when you buy a *daruma* you paint in one eye and make a wish. When that wish is fulfilled, you paint in the other eye. We wonder how many one-eyed *daruma* are floating in the canals.

Hoko-san: This papier-mâché doll has a lovely story that accompanies it. Folk tale has it that a young girl named Omaki tended to her sick mistress when no one else would go near her for fear of contracting the same illness. The mistress got well, but indeed Omaki contracted the same illness. Rather than endanger anyone else, this brave child ran away to an island, where she died. The people of her town so respected what she did that they began making dolls dressed as she had been at that time. Today the doll represents bravery and a release from illness. *Hoko-san* dolls are given to the children in a family, who are asked to hold them and then cast them out to sea. In the tradition of Omaki, this is supposed to ward off illness.

Funado-hariko: One of the more popular papier-mâché doll varieties, *funado-hariko* are the figures with the bobbing heads. *Funado* is the area where the dolls originated, and *hariko* indicates the material. These dolls come in any number of designs and sizes, depending upon the skill of the artist making them and the time taken to form the *hariko*. Some *funado-hariko* are built on molds, and some are free-formed.

Hakata doll: A clay doll that is fashioned to look like a young geisha girl, a *samurai,* or a child, the *hakata* doll is one of the most popular inexpensive dolls available.

Noh doll and Kabuki doll: These dolls represent the theater tradition of costume and mask. Usually the dolls are miniature versions of a particular type of the drama and are magnificently costumed.

Many more dolls are being made today. Some we have not mentioned still are valuable and beautiful. Look for the *Ichimatsu* doll and the *Kyo* doll. Fabric dolls that resemble the Cabbage Patch dolls also are popular. Dolls can be found in all of the major *depatos* as well as in the famous children's toy shops FAMILAR and KIDDYLAND. Three doll shops that sell only dolls are worth a visit if you are a serious shopper.

▼

SUZUNOYA: Sells its own versions of Japanese dolls that are quite beautiful and very collectible. The shop is most famous for its kimono designs. At some point they began making dolls and dressing them in their beautiful kimono fabrics. There are seven different dolls, known as the Seiko family. The doll shop is across the street from the Kabuki theater, not in the kimono shop.

SUZUNOYA, 5-10-2 Miharabashi, Chuo-ku

▼

SUKEROKU: Sells magnificent miniature reproductions of people and things that existed from the Edo Period to the present. A staff of twenty craftspeople lovingly carve these figures.

SUKEROKU, 3-1 Asakusa, Taito-ku

▼

KYUGETSU: Our favorite shop for seeing a wide selection of dolls. The *hina* dolls go on sale in February and are a wonderful buy then. The shop, founded in 1830, has over a hundred employees. Many speak English.

KYUGETSU, 20-4 Yanagibashi, Taito-ku

Fans

The Japanese *sensu* (fan) is used to denote affection, to tell a story, to finish one's outfit, and to decorate. Originally the fans were solid pieces of wood, ivory, or jade. These early *shaku* evolved from the emperor's "scepter," also *shaku.* The slatted fan, *hi-ogi,* supposedly came into existence in the Heian Period, when the emperor used it to hold messages for his court members. Soon the slatted fan was used as a decorative work of art, and from there, an art form. There are many kinds of fans. Each festival has its own fan, and each event is celebrated with a fan.

▼ Noh fans are large and have ten slats.

▼ Kabuki fans also are ten-ribbed and decorated with large designs.

▼ Miniature fans are for collections only.

▼ Tea ceremony fans are part of the ceremonial outfit and rarely used.

▼ Sutra fans are dark blue or black and have prayers inscribed on them.

Check the following shops for the best selection of *sensu:*

BUNSENDO, 1-20-2 Asakusa, Taito-ku

KYOSENDO, 2-4-3 Ningyocho, Nihombashi, Chuo-ku

WAN'YA SHOTEN, 3-9 Jimbocho, Kanda, Chiyoda-ku

Kites

The art of kite-making dates back to earliest Japan, when the nobility took up the sport. Today, kites still are handmade. The *washi* paper first is outlined with the design, then colored in. The whole process can take as long as two days. Finally, the frame and strings are put into place. Kites come in every size and design. Certain kites, designed for competition, are exhibited on Boys' Day; others have more general use. Our best kite source has been in the business of making *tako* since 1890.

HASHIMOTO, 25-6 Higashi, Ueno, Taito-ku

Masks

These are wonderful collection pieces and are very hard to find. Masks are used for the Noh and other dance forms. Masks also are used for festivals. Festival masks are the easiest to obtain. They are made from papier-mâché and wood in the form of animals. Caricature masks represent neighborhood friends. Copies of Noh masks and new festival masks are available at Bingo-ya or at Miyamoto Unosuke Shoten.

MIYAMOTO UNOSUKE SHOTEN, 1-15 Asakusa, Taito-ku

Paper

Paper-making has been a Japanese art for centuries. Many craft items are made from handmade *washi*, including umbrellas, kites, lanterns, papier-mâché dolls, and toys. Writing papers are beautiful to collect and come with many grain patterns. Specialized stationery stores carry the best varieties, but many *depatos* have a good selection. Our favorite paper shop is in Kamakura, so if you are going there for a day trip, wait—you'll be glad you did. In Tokyo, try:

HAIBARA, 1-9 Nihombashi, Chuo-ku

ISETATSU, 2-18-9, Yanaka, Taito-ku

Pottery

Ceramicware is beautiful and collectible. (See page 281 for a history of pottery-making in Japan.) Work being done today falls into different categories, according to where it is produced: *bizen-yaki* (Okayama); *satsuma* (Kyushu); *kyo-yaki* (Kyoto); *raku-yaki* (Kyoto); *hagi-yaki* (Yamaguchi); *karatsu-yaki* (Kyushu); *kiyomizu-*

yaki (Kyoto); *kutani-yaki* (Ishikawa). Look for unmatched dishes and cups with colorful designs. If you are buying teapots, a *dobin* has a half-circle bamboo handle, and a *kyusu* has a handle that is the same material as the pot. We have two favorite sources besides the usual shops:

SAGA TOEN, 2-13-13 Nishi Azuba, Minato-ku

ISERYU, 2 Ningyo-cho, Nihombashi, Chuo-ku

Swords

Every little boy's dream is to own one if not many swords. Wait till your little boy sees JAPAN SWORD. From the Heian Period on, the sword was a symbol of the ruling class. The *samurai* believed that their swords held their spirits. Sword-making is an art in which it might take months to perfect just one. Old swords are so highly valued that it is almost impossible to find one. Copies of old ones and new swords can best be found at Japan Sword. You can even buy a suit of armor to go with it. He-Man probably had his made here.

JAPAN SWORD, 3-8-1 Toranomon, Minato-ku

Pearls, Pearls, Pearls

Buying Pearls

One of the most inscrutable facts of the Orient is that $1,000 pearls look similar to $10,000 pearls. Sometimes $100 pearls look like $1,000 pearls. Egads ... what's a girl to do? Know her stuff! Diamonds may be a girl's best friend, but pearls are worth knowing.

The best pearls in the world are in Japan—they are not exported—so if you need a little something to wear around your neck, you just may want to stock up. If you have a birthday or anniversary coming—well, say no more.

Pearls are sold either loose or loosely strung and are weighed by the *momme* (each *momme* is 3.75 grams). Usually you will be shown a loosely strung set of matched pearls. Decide what finished length you wish to wear.

▼ Choker: 15 inches

▼ Princess: 18 inches

▼ Matinee: 22 inches

▼ Opera: 30 inches

Size of pearls is in millimeters. Threes are pretty small, like the size of caviar, and tens are pretty large—almost like mothballs. The average size you are thinking of is a 6 or 7mm. The larger the pearl, the higher the price. The more the matched number of large sizes, the higher the price.

The price of the pearls will depend on the size, length, and quality of the pearls. You will do better not to have your pearls strung in Tokyo. Remember, loose pearls enter the United States with a low duty. Finished pearl necklaces (with knots) are considered jewelry and taxed accordingly.

Deciding whom to buy your pearls from is the biggest problem you will face. You can buy in department stores, independent shops, back-alley shops, shopping malls, or from "wholesale" markets. You can buy more cheaply in Hong Kong, but you won't know what you are getting there (unless you buy from Miki-moto, or a reputable dealer; then the price will be the same). We have done some research among our many friends living in Tokyo and recommend checking out the shops on page 270. We can't guarantee the best price at any of these establishments. We strongly feel that when buying fine jewelry, a bargain is not necessarily a bargain. Pearls will be less expensive in Tokyo for the same or better quality by about half of what you would pay in the U.S.A. However, good pearls are not cheap. If they are, look again; you are being taken.

As far back as legend goes, the pearl has been a sought-after and rare commodity. The Chinese called the pearl "the teardrop of a mermaid." The Hindus believed that the pearl was a dewdrop that had fallen on an oyster. In the Roman Empire, pearls were considered the most valued gem. History books report that a famous Roman general paid for his campaign by selling one of his mother's earrings. Cleopatra is rumored to have crushed a pearl in a goblet of wine to win a bet with Marc Antony that she could give the most expensive dinner party. She hadn't been to Tokyo.

For centuries scientists tried to get the oyster to produce better pearls. However, not until the beginning of the twentieth century did anyone succeed in getting the oyster to make a pearl artificially. At this time three different men, working in vastly different ways, came upon the same process for culturing pearls. It was Kokichi Mikimoto, however, who put his entire future and fortune into the business of developing the right method for culturing pearls, and who made the biggest splash. After nearly going broke in the process, Mikimoto and his wife, Ume, made their discovery of a semispherical pearl in 1893. The patent for semispherical pearls was granted to him in 1896. In 1905, after a terrible disaster wiped out 850,000 of his oysters, Mikimoto discovered that five of his oysters had produced round pearls indistinguishable from the natural ones. By 1908 he held the patent for cultured pearls.

In 1952 the Japanese government, realizing what a pearl mine they had, established an export inspection office to control the quality of pearls sold overseas, and therefore the reputation of the entire industry. Pearls not passed by this office are doomed to live in Japan forever. Of course, nothing says that you can't buy inferior pearls over the counter in Japan and take them home. Also, a lot of these pearls make their way to Hong Kong via the black market. A quality-control problem arising now is the rush to get to market. Many pearl farmers are not letting their pearls mature properly, and therefore the nacre thickness is diminishing. (See page 269 for the lowdown on nacre, the substance that coats the pearl and makes it—well, pearly.) A pearl that looks beautiful might have only a thin coating of nacre and therefore will crack or discolor after a few years. Another concern of the pearl industry is the recent tendency of some pearl producers to color their products artificially. The pearls first are bleached to remove discolorations and then recolored to the desired shade. Tsk-tsk. Pink pearls are the most suspect. Although this process is only whispered about, it is widely rumored to be a rampant problem.

Culture, Culture Everywhere and Not a Drop to Drink

The process of culturing a pearl seems amazingly simple. The oyster, when invaded by a foreign substance, will either reject the substance, or cover it with the protective coating nacre. Most substances artificially introduced into the mother oyster are rejected. The base for a cultured pearl is a piece of another pearl, or a mussel. The Japanese buy their mussel shells from the Tennessee River in the United States. Here the mussels have thick inner shells (nuclei) that are cut into pieces and implanted into the oyster along with a piece of living tissue. The combination causes the oyster to secrete nacre and cover the intruder with concentric layers that will eventually be a pearl

How big the nucleus is and how healthy the oyster is determine how many layers of nacre the oyster will form.

This process, although simple, is time-consuming. The mother oyster is not big enough to be implanted until two to three years of age. At this point a technician gently opens the shell and skillfully inserts the nucleus and tissue. Then the oyster is returned to the ocean, where it sits for another two years. As technology develops, the length of time an oyster sits is decreasing. Periodically the oyster is brought up for inspection and cleaning. To protect the oysters from predators, bad weather, and poachers, they are kept in wire mesh baskets hung from floating rafts.

Originally, women divers were used to gather the oysters that were to be implanted. It was a big tourist scam to go to see the lady divers. (They were topless.) However, today, baby oysters are grown in tanks and placed in the wire baskets when large enough. The original pearl farms were around Toba, on Japan's Pacific Coast about two hundred miles southwest of Tokyo. The area now is referred to as Pearl Island because of Mikimoto's discovery there. However, the waters proved not to be good, and Mikimoto eventually moved south to Ago Bay, where today there are so many pearl farms that you can barely make your way through the waters.

Kinds of Pearls

Basically there are five kinds of pearls: Freshwater, South Seas, Akoya, Black, and Mabe.

Freshwater: Also known as Biwa pearls, these are the little Rice Krispies-shaped pearls that come in shades of pink, lavender, cream, tangerine, blue, and blue-green and that are fun to combine with other strands and wrap. The name Biwa comes from Lake Biwa, about seventy-five miles northwest of Toba, where many of the pearls are grown. They are also found in Shanghai. Instead of implanting a solid nucleus in the oyster, a piece of the mussel tissue is used to form the core of a Biwa. The pearl forms around the tissue, which then dissolves, leaving the pearl a pure nacre.

South Seas: Many of the pearls larger than 10mm are produced in the South Seas, where the water is warmer and the oysters larger. The silver-lipped oyster lives in the waters of Australia, the Philippines, Burma, and Indonesia. It produces large silver pearls that are magnificent. The large golden-colored pearls are produced by the golden-lipped oyster (really, we are not kidding).

Akoya: The pearls you are most familiar with are the Akoya oyster pearls. These pearls are from 2 to 10mm. The shapes are more round than not, and the colors range from shades of cream to pink. A few of these pearls (but not the majority) are blue.

Black: The rarest pearl is the black, which actually is blue or blue-green. This gem is produced by—you guessed it—the black-lipped oyster of the waters surrounding Tahiti and Okinawa. Sizes range from 8 to 15mm. Putting together a perfectly matched set is difficult and costly.

Mabe: Mabe pearls (they have flat backs) are very popular in the United States but not very popular in Tokyo. Most of them are exported. Discovered in 1893 by Kokichi Mikimoto, the mabe is considered a blister pearl because of how it is attached to the inner shell of the mollusk. The black-winged "mabe" oyster is responsible for the pearl. Mabe pearl farms are in the Amami-Ohshima area, which is south of Kyushu Island. These pearls are distinguished by their silvery-bluish tone. The better ones have a beautiful rainbow luster. Currently pearl farmers are trying to produce a perfectly round mabe, but so far have been unsuccessful.

Quality of Pearls

Pearls should be judged by five criteria:

Luster: The iridescent quality of a pearl is what we call luster. Look at six or seven strands of different-priced pearls. The more expensive ones will have a richer luster. This is formed by the light refraction through the translucent top layers. Luster can be measured only by your eye, so it is important to look at many strands of pearls before you buy. You will be amazed at how quickly you can see the differences among lusters.

Nacre: We have talked a lot about nacre thickness. The longer the oyster has the pearl, the thicker the nacre. The usual thickness is .4 to .5mm. Pearls form these layers only when the water temperature is above 15 degrees Celsius. It takes about one year for an oyster to form a thousand layers, with three to four layers formed a day, depending on the weather. It is very hard to tell how thick the nacre is versus how big the original nucleus was. You must trust your dealer on this one.

Color: Color really is a matter of taste. The thing to look for is evenness of color matching. Whether the pearls are cream, blue, or pale pink does not matter as to their value.

Shape: The most expensive pearls are perfectly round. The larger the round ones, the more expensive they are. You can expect to double the price of your pearls per a .5mm increase in size. An 8mm matched strand will be double the price of a 7.5mm strand. Baroque, oval, teardrop, and Biwa pearls are not as expensive.

Surface quality: Sandy finishes are not as desirable as smooth finishes. Once again we suggest that you examine different price ranges in the same size of pearls. The best test is to hold the pearl between your thumb and forefinger and roll it. You will feel any inconsistent surface problems instantly. The price goes up as the finish becomes purer.

Pearly Places

MIKIMOTO: As the leading distributor of pearls in the Orient, Mikimoto is a good place to start your search for the perfect strand of pearls. Their main shop in Ginza has floors and floors of display cases. The staff is happy to spend time showing you various qualities in the same size or different sizes. Most of Mikimoto's quality is upper end. They pride themselves on being the Tiffany of pearls, and they strive to maintain that standard. Prices are a little higher there for that reason. On very large purchases, some bargaining is accepted. Mikimoto also has beautifully designed pieces of jewelry. We suggest visiting the main store, although there are Mikimoto branches in many other locations. A top-quality 6.5mm matched matinee-length strand costs from $1,500 to $2,500. Price doubles per the .5mm increase in size. They are closed Wednesday.

MIKIMOTO, 4-5-5 Ginza, Chuo-ku

▼

TASAKI PEARL: Look out, Mr. Mikimoto, Tasaki Pearl is closing in fast. Tasaki Pearl is the most aggressive of the pearl dealers. They want your business and are out to compete. Visiting the Tasaki Pearl showrooms in the Akasaka district can be a little disconcerting until you get your bearings. When you enter the first-floor lobby, you are apt to get run down by a few tour groups. Ask to join one of the groups for the demonstration of pearl seeding. It really is fascinating. Upstairs, Tasaki has three different showrooms, where they will show you how the live oyster is implanted, how to distinguish a good pearl from a bad one, and how to take care of pearls. The demonstration takes fifteen to twenty minutes. After the demonstration, roam the many floors and study the various qualities available. The staff speaks English and will help you with any questions. Tasaki's prices are better than Mikimoto's by about 10%, and Tasaki also will negotiate on large purchases. A 6.5mm matched pearl necklace of matinee length will cost $1,000 to $2,000 there. They have one of the biggest jewelry manufacturing facilities in Japan and do a huge business in export to the U.S.A. Their "crowning glory" is the Miss Universe Pageant crown, which was made by Tasaki and is flown to the pageant and back each year. Its value is estimated at $500,000. Tasaki also carries mabe pearls. Earrings cost between $300 and $1,000. Don't forget to subtract the tax of 13%. There are showrooms in all of the major hotels, but we prefer the main one, in Akasaka.

TASAKI PEARL, 3-3 Akasaka, 1 Chome, Minato-ku

▼

UYEDA: Another famous name in the pearl business, Uyeda has its shop across the street from the Imperial Hotel (side entrance). We think the salespeople here are the best in town. We always go into a shop and play dumb. Uyeda gets the award for best sales job. We asked to see 6.5mm pearls, which is the size we had been pricing in Tokyo. They began by showing us the lowest quality and testing our eye. When we mentioned that we didn't like the particles of sand in the pearl, they immediately pulled out quality No. 2. We complained that we didn't like the luster of these (very dull indeed). Our salesman at this point figured he did not have a dummy on his hands and started to jump qualities. He still did not show us the very top quality, but the price was getting close. We figure that he could not imagine we would be buying these pearls for ourselves and therefore wanted to save us some money. (The average pearl buyer is the visiting businessman buying for his wife.) Finally, after much time and energy, we got to see the best—and they were wonderful. If you want to buy here, drag your husband with you, or kidnap a man off the street. It will save you oodles of time. Their top price was similar to that at Tasaki and better than at Mikimoto. If you know absolutely zip about pearls, you will get tender loving care and a lot of free lessons at Uyeda.

UYEDA, 1-2-15 Yurako-cho, Chiyoda-ku

▼

VICTOR'S PEARLS: Victor's was recommended by a number of expats. At one time the store was in the International Arcade. It is now down an alley beside the International Arcade and across from the side of the Imperial Hotel. Sound confusing? It is. But you can do it. Between the Imperial Hotel and the Imperial Hotel Tower is a street that looks more like an alley. Walk away from the Imperial toward the Pachinko Parlor. Across the alley from the parlor you will see a small sign for Victor's Pearls. Take the elevator to the fifth floor. Victor himself is quite a character. His son runs the business with him. There also is a staff. A 7mm matinee-length necklace there is $1,000 to $1,500. We think the quality is better at some of the other resources, but this is a good resource if you don't have thousands of dollars and don't mind medium-grade pearls. You do get a lot of value, but you should know your stuff and be an experienced bargainer.

VICTOR'S PEARLS, Yuraku Building, fifth floor, 2-11 Yuraku-cho, Chiyoda-ku

▼

YONAMINE PEARL GALLERY: Another favorite is Jane Yonamine, who runs this small but successful shop in the Roppongi area. In case you are not a sports fan, Wally Yonamine is a famous Hawaiian baseball player who was largely responsible for opening up the Japanese baseball league to Americans. Many photos of Mr. Yonamine and baseball teams from around the United States line the walls. There are also pictures of celebs such as Liz Taylor who have frequented the shop. We sat and talked to satisfied customers as they came and went. One man begged us not to print this listing and ruin his "find."

Mrs. Yonamine has a fabulous policy that serves both her shop and her customers well. Since most of her buyers are businessmen buying for their wives back home, she says, "If you don't like the quality or can match the price elsewhere, I will buy the pearls back." She has an office in Los Angeles to help her customers with stringing, or if there are problems. She keeps a computer file on all of her customers so that pearls can be matched later. Foreigners constitute 90% of her business.

YONAMINE PEARL GALLERY, 11-8 Roppongi, second floor, 4 Chome, Minato-ku

If you need help getting to the shop, call, and they will send a driver (tel.: 402-4001). Mrs. Yonamine's able assistant Yukye Yonemochi has been with the shop for fifteen years and is a certified gemologist.

9 ▾ ANTIQUES

Finding Antiques

Tokyo is a buyer's paradise for antiques. Tokyo also is a buyer's nightmare. All the confusion of this wonderful city triples when you are a serious antiques shopper. Whereas retail clothing stores have signs and addresses that are at least discernible to a taxi driver, many antiques shops pride themselves on being in "cute" and quaint locations. One of our favorite shops is in a former brothel. Another is in an alley behind the U.S. embassy. If you have weeks to spend ferreting out all the wonderful finds that Tokyo does offer, great. However, if your itinerary reads "Tokyo: Three Days," you are in trouble.

Another problem that confronts the antiquer is language. Many of the smaller serious shops are owned by Japanese collectors who do not speak English. Many of their better pieces are in storage waiting for the right request to buy. If you cannot speak Japanese, all you see upon entering is a vase or two. Even if you find a piece on display that interests you, how do you negotiate successfully? Japanese negotiations are like none other. You need to spend time and go through the formalities the culture dictates. Very few of the smaller shops are used to the Western-style, "What is your best price?"

There are a variety of ways to solve this problem and still have a successful antiques experience in Tokyo:

Our first choice is to hire a guide/translator experienced in the antiques field. All of the larger hotels have guide services. Telex the hotel and ask for a list of guides with experience in antiques shopping. Another source for guides is an antiques shop run by an American. We list them later in this chapter. (See page 290.) Very often the expat Americans are tuned into their own network of people who know the city the way you would like to. The only problem with this is that, of course, you are going to be encouraged to buy at the shop that set up this contact. Most often, however, you will not be disappointed and will find something good to purchase. The American antiques shop owners in Tokyo are more familiar with the Western look and often stock more pieces that will fit in with other styles. They also have shipping contacts to make buying easier yet. Contact two or three of the recommended guides and interview them. Pick one who has a knowledge of Japanese antiques. Set up your itinerary in advance. Doing this work ahead of time will establish a working relationship before you arrive. Let your translator know your price range and what kinds of items you are interested in buying. Decide ahead of time if you are going to be using a car or public transportation. Sometimes public transportation can save you time. Traffic in Tokyo is frustrating if you are on a schedule. Let the guide know that you do not want to go to the obvious antiques shops where you could go yourself. We have listings for these shops later in this chapter. Have your guide set up loose appointments for you. This will be a help if the antiques shop you are visiting is busy that day. The owner will be expecting you and will have set aside time for your questions and negotiations. It is also important for your guide to know that you are or are not familiar with Japanese antiques. Very often a guide will be polite when you want the guide to be honest. If you need to be protected from a bad deal, your guide should know. Doing this work ahead of time might seem excessive. Trust us, you will save yourself vast amounts of time, trouble, and money this way.

If you are a more independent traveler and like to do it yourself, there are a variety of approaches to take:

1. Concentrate on hotel arcades. By and large, hotel arcades have one if not two to three good antiques shops set up for the tourist. This does not mean that they are bad, or that you will pay more. We have encountered good deals and bad at hotel arcade antiques shops. The benefits to shopping here are convenience, shipping, and time. There always is at least one person who speaks and reads English in each shop. Very often the arcade shops stock more expensive and better items because they know they will get a good turnover and can afford to invest more in their goods.

2. Concentrate on well-known antiques neighborhoods. Kotto Dori in Aoyama and the Japan Old Folk Craft and Antiques Center in Jimbocho are two famous areas for antiques shopping. Wander these areas and take your chances. We think you will be frustrated by the language barrier, as we always have been. We have other neighborhood listings later in this chapter.

3. Wander, and discover your own finds. No guidebook will give you all the sources. If you have the time, serendipity often brings the most memorable purchases. Very often, getting lost in Tokyo pays off in this way. You may be looking for one store and in fact stumble on another because you are in the wrong spot. The only drawback is trying to guide someone else back to the same spot.

Antique Finds

U nderstanding antiques requires an education of the visual sense. Antiques first must be pleasing to the eye. If you don't like the way a *chabako* (tea box) looks, it doesn't matter that it is valued at $500. After the piece has passed the visual test, then it is important to look for value.

▼ How is the piece constructed?

▼ Has it been repaired?

▼ How many owners has the piece had?

▼ Are there any papers tracing the piece's history? Very often there are not. This is not a criterion that need stop you if you feel confident in the dealer's honesty.

▼ Will the dealer have the piece verified by a second source?

▼ Can you have the piece appraised? If the dealer has purchased the piece through an auction, this appraisal might already exist. If the piece looks too perfect, question its authenticity as an antique. Some of the newly crafted goods are as beautiful as the old ones, but they should not command the same price as an antique does. Most dealers are reliable in this way. However, it is wise to be wary.

▼ If you are buying porcelain, look for the artist's mark, very often found near the edge or on the bottom. Also look for use marks on the inside of a piece. An antique that has not been used and shows no sign of use probably is not an antique.

▼ A good antique will not be inexpensive. If you think you have found "the best buy," look again. Japanese antiques are valued by the Japanese and by collectors worldwide. Expect to pay for value.

▼ Make sure that the antique you are buying can be exported. Very valuable pieces are not allowed out of the country without papers.

Once you have satisfied the above criteria, and yourself that your deal is a good one, have the antiques dealer give you authenticity papers for Customs. Antiques are not subject to duty or value-added tax. However, you cannot expect the Customs officer to take your word. Make sure that your piece is packed so you can unwrap it easily. Some Customs officers ask to see what the papers describe. You don't want to be the one in line with wrapping paper and tape strewn all over the floor. We have stood in line behind a few of these unfortunate souls. If you are shipping your purchases home, check page 31 for hints on how to make it easier.

What to Buy

A ntiques are old objects of value. The question is, what does value mean? Some collectors think that chopsticks are valuable collector's pieces. Other collectors like *netsuke*. The problem for the collector is determining what to collect. We can't help you make that determination, but we can tell you what others collect, and why. Certain items are more popular than others and therefore harder to find. Certain items are more uncommon than others and therefore harder to find. Whatever you have decided to collect, you will find it in Tokyo—and it will be an adventure.

Books

Books interest the collector not only for their reading value (you must understand Japanese to appreciate this) but even more so for the calligraphy and illustrations contained in them. The oldest pieces of printing were religious texts and Buddhist scriptures. All early works were done by wood-block printing. The illustrations contained in these early works were highlighted with watercolor washes. After religious works, the next most popular books printed were familiar folk tales and Kabuki stories. Eventually all types of works, including educational ones, were put in print. During the Edo Period (1600–1867), books continued to be printed by the wood-block method, although European movable type had been introduced by missionaries, and Korean movable type was being used by some printers. Not until the Meiji Period (1867–1912) did movable type become widely used. This is great news for the collector, because wood-block printing is what is valuable.

Wood-block printing is achieved through the hand-lettered and -illustrated page being pasted face side down on a wooden block, oiled so that the printing shows through, and then carved into bas-relief. The wood block then is inked and laid against a sheet of paper, which absorbs the ink on the raised portion of the wood. Therefore each page is a piece of hand-carved art.

Carvings

We know architects who travel the world gathering pieces of old buildings. Tokyo is paradise for these collectors. The Japanese have utilized wood and metal carvings to decorate their homes and temples since very early times. Traced back to the Asuka and Nara periods

(600–794), these carvings were used as good-luck pieces as well as decorations. Since the Japanese home did not contain elaborate furnishings, all show of wealth had to be displayed on its doors and gables. Early feudal castles were decorated with incredible architectural sculptures. When these castles were destroyed, very often the carvings were saved. These pieces now make beautiful examples of table or wall art.

Ceramics

Pottery-making always has been a favored art form in Japanese culture. Earliest forms were utilitarian, later forms more decorative. Not until the Kamakura Period (1185–1333), however, was the form respected and taken seriously as fine art. Then, most of the production was in large urns used for storage. In the next periods (Nambokucho and Muromachi), 1333–1573, tea-ceremony utensils became popular. These are some of the pieces that the collector might find.

Six famous Kilns in the following six famous areas produce the pottery now collected:

▼ Bizen still is actively producing pottery today. Its glazes are known to be naturally colorful.

▼ Echizen produced pottery mostly for local use. It is no longer producing, but the old pieces are collector's items.

▼ Seto is actively producing pottery today. It is considered to be one of the most prolific areas. Some of the oldest pieces come from the Seto kilns.

▼ Shigaraki pottery has a distinctive look due to the quality of the clay in this hill town. Little white spots are scattered on the surface of the finished pieces. In the Edo Period, Shigaraki pottery was highly valued.

▼ Tamba is another mountain town with unusual soil. In the old pottery you can spot the erratic nature of the surface and color. There still is one kiln operating today.

▼ Tokoname no longer produces its beautiful wares. However, if you are in the area, the museum is wonderful.

Dolls

Japanese dolls, old and new, are magnificent expressions of life-style and culture. The antique dolls date back to the earliest periods of Japanese history. Originally they were made from paper or grass and used as good-luck pieces. Often dolls were made in the form of warriors and offered at the graves of nobles in place of human sacrifices.

During the Edo Period (1600–1867), doll-making became an art form, and many different types of dolls were developed. Puppetry, imported from China, quickly became popular as a story-telling tool in both everyday life and religious life. Dolls were made of wood, ceramic, or papier-mâché. Dolls were made both with and without clothing. Dolls were made for special festival days. Eventually dolls gained such prominence in daily life that a special day, March 3, was set aside as Doll Festival Day. This day has since become known as Girls' Day as well. There are fifteen dolls in all. After the festival day, the dolls are carefully wrapped and stored away for the following year. Very often families spend more than a fair proportion of their income collecting these dolls.

Another doll that is considered a collector's piece is the *kokeshi* doll. *Kokeshi* are simple forms carved from wood, cylindrical in shape, and having no arms or legs. Originally these dolls were made by roving craftspeople who wandered the countryside looking for materials. Very old *kokeshi* are cherished and passed down in families as heirlooms. *Kokeshi* dolls made today are wonderful souvenirs.

Fabric

Antique Japanese silks and brocades are valued as pieces of art. Many of the weaving techniques used are so intricate that they cannot be duplicated today. The original designs from earlier periods have distinct Korean and Chinese influences, because this is where the Japanese learned the art of weaving. The textile industry in Japan gained its own prominence during the Edo Period (1600–1867), when the nobility, who enjoyed wearing the beautiful brocades they had imported from China, promoted its growth. During this period the tea ceremony grew in importance, and beautiful brocaded fabrics were used as tea caddies and as sacs to hold the utensils. As the textile industry was blossoming, the kimono was redesigned. The outer coat became more dramatic and colorful. These antique kimonos, *obi*, and tea-ceremony fabrics make wonderful pieces for collectors.

Fans

The fan is known to be an integral part of everyday life in Japan. So many fans are produced and decorated for so many events that it is quite a bewildering adventure trying to find an old one and understand its meaning. This is where a good dealer can be invaluable. Beautiful old fans can be found in good shops and in rummagy ones. The important parts are that you like the painting and that the fan is in good condition.

Furniture

The most popular item that collectors like to buy is the *tansu* or chest. *Tansu* come in a variety of sizes and finishes. We have seen so many that we find it hard to generalize. The best ones definitely will be found through the better antiques shops. The owners of these shops are privy to private estate sales and auctions that you are not. Old *tansu* that have been kicking around too much usually are not in usable shape. Basically a *tansu* is a chest for storing clothing. The *samurai* and highest classes used very good woods and had their pieces ornately lacquered and decorated. The chests decrease in wood quality and decorative finishes with the class rank of the original owner. Today even the simple *tansu* are appreciated for their design and wood quality.

Kyodai are wooden cosmetic boxes. The typical *kyodai* has a beautiful lacquer finish and a mirror on top. It is very adaptable to modern use.

Kyosoku are wooden stands with brocade pillows on top, used originally as armrests. They were very popular during the Edo Period and continue to be popular even today. It is common to find *kyosoku* in an antiques shop without the pillow. As the wood usually is beautifully decorated with flowers, the *kyosoku* makes a wonderful footstool or accessory piece by itself.

The hibachi is well known as a stove. However, antique hibachis come in so many designs that they make delightful side tables, coffee tables, or planters. The older hibachis were made from wood; the newer ones, from ceramic. The oldest hibachis date back as far as the Heian Period (794–1185). However, hibachis did not become widely used until the Edo Period. Most of these are constructed of wood. It was not until later, 1868–1912, that the ceramic hibachis gained prominence. These were beautifully decorated, often in the blue and white motif, by the porcelain-painters of the period. Both styles make wonderful pieces for collectors.

Kimonos

There is nothing more beautiful than the kimono. Every culture has its version of "fashion art." The kimono is Japan's. Recognizing an antique kimono is not easy, as many of the new ones are made in the exact same way as the old ones, and traditional for dating methods don't work. Some antique kimonos come with papers, but this is not the rule. Mostly, you must trust the dealer. The truly ancient kimonos of the Heian Period (794–1185) come with as many as twelve layers. Each layer is color-coordinated to blend with the others. Modern kimono styles date back to the Edo Period, when the textile business was flourishing and even the merchant class considered it necessary to be attired elegantly. There are quite a few outlets for old kimonos, including the flea markets; they are used, but not real "antiques." The authenticated old ones are rare and expensive.

Lacquered Boxes

Lacquered boxes come in all sizes and with a variety of other decorations. The *keshobako* or cosmetic boxes were used by the ladies of the ancient court to store mirrors, combs, and hairpins. These boxes often have gold inlay or painted designs and still can be found in antiques shops.

Tebako, larger boxes, are harder to find because of their size, but the simpler ones still are available. The most beautiful ones, gold lacquer with pearl inlay, are rare and costly.

Maki-e is a technique used on many lacquered boxes. The design is done in a wet lacquer over which a gold or silver dust is applied. These designs can be simple or complicated, and very often inlaid mother-of-pearl is applied together with the *maki-e*.

Food boxes, or *jubako*, date back as far as the Kamakura Period (1185–1333). However, as with so many of the arts, the Edo Period saw the popularization of this type of food container. *Jubako* can be any shape and have any number of drawers.

Serving trays, also called *bon, zen,* or *sanbo*, became decorative lacquered objects during the Edo Period, when all everyday objects took on artistic importance. Trays come in all sizes and with or without legs.

Masks

Noh is a stylized dance/drama that had its beginnings in the Nambokucho Period (1333–93). Kan-ami is credited with developing Noh, which combines music, poetry, dance, and drama in a stylized form that tells a story. Noh actors wear masks that depict the character portrayed. The personality of the actor never is revealed. Early Noh masks were more dramatic than later versions. As Noh developed, it became more and more a Buddhist art form, with the subtleties being more and more emphasized. The masks are highly prized. Antique Noh masks are almost impossible to find, but copies can be obtained.

Netsuke

Netsuke are small carvings made from wood, porcelain, ivory, or metal. The most commonly found *netsuke* are carved ivory or wood. Whereas today *netsuke* are kept locked in curio cabinets, or displayed on shelves, the use is actually that of a clasp. Japanese men of the

Edo Period carried their belongings in attached sacs that were held together by the little carved figures. The artists who carved *netsuke* used images from legends, real life, nature, and history as their models. Some are more elaborate than others. Some are of finer quality than others. If you buy ivory, make sure you can bring it back into the United States (antique ivory is okay but needs papers).

Paintings

Many forms of paintings can be classified under the "antiques" category. The earliest ones were simple folk paintings done on heavy brown paper that had been washed with a clay called *odo.* The subjects depicted were those from everyday life. Pigments used were mineral-based and brilliantly colored. These paintings, called *otsu,* still are in good shape and can be found in antiques shops specializing in art and woodblock prints.

A more refined school of art called Nanga or Bunjinga was inspired by Chinese brush paintings. Subjects painted include mostly mountains, birds, and flowers. Much of the Nanga painting was done on hanging scrolls and screens and still is buyable.

Fusama are sliding doors containing fine painting, often with elaborate gold backgrounds. These are magnificent and hard-to-find works of art of the Azuchi Momoyama Period (1573–1600).

Hanging scrolls (*kakemono*) and folding screens (*byobu*) are two art forms that can be found in abundance. The painters of the Edo Period used both media to transcribe their views of religion and life. Many good examples of this art still are available.

Porcelain

Porcelain always has been appreciated by the Japanese, but it wasn't until the Edo Period—specifically, the 1600s—that a Korean potter named Ri Sanpei found the right clay to produce porcelain. Within a few decades, the Japanese porcelain business was thriving. A variety of porcelains have become known to the collector:

Kutaniware was produced for a very short time after the discovery of the porcelain process. Kutaniware is larger and more gross in style than the Imari or Blue and White of the same period. The motifs generally follow those of nature, and the colors are more dramatic and less refined than the others.

Blue and White is taken from the original Chinese Blue and White designs. Although the original Japanese Blue and White designs closely resembled the Chinese, as the craftspeople became more familiar with their art, they departed into more traditional Japanese forms. Some Blue and White is simple, with shades of blue underglazing varying from gray-blue to cobalt-blue. Other Blue and White is very ornate.

Imari porcelain was named by the Dutch for the port from which it was shipped. It dates back to the early 1600s, when it was, like the Blue and White, simple glazes over the clay. It wasn't until the 1700s, when a red overglaze was developed, that the Imari we are most familiar with came into being. The designs of Imari ware are ornate and intricate, with many glazes, overglazes, and enamels, reflective of the Edo Period.

Kakiemon porcelain is distinguishable by its delicate brushwork. The motifs are simple and feathery, the most popular being the nature motifs of fish, flowers, and trees. Kakiemon porcelain usually has a pale background, with the design covering only a portion of t area. The colors usually are clear and brilliant.

Nabeshima porcelain began as a personal pleasure for the feudal Lord Nabeshima, who liked to give pieces produced in his personal kilns to friends and other government officials. It wasn't until the 1800s that Nabeshima porcelain became available for sale. The distinguishing feature of this porcelain is that half of the area is covered by the design, which is pictoral and not geometric. This particular porcelain has been copied in modern times and still is widely popular.

Nagasaki porcelain was so named because it was of lesser quality and produced specifically for export. The plate sizes were scaled down for the European market, and the quality control was dropped. The most popular decoration of these pieces was the Imari patterns of red and gold overglazing. These pieces are not as valuable as the others.

Wood-Block Prints

Wood-block prints (*ukiyo-e*) are a very important part of Japanese art. Their history basically mirrors that of the book-publishing business. *Ukiyo-e* prints represent the growth of the literate population of the Edo Period and the Kabuki theater. Often these prints were book illustrations for books about history and cultural pursuits of the time. The characters represented in them take their style from the Kabuki characters. A popular *ukiyo-e* form is the Bijinga print, which depicts women, very often courtesans, in their everyday lives. Famous artists of this style include Harunobu, Kiyonaga, Utamaro, and Eisen.

Prints depicting actors of the Kabuki theater are called *shibai-e*. Torii Kiyonobu is credited with being the founder of this form of *ukiyo-e*. Over the years this form took many twists and turns, until the Utagawa School became popular in the eighteenth century.

Landscape *ukiyo-e* prints are called *fukei-ga* and did not become popular until the nineteenth century. The two masters of this art form were Katsushika Hokusi and Ando Hiroshige.

Sumo-e prints are *ukiyo-e* depicting the fabulous wrestlers of the late eighteenth and nineteenth centuries. The variety of these prints is wonderful. In some the sumo wrestlers are dressed in formal kimonos, and in some they are in ceremonial garb. These prints are hard to find and valued very highly.

Miscellaneous Collector's Items

There are many categories we have not gone into in any depth but mention here as other possibilities for fun antiques shopping:

▼ pillows (*makura*)

▼ pendants (*inro*)

▼ sake stands (*hai-dai*) and sake bottles

▼ shell games (*kai-oke*)

▼ chopstick holders (*hashitate*)

▼ musical instruments

▼ Japanese chops

Where to Buy

This is the hard part. There must be thousands of antiques haunts in Tokyo. You'll find it easiest to shop the "foreign" dealers. By "foreign" we mean English- or American-owned. Owners of these shops have, by and large, lived in Tokyo for years and know how the system works.

MICHAEL DUNN, ORIENTAL ART: Off on a side street in the fashionable Roppongi area, Michael Dunn exhibits a good selection of Japanese antiques, including porcelains, ceramics, tansu, and paintings. Call first to get exact directions, or have someone meet you.

MICHAEL DUNN, ORIENTAL ART, 5-16-12 Roppongi, Minato-ku

▼

THE GALLERY: Patricia Salmon and Julie Cohen own this tiny find behind the Hotel Okura and beside the U.S. embassy. To get there, find the front entrance to the Hotel Okura (on the fifth floor if you are wandering around in the hotel trying to get out), turn left as you leave the hotel, and then turn right down a very small alley that runs beside the U.S. embassy compound. Turn right again in the first alley and you will see the sign for The Gallery in front of a little house. The Gallery has been in its present location for the past fifteen years, having been previously located in the old Imperial Hotel. The clientele are very loyal, and many have been shopping with Ms. Salmon since she opened the shop. We spoke with one woman who has been shopping there since she moved to Tokyo years ago. She told us wonderful stories about how the expats used to gather at the salon for cocktails and intellectual conversation in "the old days." The Gallery carries very select items. The merchandise changes depending on what is available. You can expect to find jewelry, Oriental rugs, textiles, screens, *ukiyo-e,* and furniture on display, depending upon what Ms. Salmon and her partner have found worthy to sell. Patricia Salmon also has published a wonderful book n antiques that we highly recommend, called *anese Antiques.* If you want to speak with the owners, call first. Ms. Cohen has a shop in Palos Verdes, California, also called The Gallery.

THE GALLERY, 11-6 Akasaka, Minato-ku

▼

THE KURA INTERNATIONAL; THE TOLMAN COLLECTION TOKYO: Norman Tolman and his wife run both of these galleries from a wonderful Japanese building you would never identify as a gallery from the outside. The building has such anonymity because it was a geisha house for two hundred years. The Tolmans bought it and restored it to its present condition when they began their business. The gallery is in the Shiba Daimon area and is down the street from the Zojoji Temple.

If you are a collector of antiques, the Tolmans have a magnificent array of items. The quality is so good that this is a favorite haunt of the rich and famous.

The Tolman art collection represents some of the finest living Japanese artists. If you like the work of Shinoda, Iwami, Matsubara, Sawada, Wako, or Ryokei, to name a few, the Tolmans have files of their work for you to see. There always is an exhibit.

THE KURA INTERNATIONAL; THE TOLMAN COLLECTION TOKYO, 2-2-18 Shiba Daimon, Minato-ku

▼

KUROFUNE: John Adair is the owner of this very colorful antiques shop north of the Roppongi shopping area. Instead of walking toward the Axis Building on Gaien Higashi-dori, cross Roppongi and walk away from it. Kurofune i down two side streets and stairs. You mi want to call and have somebody at the shop meet you on the main street. Kurofune carries a selection of furniture, porcelain, and collectible items you will find interesting. Sometimes the prices are a touch higher here than elsewhere, but the selection is noteworthy.

KUROFUNE, 7-7-4 Roppongi, Minato-ku

▼

SHIROGANE: Stewart Caul always is particularly helpful to us when we visit Tokyo. His gallery is open by appointment only. He specializes in hanging scrolls, art, folk craft, and antiques of unusual quality. He deals with American gallery owners and designers who come to Tokyo to buy. If you are looking for a special something or many things, we highly recommend talking to Mr. Caul.

SHIROGANE, 5-13-38 Shirogane Dai, Minato-ku

Also see:

EDO ANTIQUES, 2-21-12 Akasaka, Minato-ku
FRAN-NELL GALLERY, Hotel Okura, 10-4 Toranomon, 2 Chome, Minato-ku
HARUMI, 9-6-14 Akasaka, Minato-ku

Antiques by Neighborhood

Aoyama

The main antiques shopping street in Aoyama is called Kotto-dori, Minami Aoyama, or Antiques Street, depending upon who is giving you directions. Take the Ginza or Hanzomon subway to Aoyama, 1 Chome. Exit the station and walk on Aoyama-dori toward the intersection of Omotesando. (You can also exit the subway at Omotesando to save time.) Pass this intersection and keep walking. The next major street you come to on your left will be Kotto-dori. To verify that you are on the correct street, a big red "books" sign should be on your left, and the Luna Park furniture store should be on your right. As you walk down the street, you will see many little shops. Some are specialized and do not have much merchandise on display. It helps to have someone with you who speaks Japanese. Some of the shops you will encounter as you walk Antiques Street are:

▼

K. MINO: Far Eastern art, ceramicware, little English.

▼

SHIMBIDO: Very small collector shop, no English.

▼

D. TANAKA: In the Sumito Building; fine art is their specialty.

▼

MORISEI: Blue and White porcelain, Imari, *netsuke,* and lacquerware.

▼

KARAKUSA: A great shop for Blue and White ware. Prices are relatively inexpensive. A large plate costs $200. Good English is spoken. The name of the shop is not written in English, so look for the Blue and White porcelain display in the window.

▼

MORITA: A good selection of ceramics, folk art, and furniture. English is spoken, and prices are good.

▼

YANAGAWA: Screens, scrolls, and porcelain are good finds here. English is spoken.

▼

ORIENTAL HOUSE: This is a shop for dealers and serious collectors.

▼

MATSUSHITA ASSOCIATES: This shop is on the corner where you turn to go to the Nezu Museum. Mr. Matsushita speaks English well and has a fabulous collection of *ukiyo-e* prints.

▼

JINTSU: A building across the street from Matsushita that houses a variety of specialty antiques shops. Take a translator.

▼

ZENRAKU-DO: Good English is spoken. A variety of antiques available.

▼

NISHIURA RYOKUSUIDO: Japanese and Korean antiques.

▼

ICHIGENDO: A good selection of ceramics; little English.

▼

OUGUCHI: Good English and good ceramics.

Ginza

Ginza antiques shopping is upscale, but rewarding anyway. The better shops are in the Imperial Hotel and nearby arcades.

▼

ODAWARA SHOTEN: In the Imperial Hotel Arcade, this shop carries a large selection of scrolls, screens, furniture, porcelains, woodblock prints, and lacquerware. The staff speaks English.

▼

MAYUYAMA: The main store is in Nihombashi, but there is enough selection here to make the trip worthwhile. This shop also is in the Imperial Hotel Arcade.

▼

M. NAKAZAWA: Across the street from the Imperial Hotel and its arcade, M. Nakazawa carries a good selection of wood-block prints.

▼

K. WATANABE: Next door to M. Nakazawa, this shop specializes in *netsuke,* Imari, jewelry, bronzes, and art.

T. SAKAI: Next door to K. Watanabe, this is another good source for wood-block prints.

▼

HIYASHI KIMONO: In the International Arcade, under the highway, this is the most highly touted shop for finding antique kimonos (see page 240).

▼

YOKOYAMA, INC.: This shop has locations in the Hilton and Okura hotels as well as on the second floor of the Sukiyabashi Shopping Center. We always have had good luck in this shop and its other branches. We especially like their collection of *ukiyo-e* prints.

▼

UCHIDA: Also on the second floor of the Sukiyabashi Shopping Center, this gallery has a small but good collection of antiques and collectibles.

▼

S. YABUMOTO CO.: A shop for the serious collector of screens and paintings. S. Yabumoto is in the Gallery Center Building (3-2 Ginza, 6 Chome, Chuo-ku, 572-2748), seventh floor. There are other antiques shops in the same building. Good if you know your antiques.

Harajuku

Harajuku is mostly a fashion area, but on the main Omotesando-dori, there are a few places not to miss for small antiques and folk art:

▼

ORIENTAL BAZAAR: Architecturally, this is a wonderful building filled with new and old antiques and folk art. The new antiques obviously are not antiques but good copies. We think the merchandise is expensive and overrated, but there always are good finds. The old kimonos are especially worth looking at.

▼

ASANI ART CO.: A well-known shop for ceramics, lacquer, *netsuke,* screens, and scrolls. You can trust the quality of what you buy here.

▼

HANAE MORI ANTIQUES MARKET: Downstairs in the Hanae Mori Building you will find a mini antiques mall. Each boutique specializes in a different type of antique. The variety includes French Art Nouveau, Chinese porcelains, American Victoriana, and Japanese porcelains and dolls.

Jimbocho

There really is only one place to go in Jimbocho, but it is exceptional: Japan Old Folk Craft and Antiques Center (Komingu Kottokan) has fifty-five shops on the four floors. You are bound to find something in one of the shops, to make your collection shine. It's at 23-1 Kanda Jimbocho, 1 Chome, Chiyoda-ku, 295-7117.

Other places for antiques in Jimbocho are the old bookshops, some of which have good *ukiyo-e* prints (see our neighborhood listings, page 167).

Nihombashi

The main antiques area in Nihombashi is around Takashimaya Department Store.

▼

TAKASHIMAYA: They have a very good antiques section in their basement. You can find a wide variety of Oriental goods, some of which are better than others. We have made some good finds here.

▼

KOCHUKYO CO.: Across the street from the side entrance of Takashimaya is one of the top antique Oriental ceramics shops in Tokyo.

If porcelain is your passion, be sure to stop there.

▼

MAYUYAMA AND CO.: Exit from the front of Takashimaya, take a right for two blocks, and before you reach Kyobashi, look for this store on your right. This is one of the famous antiques stores in Tokyo and is worth getting lost to find. The selection of goods from Japan, China, and Korea is spectacular. The owners speak English and can help you find whatever you don't see in the shop.

Shiba

This is the area of Tokyo close to the Zojoji Temple. There is one street worth walking and browsing similar to Kotto-dori in Aoyama. Tomoe-cho, a street that becomes Kamiya-cho, is reachable via the Hibuya Line subway. Both streets together have fifteen or more little shops worth visiting.

10 ▾ TOKYO ON A SCHEDULE

Tour 1: Top-Fashion/New-Wave Day

Tokyo is a combination of both new-wave fashion and established designers. And sushi. But that's another story. We happen to love the Japanese look but understand that not everyone does. This day tour will expose you to both. Skip the parts that are not your cup of sake. Linger longer over what grabs your fancy.

1. Begin by taking the JNR line to Harajuku station. This will put you right in the middle of the newest of the young new . . . in some cases, old made new again. (Remember your felt poodle skirt?) Walk straight away from the station down Takeshita-dori (this is the main drag leading away from the station and you can't miss it, even if it's not well marked; it runs perpendicularly right into the station) and enjoy the fun and feel of the street. This is definitely an area for the young or the young at heart. If you are not so young or do not have someone with you who is, concentrate on trend-spotting as you walk toward Meiji-dori. Takeshita-dori is about two blocks long and is intersected once by a cute little alleylike street. This is *not* Meiji-dori. Who knows what it is called . . . keep on walking.

2. Turn right at Meiji-dori (obviously a well-trafficked street—you'll see an Eddie Bauer to assure you that you're doing fine) and walk in the direction of La Foret, which is at the corner of Meiji-dori and Omotesando.

Don't miss any of La Foret. Then take a left on Omotesando.

3. If you turn right, you will be at the park—a must for a Sunday. But for the retailing part of the tour, go left. You are now in the heart of high-fashion Japan. Walk down Omotesando-dori toward Aoyama if you are looking at a map, and don't miss Kiddyland (we know this is not high fashion, but . . .), the Vivre21 Building (fabulous Japanese fashions, including Nicole, Junko Sagawa, and Michiko Koshino), the Oriental Bazaar (just because you should see it), Paul Stuart (we know he is American, not Japanese or European), and the Hanae Mori Building (see all the floors, even the basement). You now have seen a wide variety of Japanese fashion. Both sides of the street are good.

4. If you wish to continue in this area and don't need to stop in one of the enticing European cafes for coffee and pizza, continue on Omotesando, crossing Aoyama-dori. Check out Azuma if you forgot your Fila tennis outfit. As you walk a few blocks farther on Omotesando, you will see the Issey Miyake Plantation boutique on your left. Stop in here; check the bottom for women's and top for men's. Another block on the right side of the street is the From 1st Building, where you will find the Issey Miyake boutique along with a number of others worth browsing. Downstairs you will find the Cerutti line from Paris, and Boutique Moga. Upstairs is the Alpha Cubic Shop, where Guido Pasquali is hiding.

5. At this point we know you need a break, and the cafe in the From 1st Building is very in with the in set. If you are going on to Ginza, head back toward Hanae Mori.

6. Walk back up Omotesando and cross over to the subway in front of the Hanae Mori Building. The name of this station is Omote-

sando, which is simple enough. Take the Ginza (orange) line to the Ginza stop. Exit under the Sukiyabashi Shopping Center. Now you will be in the heart of Ginza. Don't panic. Get your bearings first. If you come out right, you should be facing the Nishi-Ginza Shopping Arcade. If you are lost already, look for the *koban*. Or take a few minutes to get your bearings. Look for the twin white tile towers next door to Nishi-Ginza and beside the elevated train tracks. This is the Hankyu and Seibu Department Store combination and a good place to find a little bit of everything. If you need refreshments, both stores have many offerings. There's a cute little cafe in Seibu on the first floor if you walk through the store.

7. After you have finished here and have seen all of Seibu and Hankyu, go under the train tracks toward the Imperial Hotel (see the map for the proper direction). The International Arcade is literally under the tracks. You will find some interesting buys in kimonos, and touristy items. Next door to the International Arcade is the Nishi Electric Center, a camera, pearls, and electronics discounter. We don't suggest you buy anything here, but in case you want to see what foreign businessmen do with their spare time in Tokyo, you can wander in here. If you still are following our tour waiting for the European designers, get out your credit cards. The Imperial Tower is next to the Imperial Hotel (side-street entrance) and across the street from the International Arcade. There's more shopping underneath the hotel, so don't confuse the tower with the arcade. The first time we tried to find the Imperial Hotel lobby, we ended up in the arcade. After a good fifteen minutes of wandering around marveling at how complete the hotel shops were, someone set us straight. Why shouldn't it be confusing? After all, Frank Lloyd Wright

built the original hotel. (It was torn down and rebuilt; the original is now in a museum.)

The tower is not the hotel but a complete office tower, with four floors filled with designer boutiques. Most of the European big names are there, high prices and all. An escalator connects the floors in the swank shopping area; you will easily think you are in Europe—until you see the prices.

8. If you are interested in looking at pearls, exit the arcade and walk straight ahead down the alley that runs beside the International Arcade. Look on the left after you pass the Pachinko Parlor for Victor's Pearls. He is on the fifth floor and worth a visit. If you're still feeling pearly, visit Ken Uyeda, across from the Imperial Tower but before the Pachinko Parlor. This is a very tony shop, but you can learn a lot here. Compare with Victor's.

9. If you are not Ginzaed out, retrace your steps back to the subway stop or Nishi-Ginza. This time walk toward Chuo-dori and Mitsukoshi Department Store. This is a good starting point. If you walk on Chuo-dori toward Mitsukoshi you will have a few blocks of fun shopping, including the main branch of Mikimoto and our favorite station-ery store, Itoya. If you walk away from Mitsukoshi, you will have more of an ad-venture. The really fun Ginza is to be found on all the little side streets that run off the major drags. Walk the 5, 6, 7, and 8 chomes and just explore. When it gets dark, settle into any of the restaurants you have passed and breathe deeply.

Tour 2: Bargains, Bargains, Where Are the Bargains?

Our bargain day will take you to Akihabara for electronic goods, under the tracks in Ueno for all kinds of goods, and to the *bashis*. If you

have truly taken our advice that there are no
bargains in electronics, totally skip Akihabara
and get off the train at Ueno. This extra hour
will give you time to see a museum or just sit
in the park and feed the pigeons—a worthwhile choice. If you just want to see the electric circus, allow an hour and then be on your
way.

1. Begin in Akihabara, home of camera and
   electronic goods. As we have stated earlier,
   the bargains here are not what you would
   expect. We know you are not going to believe us and will come here anyway. So if
   you must, here is how to get in and out fast.

2. Take the west exit, which will bring you
   into the heart of Akihabara, near the Akihabara Department Store. Pass on the *depato*
   and hit the main street, which is a half block
   away and clearly visible.

3. Look both ways. Neon everywhere. To the
   right is Yamagiwa; Laox is to the left. Wander either or both ways; check out a few
   shops, then hop back on the train. We give
   you a $30 mad-money allowance for toys for
   your kids, so you shouldn't feel like you
   didn't take advantage of the adventure. If
   you buy a CD (compact-disc player), you
   are to be penalized and kicked out of the
   Good Shoppers Club. Our monitors will be
   taking names at the train station.

4. Once you have finished Akihabara, and assuming that you do not need to return to
   your hotel with all your packages, jump back
   on the JNR line and get off at Ueno. Remember which direction your train came
   from, because basically you want to go back
   toward Akihabara under the tracks. Sounds
   strange until you have tried it. Everything
   you want at a good price is sold under the
   tracks between the Ueno and Okachimachi
   stations. If you get off the train at Okachi-

machi, look for the silver arched entry into the shopping arcade. The sign above the arch says "Shopping." It is hard to miss. We have gotten our best prices on toys and handbags here. This is a real adventure, so enjoy.

5. We suggest you endure the temptation to jump off the train at Okachimachi (the stop before Ueno) and stay on until Ueno. Explore the train station and then go "under the tracks" into the Ameyo. Walk all the way back to Okachimachi. Under normal circumstances we would not ask you to double back like this, but the junkier stuff is at the Okachimachi end and we want you to have some energy for the better part first. We love the junky part, but you'll be too wiped out to enjoy Ueno. So enjoy, already.

6. You may want to eat under the tracks—there are many noodle shops and local dives. You won't have as many choices in the "*bashis*." Okay, ready for the "*bashis*"? No, it's not a soap opera about a wealthy Japanese family. The "*bashis*" are what we call the wholesale districts. Warning: No one else in Japan calls this area the "*bashis*"; if you ask anyone, that person will think you (or we) are nuts.

7. The first "*bashi*" stop is Tawaramachi, on the Ginza (orange) line, a few stops from Ueno. This station services the Kappabashi area. Kappabashi is the wholesale district for kitchenware. The reason to go here, however, is not hibachis but plastic food. You have to like collecting unusual things to agree with us, but we think that Japanese plastic food is art. Kappabashi is only two stops from Ueno on the Ginza line. Exit at Tawaramachi station and walk past all the wooden temple shops on Kokusai-dori until you see "The Chef." He is the Japanese version of the man who ate Manhattan, and

he sits on top of the Nimi Building. This is the corner of Kappabashi-dori. You have arrived at plastic-food heaven. There are two or three shops that sell plastic food. One shop takes only plastic. Check them all out before you buy. (See our neighborhood listing on page 106.)

8. Now you have a choice. You can bail out of the continuing "*bashi*" tour and walk from Kappabashi to Asakusa, where you can pray for renewed shopping vigor at the Sensø-jogi Temple and see all the fabulous, must-see shops along Nakimasse, or you can go back to the subway and continue with the *bashis*. To help make this decision the right one for you, see both neighborhood listings for these two various areas (pages 106 and 109) and figure out your other days in Tokyo. If we had to choose for you, we'd walk on to Asakusa and *then* do some more "*bashi*"-hopping by ending up at the Kurame station, which is only one stop from Asakusa on the Toei-Asakusa (rose-colored) line. But we're gluttons. The neighborhood text portions will guide you through the rest of your tour. The choices are yours.

9. When you return to your hotel, book the masseuse who walks on your back. You're going to need it.

Tour 3: With Six, You Get Eggroll

Since Tokyo is so automatically divided into neighborhoods, the best tours are the ones you make up according to your own interests. Depending on your fortitude, combine two to four neighborhoods in a day tour. These are our suggestions for some good combinations, based on transportation and the need to see (and buy) a lot in a short time. Look up each section in our chapter on neighborhoods for more specific information.

1. Suburban Shopper's Delight: A.M., Ikebu-kuro; P.M., Shinjuku

2. Get It All Day: A.M., Ueno, Ginza; P.M., Harajuku, Aoyama

3. Great "*Bashi*" Day: A.M., Nihombashi; P.M., Bakuro-cho, Asakusabashi, Asakusa, Kappa-bashi

Tour 4: Out-of-Tokyo-and-Out-of-Your-Mind-with-Joy Tour and Treasure Hunt (Kamakura and Yokohama)

Not that you'll be happy to give up a day in Tokyo, but if your schedule permits, we think you owe it to yourself to see two other cities. You could do each of these cities as separate day trips, of course, but we combined them because we understand how precious your time is on a big trip like this. If you are a true shopper, no matter how limited your time in Tokyo, you will not miss Sogo in Yokohama. If you have to choose between Ginza and Sogo in Yokohama, we say Sogo! The trip alone back and forth to Sogo can be done as a half-day excursion, naturally. But this is our day trip, so you can improvise as you see fit:

1. Board the train for Kamakura at either To-kyo station or Shinagawa. If you are staying in Shinjuku, it's crazy to go back into town to Tokyo station; just zip over to Shinagawa. It's easy. Take the JNR.

2. When you inquire about the train to Kama-kura, note that some trains require changing cars at the end of the line; an easy step. You will get off and change to another track for the two more stops into Kamakura. We sat on the train a long time (long after everyone else had gone) before we figured it out, but

KAMAKURA

● STORE
□ STATION

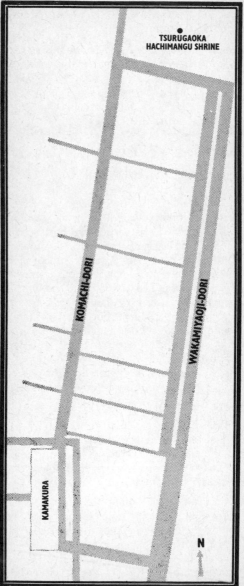

TSURUGAOKA
HACHIMANGU SHRINE

KOMACHI-DORI

WAKAMIYAOJI-DORI

KAMAKURA

N

our guidebook didn't tell us that all the trains weren't through connections. It's not a big deal, but it is nice to know if you're going to change.

3. The train ride is not very eventful; if you expect to see the old Japan of your dreams, forget it. You will pass through Kawasaki (letting the good times roll) and Yokohama. The ride is about an hour from Shinagawa. (If you get on at the Tokyo station, your train may not stop in Shinagawa—there are two routes.) You won't see quaint until you search for it in Kamakura, but it is there.

4. Kamakura briefly was the capital of Japan. It is filled with shrines and magnificent temples and a lovely set of cherry trees, as well as two shopping streets: One is touristy and fun (as in any beach community); the other is more funky and has lots of good antiques shops. When you get off the train and see more of modern Japan, don't panic.

5. While you can spend years in Kamakura taking in the culture, we leave early in the morning; arrive when the shops open; and take in stores, lunch, a divine shrine, coffee, some more stores, and a 3:00 P.M. train so we can get to Yokohama. If you want more shrines, look in any of the many guidebooks. Kamakura is well covered and quite the tourist spot. We go for the combination of culture and shopping. Follow our square pattern (see the map) that begins and ends at the train station.

6. Walk forward from the train station one block to Wakamiya Avenue. This is the main drag of town and is like the main drag of any small quasitourist town. It reminds us of Deauville. The street has restaurants and shops on both sides, with an island of cherry trees and a few torii running down the middle. Even when the trees are bare, it's picturesque. There's a wonderful children's shop

(clothes, no toys) on the side street that connects to Wakamiya Avenue. Wakamiya Avenue has a few clothiers (don't miss Kamakura Kent for the preppy Japanese look) but mostly is craft, souvenir, and folk-art stores. While there are many nice shops here, the more important works are sold in shops on another street.

7. Wakamiya Avenue will dead-end at a plaza that leads to a shrine. You don't want to miss the shrine. A shop there sells wooden placards for writing prayers; there will be two more stalls closer to the shrine. We won't give you the guided tour of the shrine but will tell you that there is a small hut for you to leave your shopping bags so you can wander around unencumbered. No one (almost) in Japan steals anything. As you approach the shrine, you'll see the Museum of Modern Art to the right. We saw a Paul Klee show there. Farther up is the Hachiman Shrine. It is breathtakingly beautiful. We were lucky enough to catch a wedding there.

8. As you are leaving the shrine and its park area, you'll see a coffee shop by a pond and next to the Museum of Modern Art. While it can be mobbed in season, if it's not too crowded, you may want to stop for ice cream or coffee. The bathrooms there are very clean.

9. When you get to the street, turn right rather than go back to Wakamiya Avenue. Go one block to a small, alleylike street and turn left. You are now on Komachi-dori, which will lead you right back to the train station. And what a way to be led—antiques stores, stores for paper, a lovely kimono shop, many stores for ready-to-wear, etc. This is the Japan you've been waiting for.

10. Get back on the train and go to Yokohama. This will take about half an hour, so you can rest up from your hike in Kamakura.

You can buy the ticket to Yokohama rather than to Tokyo and then buy a new ticket when you leave Yokohama for Tokyo.

11. When you get off at the train station in Yokohama, you will see numerous signs in Roman letters for various department stores you have heard of. This will be a bit confusing, but Yokohama wasn't born yesterday, and it is a key retailing area. And you already know about train-station retailing. Follow the signs to Sogo—they have arrows as well. You may get lost; ask people. Just keep saying "Sogo." You will leave the train station and enter a shopping mall, although it will feel like you still are in the station. As you enter the new mall you may think you have found Sogo. Not quite. You may want to shop these new shops (an entire boutique devoted to Anne Klein clothes) or go right into Sogo, which has a façade you can't miss and a gigantic clock made up of a village of international children who come out and dance on the hour and sing (in English) "It's a Small World." People gather to watch the clock much as they do in Venice to see the blackamoors come out.

12. Once in Sogo, you're on your own. We don't like to get soppy and goopy and disgusting in our rave reviews, so we merely say this is the best store in the world. Send us a postcard.

At Sogo Yokohama: B3, parking; B2 (subway, train, and bus entrance), best foods; B1, young (not kids); 1, accessories; 2, ladies'; 3, ladies'; 4, men's; 5, kids'; 6, life up; 7, home; 8, hobilot; 9, civil (community offices); 10, gourmet (numerous restaurants); 11, roof garden (Kiddy Playland, bonsai).

13. The store closes at 6:00 P.M. during the week, 7:00 P.M. on weekends. You'll find

you are exhausted by closing and are quite ready to sit on the train for a half hour to get back to dinner in Tokyo. Or, if you are really strong, you can take a taxi to Chinatown in Yokohama and have dinner there.

14. Hot bath.

Japanese and American Sizes

WOMEN'S CLOTHING

Japanese	9	11	13	15	17	19	21
American	6	8	10	12	14	16	18

MEN'S SWEATERS

Japanese	S	M	L	XL
American	34–36	38–40	42–44	46

MEN'S SHIRT COLLARS

Japanese	36	37	38	39	40	41	42
American	14	14½	15	15½	16	16½	17

WOMEN'S SHOES

Japanese	23	23½	24	24½	25	25½	26
American	6	6½	7	7½	8	8½	9

INDEX